RISING ON THE WINGS OF THE DAWN

Simon Rutembeka Ninsiima

Grosvenor House
Publishing Limited

The right of Simon Rutembeka Ninsiima to be identified as the author of this
work has been asserted in accordance with Section 78
of the Copyright, Designs and Patents Act 1988

Book cover photo is courtesy of Jim Leppard

This book is published by
Grosvenor House Publishing Ltd
Link House
140 The Broadway, Tolworth, Surrey, KT6 7HT.
www.grosvenorhousepublishing.co.uk

A CIP record for this book
is available from the British Library

ISBN 978-1-78623-802-3

For my beloved parents,
Petero and Ruusi Rutembeka,
whose steadfast love and faith
have been my rock and inspiration.

"If I go up to the heavens,
you are there;
if I make my bed in the depths,
you are there.
If I rise
on the wings of the dawn,
if I settle
on the far side of the sea,
even there
your hand will guide me,
your right hand will hold me fast."

Psalm 139: 8-10

CONTENTS

Foreword   *vii*

Acknowledgements   *ix*

Glossary   *xi*

Introduction – How it all began   *xiii*

Chapter 1.	Just another day	1
Chapter 2.	Dancing with butterflies	16
Chapter 3.	In heaven?	26
Chapter 4.	Way out	39
Chapter 5.	Stranger	52
Chapter 6.	A charcoal landscape	67
Chapter 7.	The cornfield	78
Chapter 8.	A permanent home	99
Chapter 9.	Prophecy	127
Chapter 10.	New Mulago	143
Chapter 11.	Not forsaken	160
Chapter 12.	Threats and thrills	177
Chapter 13.	Like the others	197
Chapter 14.	Moving on	214
Chapter 15.	A useful son	232

FOREWORD

This is a delightful story about a young boy with polio in rural Uganda in the 1960s. The story itself is harrowing at times and yet the love of God shines through on every page. Uganda may be far away and you may not be able to imagine the terror of hiding under the bedclothes because there is a lion outside, but Simon describes his life in such a way that you can easily picture it in your mind.

He was an adventurous, courageous and happy child. Then at the age of 6 he is struck down with polio and we feel his bewilderment as he becomes paralysed. He doesn't know what has happened to him. He cannot move his arms and legs. He cannot move his head. His body is racked with pain and he is unable to breathe. But even in this helpless state he understands that if he just "whispers" a prayer, God will hear him. He has learnt this from his parents; now it is time to find out for himself if it is true.

We feel his mother's anguish as she watches over her child in an "iron lung" machine, entrusting him to God's care whether he will live or die. After 3 months when he is able to breathe on his own, she takes him the 80 miles home on the bus, a totally paralysed child in her arms.

A year later, with the best of intentions, his parents leave him in the "care" of a traditional healer for several months while they try to find new pastures for their cattle and a new home for themselves. We cannot describe the horror we feel at the way he is treated: left in a filthy room to be bitten night after night by fleas and bed bugs and then held down and burnt with red hot metal rods and cut with razor blades. The "healer" ignores his screams and makes no attempt to comfort him. Only God hears his cries.

By the age of 9 he is able to crawl around on his hands and knees. He goes back to the big hospital in Kampala and after several operations and months of traction he is able to stand upright and take a few steps with the aid of callipers and crutches. But it is one thing to do this in a hospital in Kampala, quite another to walk back home in the village where there are no roads and no level ground. Eventually he discards the callipers and goes back to crawling just so that he can be mobile. That enables him, one day, to crawl the 3 miles to school to join his brothers and sisters – only to arrive just as the day's classes are over. A heart-breaking end to his hopes of getting an education.

The faith of Simon's parents shines through the whole book. The Christian community is very much like that of the early church where the believers meet and pray together, hold everything in common and give to anyone who has a need (Acts 2:44-47). As Tertullian said, "See how these Christians love one another." Here in the West we have much to learn from our African brothers and sisters.

Barbara Leppard

ACKNOWLEDGMENTS

I would like to thank all those whose guidance and support have enabled me to bring this book to completion, especially:

My parents and elder sister Phoebe Mushuku for filling in the gaps in the memories of my childhood and other events in the distant past.

Colin and Jill Day and Pauline Spiers for their time and encouragement at the early stages.

Barbara Leppard for taking such a keen interest. Thanks to her proactive attitude this book has finally been published. My deepest gratitude also to The Listeners for kindly investing their financial resources in this project.

Bishop Tim for his gracious commendation on the back cover.

My wife Gerdine. As my practical right hand, she has been instrumental in the bringing about of this book.

Our children Efraim, Leah and Esther for their moral support. They have been so patient as Gerdine and I spent many hours drafting and redrafting numerous manuscripts. Also my daughter Tabitha for her persistent prayers and encouragement.

Everyone else who has been involved through well-wishing and prayer over the years.

Most of all I would like to thank the Lord for carrying me over every hurdle in my life and blessing me beyond my wildest dreams.

GLOSSARY
(Excluding indigenous names)

Abeen'iguru	Beings descended from heaven
Akoojo	Little boy
Ankole	Region in western Uganda
Baganda	One of the largest tribes in central Uganda
Bahima	Semi-nomadic Banyankole tribe, originally from Ankole, western Uganda, sharing language and ancestral land with the Bairu
Balokole	'Saveds' or 'Set free' (from sin) – name for Christians converted by the Revival
Bairu	Peasant Banyankole tribe, mainly in Ankole, western Uganda, sharing language and ancestral land with the Bahima
Buganda	Region in central Uganda
Chwezi	(also Bachwezi) Legendary people with supernatural powers
Enchwera	Deadly venom-spitting black snake
Ghee	Clarified butter
Hajji	A Muslim who has been to Mecca as a pilgrim
Iteka	Lit. 'Commandments' – a booklet outlining the basics of Christianity, combined with a crash course in reading

Kabaka	King of Buganda
Kabaka Yeka	Political party supporting the King (Lit. 'The King Alone')
Kijana	Young man (Swahili)
Luganda	Language spoken by the Baganda
Mandazi	Small, sweet, deep-fried breads, quite like doughnuts
Matoke	Type of green bananas used for cooking
Muganda	Singular for Baganda
Muhima	Singular for Bahima
Mulokole	Singular for Balokole
Murram	Rusty-red tropical soil consisting of sand, clay and stones
Muzungu	'White' person (Swahili)
Okukund'abantu	Love for people
Orokongoro	Large bird of prey
Orunyankore	Language spoken by the Bahima and Bairu
Tonto	Traditional wine made from sweet, fermented bananas and sorghum
Tukutendereza	*'We praise You [Jesus]'*. The Balokole song of praise, also referred to as the Anthem of the Revival
Tutsi	Rwandan tribe. Traditionally and historically the Tutsis have a lot in common with the Bahima
Yesu	Jesus

HOW IT ALL BEGAN

"This one is enormous," the women gasped as they crowded round the bed where my mother lay recovering, trying to get a glimpse of the newly born child and the woman who had produced it.

Apparently I was the largest baby ever delivered in this hospital in Uganda. The midwife pulled me from my mother's arms and proudly paraded me around the maternity wards with an ever-swelling number of people in her wake – visitors, members of staff and anxious, expectant mums, all with one question foremost on their minds, *"Has the poor mum survived the birth?"*

I was born in 1957 but it may well have been a year earlier as in those days no formal records were kept. Had I been born some two decades earlier, no doubt my parents would have given me an evocative, traditional name. Something like *Rubanozya* for example, which in my mother tongue means 'The one who obliterates his foes'. As it was, they named me Simeoni Ninsiima. Simeoni after Simeon in the Bible, and *Ninsiima* meaning 'Gratitude to God'.

In the 1930s Christianity already existed in many parts of Uganda but it was as if the fire of the gospel had fizzled out. Although native people were converted, baptised and given Biblical names, not all had adopted the teachings of the Bible. Over time many returned to their old ways of life. Several indigenous societies had never even been reached. In western and central Uganda the *Bahima* tribe largely continued to live as they had done for centuries. And among these traditional, superstitious people were my parents.

The *Bahima* were a semi-nomadic tribe whose lives revolved around the keeping of beautiful, tall, long-horned *Ankole* cattle that they loved and cherished like members of the family. They lived in grass huts in communal settlements, at times large enough to contain as many as fifty families and thousands of head of cattle. Settlements were fortified with strong enclosures made of felled thorn trees and shrubs to keep out predators like lions, leopards and cheetahs.

During the day the men herded their cattle into the surrounding fields for grazing and watering. At night people and livestock retreated within the settlement where bonfires were lit to repel insects and deter wild animals from trying to break through the enclosure. Whenever pastures were exhausted or an area threatened by disease, drought or pests, the settlement was broken down and rebuilt in another location.

The *Bahima* believed in the existence of *Kazoba*, a mysterious, illusive god, creator of the sun, though they mainly worshipped *Nyaburezi* and *Nyabingi*, the supreme spirits of their ancestors. These were the supernatural authorities to which they would turn with their problems.

They were generally tall people with fine features who idolised each other's beauty in poems and songs. Their looks were quite envied by other tribes but marriage outside the *Bahima* tribe was strictly forbidden. Like the Tutsis of Rwanda they descended from the *Bachwezi* (or *Chwezi*) who, according to oral myths and legends, were a people shrouded in mystery with extraordinary supernatural powers. They were said to communicate by telepathic means and could vanish in thin air. Battles were fought by telekinesis whereby spears and arrows were propelled with great precision from a distance through the power of the mind. Some were so renowned for their mystical powers that people referred to them as *'Abeen'iguru'*, meaning 'beings descended from heaven' who just appeared on earth one day.

One *Chwezi* king, Bugaro, was said to have been in direct contact with god, the giver of life and creator of the universe. In times of calamity people turned to him for prayers. A famous legend tells how once in a time of drought the *Bahima* were dying and their *Ankole* cattle facing extinction. Bugaro prayed, sacrificed one of his last remaining cows and shot an arrow into heaven, signifying that he committed himself and his subjects to god. Following his actions amazing things began to happen. All of a sudden it poured with rain. *Abeen'iguru* appeared in the fields with herds of cattle as though delivered from heaven.

The *Chwezi* dynasty dissolved into subsequent *Ankole* kingdoms with the *Bahima* as the ruling class over their fellow *Banyankole* tribe, the *Bairu*, just as in Rwanda the Tutsis traditionally ruled over the Hutus. Whereas *Bahima* herded cattle, the *Bairu* were largely subsistence farmers, traditional craftsmen and traders. The two tribes shared ancestral land and language and depended on each other by bartering cattle produce for crops and other necessities. The *Bahima* generally coexisted well with surrounding tribes but their exclusiveness and self-content were sometimes viewed as arrogance and conceit which could lead to resentment, in particular among the *Bairu*.

Bahima society was governed by a strict code of conduct and rigid moral values, all of which revolved around respect, dignity, honour and love for one's family in the widest possible sense. Distant relatives and clansmen were treated as part of the immediate family. Cousins were so close that no one could distinguish them from the real brothers and sisters. Love for people (*'okukund'abantu'*) was regarded the greatest virtue a *Muhima* could possess. In practice this meant a whole range of traditionally admired qualities, such as humility, hospitality, generosity and compassion, as well as being receptive, helpful and caring. '*Okukund'abantu*' was so important that a person's status and respectability were not just defined by his wealth in terms of cows but also by his ability to love his fellow *Bahima*.

A *Muhima* showed unconditional hospitality to all *Bahima*, even total strangers. Adults were collectively responsible for the care, discipline and safety of *every* child and not just their own. Children respected and obeyed *all* adults, in turn receiving abundant love and affection. Sons and daughters showed obedience to their parents and avoided doing anything that could embarrass or disgrace them. Boys worked alongside their fathers, thus proving that they were useful sons and worthy heirs. This created a good image and increased their own chances of marrying well. In fact, every family member was expected to contribute towards elevating the family's good name and standing within the clan and society as a whole. Young men could be assured of a good reputation as long as they were seen to honour their parents, love people and adore cows. Unmarried women also had to be dignified and keep themselves pure.

Parting with these cherished customs and traditions would amount to a scandal and expose the perpetrator to public ridicule and disgrace, which in turn could tarnish the reputation of his or her entire family. Strong cultural values and high expectations kept people in check. Although society was not free from mischief, there was a relatively low incidence of crime.

On the whole, the *Bahima* were a peaceful people, thoroughly content with their pastoral lifestyle and fiercely protective of their culture. They certainly did not see a need for change, nor were they readily going to embrace it when it came.

Yet, change was on its way. In Rwanda, in a place called Gahini, Christians turned to the Bible and realised that it was not enough just to be baptised and belong to a church. Being a Christian required obedience to the Word of God and therefore a total turning away from sin. It meant aspiring to being holy, just as the Lord is Holy! So they openly confessed their sins, abandoned their old ways of life and set out to spread this 'revived' gospel with great self-denial, power and joy. They called themselves *'Balokole'*, which means 'Saved'. This revival in Christian faith rapidly spread from Rwanda into Uganda and beyond and became known as the East African Revival.

My mother used to liken the Revival to a bush fire. It was just unstoppable. Even if the flames died down in one location sparks caused more fires to break out further afield. Every time Christianity lost momentum (as eventually happened in Gahini), the fire of the Holy Spirit ignited Christians elsewhere and these not only continued spreading the Gospel but also rekindled existing believers. When the Revival reached Rujumbura in Ankole, western Uganda, it almost ground to a halt. There was stiff resistance from the *Bahima* and other local tribes who saw it as a threat to their indigenous beliefs and culture. A certain *Balokole* missionary named Kutyamukama (meaning 'The one who fears the Lord'), who had come to Uganda from Karagwe in Northern Tanzania, saw the Revival fading in Rujumbura. Determined to take the Gospel to communities beyond Ankole he moved on to Bweera in central Uganda. There he started preaching in a small mud-built church in Kikoma, close to the area where my parents lived.

The year was 1939 when Kutyamukama reached their settlement. My mother was eighteen years old and my father twenty-two. Both of them were orphans. My mother descended from the aforesaid *Abeen'iguru*, the so-called 'heavenly beings'. Her grandmother was a princess in the Bashambo dynasty that was defeated in a war with the Basongola and annexed by a larger Ankole clan, the Bahinda. While most of the royals were wiped out she was captured and given as part of the plunder to a nobleman at the

Bahinda court, my great-grandfather. My mother's father was a traditional hero and envoy to the king. He was so highly favoured and regarded that the royal family rewarded him for his services with many gifts, including herds of cattle.

My father's maternal line leads back to *Nyakahima*, the last known *Chwezi* whose statue now features as a tourist attraction in the Ugandan Museum. He was born into the Basasira clan that descended from the ancient *Muganga*, a powerful traditional leader related to the *Chwezi*, who is said to have introduced the first *Ankole* cattle.

Although my parents already knew each other in those days, another man had proposed to my mother. According to *Bahima* customs the process of marriage proposal could easily take a whole year. The groom first had to be vetted by the bride's parents (or in mother's case, being an orphan, her older brothers) and then by her extended family, like all the aunts and uncles. Only when all parties had given their approval could the wedding take place. Then the groom's parents paid a dowry to the bride's parents and she moved in with her husband and his family.

While marriage consultations were still going on, my mother and several other youngsters from the settlement went to listen to Kutyamukama. He told them about God, the creator of mankind, whose love for human beings was boundless. He even gave His only son who died a cruel death on the cross to save people from sin.

"The Bible tells us that Jesus wants you to open your eyes and turn from darkness to light and from the power of Satan to God," Kutyamukama preached (Acts 26:17). "Through faith in Him you will have your sins forgiven and receive your place among God's chosen people."

Hearing this, they were deeply moved and anxious to find out more about this Jesus. What was it that they were doing wrong? How did God want them to live? The moment they confessed their sins the Holy Spirit came upon them and their lives were totally transformed. As they turned their backs on everything to do with traditional worship, superstition and ignorance, almost overnight they became humble, selfless and God-fearing people. No one needed to tell or teach them what to do; the Holy Spirit gave them the conscience and wisdom they needed.

But the *Bahima* community saw their changed behaviour as embarrassing, rebellious and terribly shocking. My mother's relatives were worried that, once it became widely known how much she had changed, she would be publicly disgraced and lose her chance of ever getting married! To save her face as well as their own they quickly married her off to the man who had shown interest in her, without finishing the usual proposal consultations or a formal wedding. They even allowed the groom to come and live with them, rather than mother moving in with his family and exposing her 'delusions' and 'scandalous behaviour'. This, so they hoped, would help mother settle back into traditional life and protect her from 'bad' influences. How wrong they were! Despite family pressure, threats and ill treatment, my mother refused to go back to the traditional lifestyle and beliefs. Instead, she continued to openly declare herself a *Balokole* Christian, much to the horror of everyone around, including her new husband.

My father was also among the people who had gone to listen to Kutyamukama in the little mud-built church but he was sceptical about this new faith.

"How can anyone give up their worldly pursuits for an illusive dream?" he wondered. He was young and trying to make a start in life. Rather than joining the *Balokole* he decided to go and visit some relatives in another settlement to ask whether they could lend him a few cows. This was not an unusual thing to do for a *Muhima*, as society cared for orphans, widows and the poor. If, for example, due to disease or misfortune a man's cattle were dwindling, his relatives and friends could give or loan him a milking cow so that he and his dependants would not suffer. Starting in this humble way, father hoped to build up a herd and establish himself, get married and so continue the respect and honour of his father's name. As it happened, the very first relative he approached had recently become *Balokole* and was learning to read the Bible.

"I don't have any cows for you," the man said to father, "but I'll give you my *Iteka*." He handed him a booklet. The *Iteka*, meaning 'Commandments', was introduced by visiting preachers and provided the basics of Christianity combined with a crash course in reading. Father was totally smitten.

"It was as if Jesus had cast a net around me," he told me later. "There was just no escape. I could have gone to any relative but instead went right to the person who had already been converted and was reading the Bible!" So father returned to Kikoma without cows but with an *Iteka* and this became a great tool in further advancing the Word of God.

Traditionally, *Bahima* people ended their day with storytelling, singing and dancing around bonfires, and showing off with their good looks. However, rather than engaging in such activities, the young Christians spent their evenings in fellowship. They put bamboo torches in front of their huts to provide light as they studied the *Iteka*, listened to Bible stories and learnt to read and write. They were filled with great joy, praising God in spite of the hostility around them. Their behaviour was so unusual that their clansmen thought they had gone mad, eventually casting them out of the settlement.

"The *Muzungu* (white man) spirit has bewitched you!" people cried out in shock and rage. "You have become a disgrace to your clan!" They subjected the *Balokole* to insults and mockery, beating them with sticks and pelting them with stones. In the eyes of traditionalists these young men and women had brought disgrace upon their families and clans, simply by becoming Christians. The men were beaten up and chased, the women sent away through a hole in the enclosure surrounding the settlement amidst the sounding of drums. Such public humiliation was normally only displayed in severe cases of misbehaviour, for example when a girl had become pregnant before marriage. Such a girl was not sent away through the gate but through a purposely made hole in the enclosure to symbolise that she had broken with society. Unless an influential relative like an aunt was willing to take her in, she would be unprotected and either try to survive alone in the wild or risk being killed by angry relatives. Even if a forced marriage was later arranged she would not be accepted back by her family and clan for many years, not until she had raised several children. In the same way, my mother was chased away, disowned by her community and rejected by her husband, even though she was expecting their first child.

Nothing though could extinguish the fire of the Holy Spirit. Away from the settlement the new believers cared for each other, grew stronger in faith and kept on rejoicing and praising Jesus, their Lord. Among them were my father and his sister, as well as my mother, her brother and their eldest sister who had also been thrown out by her husband and forced to leave her two children behind.

Father could not rest until he had gone back to the settlement to look for his best friend and blood brother whom I came to know as Uncle Thomas. In *Bahima* society men could seal a strong friendship by becoming 'blood brothers'. This meant that following a special ritual they swore an oath of allegiance to never let each other down. Even in this modern age the grandchildren of blood brothers still respect this type of family connection. They arranged to meet in secret somewhere outside the settlement.

"How could you, of all people, succumb to this craze?" Uncle Thomas chided my father. Father was undeterred.

"We have made a vow to protect each other in danger," he answered. "How could I ever be at peace knowing that I have been saved while you still live in darkness and sin? I don't want you to perish. I must share with you this new message of Salvation!" They spent many hours talking and arguing about the Scriptures. Uncle Thomas was fiercely opposed but somehow feeling restless. He had noticed that something spectacular, life changing had happened to my father and was curious to know what it was. Before long he too began to believe. As the Revival spread and gained a foothold he was to become one of the pillars of faith in Bweera.

Once my parents and the other young believers had mastered the *Iteka*, the preacher Kutyamukama took them to the house of Mondo, one of the leaders of the Revival in the Buganda region. From there they went to a missionary school in Katare, Nsangi, near Kampala, for adult literacy classes and Bible study. Before being baptised into the Church of Uganda they had to be able to read the Bible, interpret scriptures and learn the Catechism by heart. In Nsangi other prominent Revivalists joined them, like William Nagenda, Simeoni Nsibambi, Erica Sabiiti and Festo Kivengere. Here my mother gave birth to her first child, but the baby girl died shortly afterwards.

At that time *Kabaka* Chwa, the king of Buganda and father of Sir Edward Mutesa, had just passed away. The general mood was subdued in Buganda with the period of public mourning yet to be concluded. In spite of this, the Revivalists were glowing. The Holy Spirit was upon them and they kept increasing in number. They had their own special song for praising and thanking the Lord, a *Luganda* hymn that was to become the anthem of the East African Revival. It has been sung in parts of Uganda, Kenya, Tanzania, Rwanda, Congo and Sudan up to this very day:

Tukutendereza Yesu,	We praise you, Jesus,
Yesu Mwana Gw'endiga.	Jesus the Lamb.
Omusayi gwo gunaziza,	Your blood cleanses me,
Nkwebaza omurokozi!	I thank you, Saviour!

The missionary course lasted eight months after which the *Balokole* were baptised and confirmed into the Church of Uganda. They were given new Christian names, primarily based on the Bible: my father became Petero (Peter) and his sister Miriamu (Miriam); my mother was named Ruusi (Ruth), her brother Kosiya (Hosea) and their elder sister Elizaabeesi (Elizabeth).

Kutyamukama, who had led them to Christ, did not want to belong to any particular denomination or church.

"I am only a messenger," he declared. "I just wanted to deliver this wonderful news about a new way of life in Christ." He returned to Rujumbura before they could convince him to be baptised too and they never saw him again.

When the course was over, some Christians continued their education in Nsangi, later helping to translate the Bible into their mother tongue *Orunyankore*. My parents and several others stayed on for a further two years to be trained in evangelism and preaching.

The *Balokole* lived together as a family, referring to each other as *'abeishemwe'* – 'children of the same Father' or 'brethren'. Having been rejected by their own families and clans they were now one clan in the Lord. This meant that they themselves had to solve issues and disputes without the support of their natural families and clan elders. One difficult issue was that Kosiya and Miriam were engaged before being chased from the settlement, and their families had now nullified the arrangement. As they still wanted to get married it was decided that, under the circumstances, my father and some other brethren could give the bride away, regardless of the families' objections. Nothing like this had ever happened before in *Bahima* society. When it became known back home, the clan elders were furious, wasting no time to disinherit the young Christians. Miriam's dowry was recalled as punishment for the couple joining the *Balokole* and deciding to go ahead with their marriage. My mother's cows were also confiscated, including the ones given in gratitude for her father's services rendered to the Bahinda royals. In some cases, where only the husband had become a Christian, his wife was taken back by her family and married off to someone else.

In 1942 my parents graduated from Nsangi. They got married and a year later my brother William *Karanzi* was born, named after the great evangelist William Nagenda who was a close friend of my parents.

The Revivalists went their own ways, wherever the Spirit led them. Some travelled as missionaries to parts of Tanzania and Congo where the Revival message had not yet reached. Erica Sabiiti was to become the country's first African-born Archbishop. Festo Kivengere ended up preaching alongside Billy Graham. My parents, Aunt Elizabeth, Uncle Thomas and several others returned to their homestead in Bweera to preach the gospel to the *Bahima* there. They joined hands with a Christian called Yosiya Kyinuka who was the only *Bahima* evangelist in the area. He became their mentor as they faced the difficult task of returning to the people who had chased and humiliated them. People who were now even more angered by the 'disobedience' the *Balokole* had shown to their much valued *Bahima* customs and traditions.

Unable to return to their homes and clans, the *Balokole* built a permanent settlement of their own. It had lasting huts, large kraals and a formidable enclosure. Here they could safely raise their families and worship the Lord. To traditional *Bahima* such a settlement meant breaking with their semi-nomadic lifestyle, which was considered terribly shocking. Land was abundant in those days and there was freedom of roaming. Critics were convinced that in order to care for cows one had to be prepared to keep moving in search of greener pastures.

"These crazy people have decided to go and live in one place," they scorned. "How can anyone be so cruel towards cattle? They will destroy themselves with their mad religion." So they eagerly waited for the *Balokole* and their livestock to be struck by diseases and die.

The believers had their weekly routine. On Saturday they carried out domestic chores. On Sunday they gathered for worship in the little church in Kikoma where Kutyamukama had led them to Christ. On all other days they woke up very early and, after meeting for fellowship in each other's homes, went out in teams to spread the Good News of Salvation. Walking from home to home and village to village they told the occupants how believing in Jesus had transformed their own lives.

"In the past we used to be slaves to drunkenness, lust and other sin," they testified without fear of tarnishing their image. "But now we have been cleansed and set free through God's saving grace in Jesus.

"We are not bewitched by a *Muzungu* spell nor have we lost our senses. In fact, the Holy Spirit of God has opened our eyes. He is helping us to see more clearly.

"Repent of your sins. Accept Jesus as your Lord and Saviour. He will do for you what he has done for us. He wants to redeem your life right now!" They asked onlookers whether they could pray with them but the response was usually one of hostility and resentment. Not only was the behaviour of these *Balokole* totally unacceptable in the eyes of traditional *Bahima*, they also looked very strange with their short hair and *Muzungu*-style clothing – the men in shirts and trousers and the women wearing dresses or blouses and skirts. Particularly shocking for the traditionalists was the sight of *Balokole* women exposing their ankles and not covering their hair and shoulders with a veil.

"Christians bring bad luck to our homes," they cried out. Husbands even hid their pregnant wives to prevent their offspring from catching the '*Muzungu* curse'. Wherever they went the *Balokole* were despised, harassed, threatened and cursed. But as people watched them their aggression was mixed with curiosity and wonder. Weren't some of those *Balokole* men once known to be irresponsible drunkards? Now they managed their homes in an almost enviable way. Similarly, notorious womanisers had been transformed into faithful husbands; sad and troubled people like widows, widowers and orphans were filled with joy and the chronically sick and ailing revived with inexplicable strength and hope. There were also many testimonies of physical recovery. People with mental illness, epilepsy, leprosy, tumours and other medical conditions were miraculously healed. However, the *Balokole* preferred to focus on Jesus and the Holy Spirit rather than on these miracles. Miracles just tended to happen when you decided to wholeheartedly serve the Lord. Among all the transformations one thing was particularly puzzling to that proud *Bahima* society. Strong traditional fighters, renowned for their toughness and courage, refused to fight back when humiliated, beaten and chased!

"Christians are not only mad, they're also cowards," people mocked. "They don't even defend themselves or fight for their honour!" Time and time again the *Balokole* were chased away. Yet many traditional *Bahima* could not help feeling drawn to them. Some even secretly camped overnight outside the *Balokole* settlement, just to see what would happen to this jubilant group of people so united by love and their 'crazy belief'. They never seemed to be disheartened by rejection and abuse, not even by the confiscation of their property!

The believers also went out in teams to spread the Gospel to other tribes in the country. Some travelled all the way to Karamoja in north eastern Uganda. They even crossed the borders into Kenya, Tanzania and Congo using any means of transport they could find: buses, lorries, bicycles or on foot. My parents, among others, were called westwards to places like Rujumbura, Kigani, Kinyasano and Kabale where God did amazing things. In those days the roads were rough.

Only one vehicle travelled once a month from Kampala to western Uganda – a lorry transporting passengers, mail and goods. My mother described how they used to walk many miles a day through wild and difficult terrain, climbing steep hills and crawling on hands and knees over precarious, slippery rocks, while she carried little Karanzi in a sling on her back.

One day, the leader of a settlement in the Bweera area invited the *Balokole* to come and explain more about 'this Jesus thing'. Unsure whether this was genuine interest or a trap my parents and some twenty other Christians entered the settlement. There they preached the gospel, prayed and sang praises to God well into the evening. They did this with such power that several bystanders were moved. The elders, however, became extremely alarmed.

"Stop this madness at once," their leader shouted at the top of his voice. "We don't want to hear anymore! You people are doomed. Get out and let the wild beasts finish you off!" With sticks they chased the *Balokole* all the way into a notorious valley where lions, leopards and hyenas were known to roam. If a cow strayed there in the dark, its dying screams would be heard at night and nothing but bones found in the morning. In the pitch-dark and pouring rain the young Christians managed to gather wood and light a bonfire. There wet and hungry, surrounded by fierce predators, they spent the night out in the open, singing and praising God.

Back in that settlement hardly anyone was able to sleep. Some inhabitants felt concern for those poor, deluded souls, while others were simply too excited. Everyone waited for cries of pain and terror to rise up from the valley but these never came. All that was heard was the roaring and howling of wild animals mixed with joyful singing that continued throughout the night. The following day the *Balokole* made their way home, unharmed and with another experience to add to their testimonies. Now they could prove to unbelievers that Christ really does save and that their new faith was indestructible.

In the meantime the Gospel had touched a number of youngsters in that settlement. Keen on hearing more they decided to visit the church in Kikoma but their families refused to let them. Those who dared to defy were beaten with sticks. Some were confined to their huts and starved for days on end. Others were tied up and left out in the scorching sun, until they denounced their interest and promised never to join the Christians!

Notwithstanding such stiff opposition the *Balokole* congregation kept growing. When the little thatched church in Kikoma could no longer contain them they decided to build a new one. It was to be a large, semi-modern building made with timber, mud-plastered walls and a corrugated iron roof. Father and Uncle Kosiya headed the project. Everyone contributed, either by selling cows or volunteering building expertise or going out into the fields to cut down trees and bamboo. None of them had ever built anything on such a large scale before but somehow God provided the skills and know-how. They put money together to buy a *karatutsi* plantation. *Karatutsi* is a type of tall, straight tree used for constructing robust buildings. Skilled experts were paid to cut down the trees and deal with the more complicated work, like roofing.

Traditionally among the *Bahima,* men would do tasks that were physically demanding while women carried out lighter duties in and around the home. However, these newly converted Christian men and women worked alongside each other, carrying felled trees on their shoulders and heads, digging trenches and working the soil with their feet to make a sticky clay mixture used for plastering walls! It turned out to be quite a spectacle: men in trousers and women in dresses working together to erect a building that was larger and more modern than any other known in Bweera. From all over the area people gathered to find out what was happening, only to find these shining, jubilant and yet highly disciplined Christians at work and to hear them worshipping and preaching.

The new church in Kikoma became a focal point for criticism and opposition, but also a springboard for the believers to reach out to the community and spread the Good News. Its impact was huge. Every Sunday large crowds gathered either to worship or to protest. People besieged the church to harass and threaten the worshipers entering or leaving the building. Others just listened from a distance to the singing, Bible reading and preaching in their own language as it resounded through the church windows.

Gradually people began to draw closer until they dared to enter the church. To their astonishment, none of the Christians blamed them for their hostility. Instead they were warmly received and made to feel welcome. More and more people began to admire this new way of life and accepted Jesus Christ as their Saviour. After being taught the basics of their new faith and learning to read the Bible, they and their children were baptised and joined the congregation. And so, despite continued resistance from hard-liners, Christianity gained a foothold among the *Bahima*.

Christianity did not entirely break with the *Bahima* culture and customs. In fact, it enhanced and purified many traditional values, the way it instructed people to love each other, respect their parents, care for the widows and orphans and show compassion to the poor and the needy. Even aiming to live a holy life was not very dissimilar from the traditional discipline of staying clear from scandals, which made it easier for new believers to grasp the concepts of righteousness and sin.

The gospel preached by the *Balokole* was frank and did not try to appease. People had to confront their sinful nature and repent. Only then could their lives be transformed by the Lord's saving grace. The *Balokole* openly confessed their sins before God and to each other, exposing any ungodly actions, feelings and thoughts. This was not an easy thing to do but it paved the way for genuine love and helped the believers not to fall back into sin again. New believers not only asked for forgiveness from God but also from the people they had offended or wronged. In this way relationships were restored, conflicts resolved and clans reconciled without need for traditional courts or elders. Stolen goods were voluntarily returned to the rightful owners, including cattle and property initially confiscated from the early Christians.

Part of the *Balokole* discipline was to refrain from anything that could make people falter in their faith, such as lust, greed and drunkenness. Just as Jesus once said, *"If your right eye causes you to sin, gouge it out and throw it away"* (Mat 5:29) they strived to stay clear from worldly temptations. They did not flirt, glorify earthly beauty or seek to accumulate wealth on earth. They also abstained from alcohol consumption as this could easily lead to misjudgement and sin. The *Balokole* conscientiously tried to live according to God's will in order to be prepared for his Kingdom. And because the words they preached were evidenced by their actions and love they were able to make a huge impact on the surrounding communities.

Without moving from place to place in search of fresh pastures, the *Balokole* community became very experienced in looking after cattle. Living in a permanent settlement had many advantages. The traditional semi-nomadic lifestyle was often wrought with dangers; it was rough on vulnerable people, especially the elderly, sick and disabled. Even cattle often suffered. Nature had to be conquered before a new settlement was habitable and safe, which required a lot of time and effort. In the meantime everyone was exposed to predators, snakes and diseases.

By staying in one place the *Balokole* were less exposed to risks and had more time to devote to their families and livestock. They taught their children to read the Bible.

Alongside their new faith they adopted a more modern lifestyle with a varied diet and improved hygiene. For example, they now first boiled their milk rather than drinking it straight from the cow. The beneficial effects were evident – children flourished, cows multiplied rapidly and the incidence of stillbirth went dramatically down. Christianity actually paved the way for modernisation in a sense that it made people more receptive and adaptable to programmes and initiatives promoting education, hygiene and health, including immunisations.

"Surely, if these people were really cursed or bewitched, their cows and children would have been dead by now," *Bahima* hard-liners wondered. "Their lifestyle is self-destructive. Yet, they are better off than we are!"

Finally, in an attempt to find out what secret the *Balokole* were harbouring, they too began to draw closer and slowly got used to this new way of life. Although not every traditionalist became a Christian, the attitude changed from fierce hostility to mere cynicism and disapproval. By the late 1950s the *Balokole* were no longer outcasts but warmly welcomed back into society as respectable citizens, and many more people accepted Jesus Christ as their Lord.

Following the birth of their first child Karanzi, my parents had three daughters: Phaibe, Eseza and Miriam. My brother Karanzi was a keen Christian who from a very young age enjoyed engaging in spreading the Gospel among fellow youngsters. He was a loving, caring and dutiful son who always passionately aimed to do well in everything in order to please the Lord. When he was in his early teens his stomach suddenly began to swell up to an enormous size. He suffered excruciating pains. The cause was unclear but my parents thought that it might be the screw he had once accidentally swallowed while helping someone repair a bicycle. Every local treatment failed. Father sold several cows, spending the money on taking him to one hospital after another and finally to the national referral hospital in Kampala. Doctors, however, were unable to make a diagnosis and his condition deteriorated further.

In these months of terrible suffering, Karanzi grew even closer to the Lord. When distraught adults and children came to his bedside, he was the one to comfort and counsel them, encouraging them not to be troubled but to put their trust in the Lord.

Even as he was slowly dying he urged my parents not to give up.

"My journey has been short... I am going to be with my Saviour in heaven. Keep holding onto your faith. Always remember his love! God will reunite us again." When he heard that mother had given birth to another boy he was relieved and delighted.

"Now I can be totally at peace," he said, "because God has given you a son in my place." He died shortly afterwards from multiple organ failure.

My parents named their newborn child *Samwiri* (Samuel) *Mwebaza*, which means 'Praise the Lord'.

Two years later I was born.

CHAPTER 1

JUST ANOTHER DAY

"How clearly the sky reveals God's glory!
How plainly it shows what he has done!
Each day announces it to the following day;
each night repeats it to the next...
God made a home in the sky for the sun;
it comes out in the morning like a happy bridegroom,
like an athlete eager to run the race."

Ps 19:1-2,4b-5 (TEV)

Every morning we were woken up before dawn to prepare for the day. Having a lie-in was a rare treat and only happened when our sleep had been seriously disrupted. Like the night a heavy thunderstorm ripped off part of our grass roof and we were drenched by rain, or when safari ants invaded our hut and we got terribly bitten. On more than one occasion a lion tried to jump the thorny enclosure around our settlement. Then father and the other strong men had no choice but to go outside to bring our panic-stricken cattle under control and keep guard till morning. Meanwhile my siblings and I lay petrified under our bedding, listening to every sound.

Surrounded by the spectacular wilds of central Uganda, life was ever so eventful. In the early 1960s we lived in huts made of sticks and grass, at the mercy of nature with its abundant wildlife and temperamental climate. Yet, in our close-knit *Bahima* community, where life was characterised by a beautiful blend of traditional African sociability and selfless Christian love, we were ready to face anything nature threw at us.

Our lives revolved around our Christian faith and the keeping of tall, long-horned cattle. My parents had been converted some twenty years earlier when the East African Revival swept Uganda. The revivalists, called *'Balokole'* (meaning 'Saved'), devoted their lives to emulating Jesus, sharing God's love in a practical way and spreading the message of Salvation. Therefore, whatever challenge the night might have brought, each new day was begun with thanksgiving and praising God. As we stumbled out of bed, father, mother and any *Balokole* guests were already assembled near the fireplace where the following hour was spent in worship. Whether old or young, everyone was given a chance to share how we had seen the Lord's hand at work. This was also a time for confessing any grievances and worries – anything that could hinder us from having close union with each other and the Lord in the course of the day. Together we prayed for forgiveness and strength. We read the Bible, sang worship songs and encouraged each other in faith, and then it was milking time.

First we groomed the cows with an *enkuyo*, a soft sisal brush, to reduce the dust and dirt that tends to attract flies. This made the animals feel more relaxed when feeding or being milked. While the adults were busy milking, it was the task of children to keep the calves at bay. Calves were allowed to drink some of the milk but most of it was kept for people. Cattle were our livelihood and their produce our only source of food and income.

Every child had a role to play in the running of a *Bahima* household. In turns we cleaned out the pen for the tiniest calves and cut fresh grass for them to lie on. Other early

2

morning chores included fetching firewood and water if the well was within a safe walking distance from our home. Grazing was a communal activity and usually adults and children from different families joined up. The men and teenage boys herded the cows to faraway pastures, while younger boys took the larger calves out for grazing and watering in the fields around our settlement. Girls also looked after calves but they usually stayed closer to home.

By the time I was five I was regarded as old enough to be out in the fields with the boys and a herd of playful calves. I absolutely loved it! Early in the morning the earth was revitalised by the cool of the night, and the early dawn revealed a glorious freshness. Dew glittered and sparkled all around us like a silver sea, soaking our legs as we waded through the tall grass. In the distance the hills and valleys were covered by mist. For a brief moment nature seemed to be harmonious, almost benign. Then, slowly, the gentle sunrays intensified and turned into a scorching heat. The hazy clouds on the horizon lifted as though climbing up the hillsides, unveiling breath-taking scenery thus far kept hidden from our sight – a landscape littered with animals of different kinds and colours. Most easily recognisable were the agile zebras with their black and white stripes; they loved to run in the morning sun. There were herds of buffalo, wild pigs and antelopes, joined in the course of the morning by our own *Ankole* cattle with their striking colours and long white horns.

My eyes scanned the fields.

"Where are we taking the calves today?" I asked the bigger boys. "Can we go to the foot of the hills to watch the animals from nearby?"

"A little later," they replied. "First we must go to our favourite spots to look for fruits and roots."

Most bushes were littered with edible fruits. We especially loved *binyamakara*, a type of small berry that turned from green to purple to velvet-black when ripe, sweet and juicy. Nicknamed 'black passion' they were used as a romantic gift from a young man to his girlfriend. Even beautiful women were named after them in traditional poems and songs.

After the rains water flowed from the hills, causing fresh vegetation to spring up everywhere. The abundance of wild flowers and fruits attracted numerous insects and birds. Beautiful birds with glittering feathers in all colours of the rainbow; snow-white ones that landed on our calves to feast on the flies. An overwhelming choir of birdsong filled my ears with an endless variety of melodies resounding from the treetops. I felt a cool breeze in my face, seemingly blowing right through me, clearing my lungs and head. All of nature rejoiced in the early morning freshness and together with God's creation every fibre of my being stretched out to welcome the new day.

Our calves ran ahead, kicking with their rear legs in the air, jumping with joy. We dashed after them. Looking after cattle might have been a daily chore but for us it came with countless pleasures. Nature was unspoilt and provided us with an inexhaustible source of entertainment, adventure and fun. While the calves grazed we kept ourselves busy playing. With clay and sand we made mini-settlements, using speckled beans and little sticks for cows. We built grass huts to shelter from the sun, dug up edible roots, picked berries and climbed trees to reach rare fruits that only grew in the highest branches. By the age of six I was so good at climbing that I could get to the top of almost any tree. I even had a go at the thorny enclosure surrounding our settlement but that was very risky and the adults told me off. Whenever I wasn't playing or climbing I ran after butterflies or tracked small animals and birds, trying to discover their hideouts. If I found something special, like a tree laden with fruits or an abandoned nest, I marked the area with a stick so I could find the place again and show my friends that I had got there first.

Once I found a burrow with baby rabbits left abandoned – their poor mother probably devoured by a stray dog. With thorny branches I built a fence around it to protect the little ones and put some milk in a piece of calabash for them to drink. In my own childlike way I wanted to protect and care for our natural environment, as I loved its beauty and knew that the Lord had made it. I adopted young, orphaned animals, like hare, pheasants, crown birds and cranes, trying to find ways of keeping them safe. I loved to tame them and take them home but, unfamiliar with human touch, they often died from shock. This was so heartbreaking that I soon learned to look after these precious creatures in their own habitat.

Occasionally my friends and I stumbled across the remains of an animal that had been killed by a predator the previous night. Then we quickly ran off to tell the older boys. From the carcass they were able to identify what animal had killed it and warn us not to stray in a particular direction. From a very early age we were taught how to survive in that untamed nature. *'Run and call for help whenever you sense danger!'* was the golden rule for us children to keep safe. We learnt about habitats and the behaviour of animals that posed a threat to cattle and human beings, and how to recognise their tracks and scents. Some animals displayed extraordinarily cunning behaviour. A female buffalo could dig a hole with her hooves in which she released a bit of milk. When an animal or person stopped to investigate the puddle of white fluid on the ground she would emerge with terrifying speed, crashing into the unsuspecting victim and inflicting horrendous injuries with her horns. Growing up we became skilled in defending ourselves with sticks cut from a special tree and treated with fire for additional toughness. *Bahima* carried one with them wherever they went. Our men were able to defeat leopards and lions with nothing but a stick! Spears were only used as the last resort, as we were well aware

5

that a non-fatal injury could make wild animals even more ferocious.

On the brow of a hill we spent many hours playing traditional sports and games. We held competitions in running, high jumping and archery with handmade bows and arrows. We hurled sharp pointed sticks at rolling hoops made from flexible branches tied together with sisal. Such 'javelin' games prepared us for using a spear in adult life when we would be the ones to defend our homes and cattle from danger.

Around midday one of the mothers brought us pots of milk or yoghurt that we drank in the shadow of a tree. The *Bahima* were not used to eating food during the day, except that children often enjoyed indulging in wild fruits and roots. Milk was our staple diet and it was readily available. If we wanted to eat anything else we bartered milk, butter or meat for agricultural produce with peasants from surrounding tribes. By two o'clock, when the sun was at its fiercest, we led the calves into the valleys to drink from rainwater ponds. Hot and dusty we threw off our clothes, jumped in and swam among the water lilies and butterflies. Some days an older brother or sister joined up with us to give us a good wash.

Towards mid-afternoon the youngest boys and I went back to the settlement with the smallest calves, collecting firewood along the way if our mothers had told us to do so. The other boys stayed out a little longer with the rest of the calves. By now it was time for the herders to start moving the cattle towards the watering place. This could be a well or a lake where women also gathered to fetch water, wash clothes and bathe their youngest children. Places like these were important meeting points for people from all over the area. Unless mother had specifically instructed me to stay home and rest I spent the remainder of the afternoon watching the watering of the cows. Adjacent to the watering place was an *obwato*, a large man-made water basin built with clay. A few

6

men filled the *obwato* with an *icuba*, a traditional bucket carved out of wood. With a special loud cry they alerted the herders when the basin was full. Once the cows sensed where they were heading they became excited and began to run. Before long hundreds of thirsty, mooing animals came charging towards the water. To prevent them from trampling the *obwato* and stirring up mud, youngsters were put in place to drive them towards a holding area from where small groups were released to drink at any one time. Meanwhile the men kept topping up the *obwato* until all the cattle had drunk, which could easily take several hours.

When I was six I managed to convince my uncle Yokana that I was big enough to help the youngsters drive our cattle towards the well. I was quite tall and advanced for my age and sometimes he allowed me to try out a task normally allocated to much older children. Bursting with pride I walked in front of the herd, but the animals were impatient and raging with thirst. As they rapidly gained momentum the earth trembled under their hooves. Soon I needed to pull out all the stops to keep up with their pace! A few zebras jumped from a nearby bush and galloped alongside me. Distracted by their presence I stumbled over an anthill, falling flat on the ground with hundreds of mooing cows hard on my heels. Fortunately Uncle Yokana had been keeping a vigilant eye on me and hastily came to my rescue. Fending off the cows he pulled me from beneath their trampling hooves.

"Is there nothing that can stop this child?" I heard him mutter under his breath as he busily brushed the dust off my face and hair. Like many adults he seemed to wonder what would become of me. "This boy is so strong, so active and daring," people used to say, "He certainly is a promising man in the making!"

Once watering was over, our cattle continued grazing around the settlement while young men entertained themselves with games of stick fighting, high jumping and wrestling. Besides practising their skills, this was a good opportunity for them to show off their agility and strength in front of admiring young women. While *Balokole* children and teenagers were discouraged from taking part in such a worldly display, we were not prevented from watching.

Sunrise always brought the promise and excitement of yet another day, but with sunset came the climax. At this time the fields were basking in brilliant colours. Nature buzzed with activity as animals and birds hastily sought cover from the encroaching darkness. As I watched the creatures disappear in different directions I tried to memorise where they went.

"The deer hide in that clump of trees ... The crown birds sleep in those shrubs."

Golden clouds surrounded the sun as it touched the horizon like a huge luminous yolk. The hills, alight in orange glow, briefly merged with the skies beyond. I imagined climbing up from the hills into that heavenly landscape. I wanted to cling onto the day, using every remaining moment of daylight to run and play in the fields before nightfall forced us to retreat within the safety of our enclosure.

At such a time it wasn't always easy for children to remember their responsibilities and chores. One of those glorious evenings my elder brother Sam and I were so engrossed in our games that we failed to notice that five of our calves had gone astray. They had probably heard the mooing of cows in the distance and followed the sound. Unfortunately we did not realise this until back in the settlement. Dreading father's rebuke we rushed back to the fields with one of our cousins in search of the calves, still carrying the javelins and sticks that we had been playing with. First we looked around the settlement in all the obvious places. Then we walked further afield, asking anyone we met along the way whether they had seen our calves.

"I am going to check near the well," our cousin announced. "If they aren't there I will quickly run home and call for help." With that he left us alone.

Daylight was disappearing fast and Sam and I were getting increasingly worried. The day usually brought out harmless creatures (except for snakes) but predators owned the night. Under the cover of darkness they emerged from their hiding places to embark on their vicious pursuits. Hyenas and leopards first – we especially feared the latter as they liked hiding in bushes close to human settlements and were able to climb trees, making it hard for people to get away from them.

We heard the mooing of calves in the distance but weren't sure whether these were ours. Although the sound moved further away we decided to follow it. By now the last rays of sunshine had given way to the soft glow of the moon.

"Look, over there," Sam suddenly whispered. "There is a cheetah. It is staring at us!" It turned out to be no more than an anthill. In the dim moonlight everything around us seemed to come to life. In our fearful imagination each tree and shrub looked like a dangerous creature. Walking along we hurled sticks and stones in the dark shadows around us to check whether anything was lurking there.

At last we spotted the missing calves. They were still moving further away from our settlement and we had to chase after them. All of a sudden two of the larger calves bolted off in different directions, not to try and get away from us but from something they had smelled. Something that caused them to panic.

Sam and I heard the vicious creatures even before their shadowy images appeared. Hyenas – a pack of three! For a moment they stood motionless when detecting us with the calves. Then, crouching down in the tall grass, they started creeping towards us. We knew we had to run home for help but by the time we got back with an adult the calves would be injured or killed! How could we ever tell father that first we had lost his calves, then found them, only to run off and leave them at the mercy of those horrid, cruel beasts? Being young boys of eight and six we were certainly not very imposing but we decided to try and frighten the hyenas away while rounding up the calves. We frantically hit the bushes with our sticks, making loud and threatening noises, even though inwardly we were terribly afraid. The hyenas became nervous and howled. Just as we thought we were making an impact they suddenly moved in on us, one from the left and two from the right close to where Sam was standing. We could clearly distinguish their hairy outlines and yellowish eyes glittering in the glare of the moon.

Hyenas were known to be opportunistic, cowardly creatures that normally took advantage of vulnerable prey. However, in a pack they could easily kill a strong adult if he became an obstacle between them and their prey. And these hyenas were getting angry. We screamed in the hope someone would hear us, perhaps one of our neighbours. The calves panicked and started running towards the hyenas. We shouted even louder to try and direct them away. I threw my stick at one of the predators and managed to hit its flank. It briefly withdrew.

"Simeoni, how can you let go of your stick when you need it most!" Sam rebuked me. He was right of course; our sticks were our main means of defence. Only moments later he thrust his own javelin at another hyena and it backed off too.

"And you know you should never throw your javelin at a wild animal," I retorted. We almost got into an argument.

With the hyenas prowling around us we managed to gather the calves and steer them towards the path. Then, out of nowhere, Simba appeared, jumping over bushes and barking like mad. Simba was our shepherd dog, a gentle giant, very protective of his owners but also a fierce hunter.

Under normal circumstances I would not have been happy to see that dog; we were not on good terms, Simba and I. He always turned up at the wrong moments. Whenever I tried to get close to a beautiful bird by sitting still for hours, almost holding my breath, he barged in and chased it away. And how could I ever forget what he had done to Mama Nunu!

Mama Nunu had been an uncommonly large and beautiful wild hare. While she hopped around I used to lie in the grass and tempt her with soft, juicy leaves until I could almost touch her. She was so special that we first named her Queeny. When she had given birth we called her young ones 'Nunu', meaning 'precious little things', and Queeny became 'Mama Nunu'.

But Simba had been eyeing the hare all along – he was obsessed with her! However much I tried to keep him at a distance, one day I saw him proudly emerge with his catch – Mama Nunu dangling from his mouth. Staring at me as though expecting a compliment he dragged her to the back of our hut and began to tear her to pieces. I looked after the baby hares as well as I could. A few of them did survive, but for a long time I could not help resenting Simba.

On this occasion, though, he was a welcome sight. Unknown to us Uncle Yokana had gone to look for us with the dog and one of our herdsmen. Upon hearing our screams in the distance, our cousin had rushed back to the settlement to call for help, only to bump into them on the way. While he was still busy showing them the direction in which we had headed, Simba had already found us.

"Go, get them, Simba!" we shouted, pointing at the hyenas. The dog bared his teeth. His growling and barking kept the hyenas at bay, giving us the opportunity to escape with the calves. Then we heard Uncle Yokana's voice calling out to us in the distance.

"Hold on, Sam, Simeoni. You are not alone! We are coming!"

We were so happy and relieved to see this tall, strong adult approach, but my uncle did not seem to reciprocate our feelings.

"Boys, how could you have done this!" he angrily exclaimed. "You should have gone home and alerted your parents. Being told off is not as bad as putting your lives at risk." But at the same time he could not help complimenting us. "The calves are alive; they haven't even been harmed. It's a miracle. Well done!"

For a while we were heroes to our friends when they heard that we had defended our calves against a pack of hyenas, but in reality we were terribly shaken. Back home an anxious mother awaited us, as well as a furious father. Thanks to a good word from Uncle Yokana we got away with only a serious warning. Not that there was a need for this though. The experience taught us a better lesson than words could ever have done. From that day on we made sure not to stray far from home at nightfall. We had learnt to be more cautious and respectful of time and nature.

Now our world had shrunk to the area within the enclosure where we found father and the other men busy milking the cows amidst smoky bonfires. It was ancient *Bahima* practice to burn heaps of dried cow dung, twigs and grass during milking time. This produced a dense smoke that helped repel the flies, thus preventing them from unsettling the cows.

Occasionally mother prepared us an evening meal from cassava or *matoke* (a type of banana only used for cooking) mixed with beans, greens or mushrooms. If someone in the neighbourhood had slaughtered a bull we also ate meat as meat was always shared out amongst the neighbours. While we sat cosily around, father roasted it in the fireplace. Sometimes we ate *enjuba*, a kind of black pudding made from cow blood. Traditionally it was believed to be beneficial to bleed cattle when they were very fat and only a really experienced herdsman, like father, was allowed to carry out the bleeding. He did this by tying two sisal ropes round the animal's long neck and darting an arrow from close range into a specific spot. Then, pulling out the arrow, he caught the flowing blood in a wooden vessel. Once he had collected enough he pressed on the vein and rubbed herbs into the wound, thus instantly stopping the bleeding. Mother boiled the blood with butter and spices into a delicious thick pudding that we shared with neighbours and friends.

On other evenings we just had milk. Adults could easily drink several litres and unless there was scarcity we never went hungry. We each had our own wooden milk pot, smoked by mother with a special type of grass to give the milk an even more delicious flavour. We also had a milking cow especially allocated to us. When father called out its name you knew that your supper was near. One by one he filled the pots with the rich, creamy milk that foamed and was still warm. When it was our turn to fend off the calves we had the additional treat of drinking the warm milk right out there in the open.

Uganda is situated right on the equator. This means that it always falls dark around six o'clock. Days and nights are equally long, regardless of the seasons. Our evenings were a time for socialising and having fun, with youngsters joining up with friends in each other's huts. Ours was especially popular. The place often resounded with laughter as we told stories, joked and sang worship songs, harmonising in multiple voices. While youngsters exhibited their comic talents the elders looked on and relaxed. Sometimes we sat together outside in the compound, our eyes glued to the deep blue sky – a magical expanse with countless stars sparkling above our heads like crystal chandeliers. Now and then we spotted one moving slowly or suddenly shooting by. The ground too was alive with tiny specks of flashing light, as numerous little fireflies known as *Enyonyozi* mirrored the twinkling of the skies.

"It is getting cold," mother called from inside the hut. "Won't you come inside now?" Unwilling to go indoors yet we looked for our favourite cows and snuggled up against their warm, glowing bodies, ever watchful of the massive horns. Our settlement was not totally protected. Leopards and cheetahs could climb over the enclosure or find a weak spot and break through. When cows caught their scent they restlessly sniffed the air, giving us an early warning sign to run inside and call the adults. The nights were filled with sounds: a chorus of crickets chirping all around us, joined by croaking frogs when the ground was soaked with rain. Large rodents scurried around our feet, looking for food. In the distance a lion roared and hyenas howled.

Without electric lights our world was a dark, intimidating place but when the moon was full our settlement and the surrounding fields were bathed in a dreamy, silvery glow. The brightness could give a false sense of security, enticing people to leave the settlement to go and visit friends, even if it meant walking through dangerous and overgrown terrain. Sometimes the men dared take our cattle out into the fields in the dead of the night for a stint of further grazing. The moist grass, softened by dew, was a special treat for cows and helped increase the milk flow. However, on such a moonlit night people could easily be attacked by predators lurking in nearby bushes!

Every hut had an indoor fireplace for cooking, warmth and light. Occasionally one of the households lit a large bonfire in the compound and that meant party time! We gathered round the fire, making ourselves comfortable in its warming glow. While the older men lit their pipes, the younger ones roasted meat and wild mushrooms. This was a perfect environment for telling thrilling stories. If we had elderly guests we could be assured of an interesting evening. Storytelling was our way of passing on history, knowledge and lessons of life from one generation to the next. We learnt about our *Ankole* dynasty and our ancestors, the *Chwezi*, with their extraordinary supernatural powers. Adventurous tales involving bravery, loyalty, friendship and love taught us that wisdom and decency were ultimately rewarded but that ill-fated decisions could lead to disaster.

Sometimes stories were so scary that my Aunt Esther, small and frail as she was, made a point of staying close to me and holding my hand in affectionate protection. As the plot unfolded, her eyelids drooped, her grip tightened and she brought my hand right up to her chest, looking increasingly anxious. It always gave me great comfort to notice that my aunt was even more frightened than me! However, on the day of our encounter with the hyenas Sam and I skipped storytelling and went to bed early. We had had more than our fair share of thrills.

As the evening progressed, *Balokole* families retired to their huts. Now the bonfires became a romantic setting for traditional *Bahima* men and women of marriageable age. According to our customs it was inappropriate for an unmarried woman to be seen intimately chatting and flirting with a man but within a group around the fire she could be more spontaneous and even dance without it being regarded as disgraceful. While young men danced and showed off their physique, women remained seated and displayed their elegance by seductively moving their upper bodies, arms and heads.

Grown-up *Balokole* preferred the calmer environment of their homes where they cosily sat together, talking, sharing testimonies and singing worship songs. Before long our evening drew to a close. The fires were put out and charcoal left to smoulder as smoke was known to have a calming effect on the cows. As we prepared for bed, my parents concluded the day with Bible reading, prayer and song. Unless something unusual was to happen that night, we would all be up again at the crack of dawn. Up for another day – days full of routine and yet always eventful. We might have been exposed to the challenges of nature but life was enjoyable and good. Surely, as a six-year-old child I could see no reason why it should not remain like that forever.

CHAPTER 2

DANCING WITH BUTTERFLIES

*"And we know that in all things
God works for the good of those who love him,
who have been called according to his purpose."*

Rom 8: 28

We lived in a remote part of central Uganda where cars could not easily reach. There weren't even roads. If we wanted to go to the market, visit relatives or attend a fellowship meeting in faraway places we mainly travelled on foot. Only a few *Bahima* were in proud possession of a bicycle and they did not always know how to ride it!

Whenever my parents had to walk a long distance they would ask one of their children to accompany them. This time mother intended to visit her sister Elizabeth in the *Balokole* settlement of Kikoma some ten miles away and I was chosen to come along. I was born in Kikoma but we had moved from the area when it became overcrowded and could no longer sustain everyone's cattle. Now we lived closer to my father's relations where there was still sufficient grazing land and water.

My father was usually out of bed first, way before the cock crowed, but this time I beat him to it.

"Are you well enough, my child?" mother asked me with some concern. "Do you really feel up to the journey? You boys have been so restless all night."

A few weeks ago Sam and I had swum in a pond and subsequently succumbed to a serious bout of fever. Even now we were suffering from headaches and pains in our limbs, only I seemed to be improving faster. While Sam was still bed-bound I was up and running, thrilled at the prospect of an outing with mother. In fact, my restlessness that night had not just been caused by fever but also by sheer excitement at the thought of seeing my cousins and friends again.

"Yes, mama, I'm fine" I eagerly cried. Had I admitted I was actually feeling quite poorly my parents would never have allowed me to go.

To prove my point I jumped out of bed and began my morning chores. First I helped fend off the calves which enabled father to milk our cows without their interference. Having impressed him with my help I now had to convince mother that I was fit enough to accompany her. I rushed out to fetch firewood even before she could allocate the task to any of her other children. Searching through a nearby bush I discovered some purple berries looking so irresistible that ignoring them would have been rude to Mother Nature who had brought them so close to our home. After feasting on various wild fruits I hastened my efforts to collect as much firewood as possible and hurried home with a huge bunch of dry sticks and branches.

My sister Miriam could not believe her luck.

"Mama, Simeoni is here with firewood!" she cried out in surprise and delight. With Sam ill in bed and me escorting mother she had clearly been concerned that she would be the one to carry out most of our chores.

"Well done, my child," mother praised me. "I cannot remember any of you ever going out this early to fetch firewood without having to be asked several times. If you still have any energy left, you had better get cleaned up. We should be on our way before the sun gets too hot."

Mother had carefully planned for our visit to be on a market day. The journey would take us through some densely over-grown and isolated terrain where leopards and cheetahs had been spotted. There were even rumours of man-eating lions. At least on a market day we had a chance of meeting up with other people. Their presence could help us brave areas that would otherwise have been extremely lonely and unsafe for a woman and young child travelling on their own. As we set off on our journey I endlessly chatted about all the scary things that could possibly happen to us. Clenching my small *Bahima* stick I was determined to protect my mama from danger. She herself did not seem too worried.

"As long as we walk with the Lord nothing can really harm us," she now and then interrupted my chatter. "Without his protection, the strength and skills of human beings are useless.

"Nothing happens without God's knowledge. Just remember, my boy, if anything terrible were to happen to us, he will use it to serve his ultimate purpose."

Her words turned out to be very true indeed, although at that time we had no idea of the kind of troubles awaiting us.

Our progress was slow. Mother was a heavy woman and we were carrying a lot of weight. Gifts for Aunt Elizabeth: a large calabash with homemade butter, a wooden pot of milk and another one for us to drink along the way. I helped mother carry our pot but my boundless energy and excite-ment made me almost spill the milk. She hastily took over. Now and then we took a long break to enable mother catch her breath. When people passed by on foot we resumed our journey, trying to keep up with our fellow travellers. The breaks gave me a chance to venture out and explore the terrain around us while mother rested in the shade. I climbed trees to look out for zebras and other animals that usually stayed clear of the paths. I chased after rabbits, searched for bird's nests and, of course, for wild fruits, roots and seeds. My favourite were *bihobohobo* – tasty, crunchy, oval shaped roots, like small potatoes, with a lovely scent. I discovered a *binyamakara* bush and filled my pockets with ripe, juicy berries. After all, I had promised my sisters to bring them some nature treats, to make up for their disappointment of having to stay home.

We passed through an area I had never seen before but I had heard much about its beauty.

"Please, Mama, can I climb that hill to see the view?" I asked mother, begging her to divert from the path. "Can't I go and find out what lies behind those trees?" The urge to venture out and absorb nature was overwhelming. I felt emotional in a way I did not understand. Running back and forth I asked her the names of everything new and was surprised at how much she knew.

"We'll only be gone for a day and a night," mother observed me amused as well as a little puzzled. "Tomorrow you'll have plenty of time to explore these places further!" Later she told me, "I always knew how much you loved nature but there was something unusual about the way in which you were indulging that day, almost embracing the hills and fruit trees. It was as if you were saying good-bye, like someone who is about to go on a long journey and knows he may never return."

The area was getting busier now with a network of paths leading up to the local market. Soon we found ourselves surrounded by scores of women balancing huge baskets with crops on their heads. Men were running up and down to keep their unruly livestock in check, their voices blending with mooing, bleating and the clattering of horns reverberating from all directions. The market took place only once a month and people came from far and wide to buy or sell cattle, food and goods.

A young woman approached with a large pot of *ghee* that she intended to sell at the market. *Bahima* women could use excess milk to make butter and *ghee*. Once they had accumulated enough they visited the market to meet up with relatives and friends and buy themselves something from proceeds of the sale. From a distance I heard mother and the woman exchange greetings with *Tukutendereza Yesu ('Jesus, we praise you')*, the widely used *Balokole* song of thanksgiving. Before long they were absorbed in conversation.

"At last something to distract mother," I chuckled. "Now she won't ask me to stick around all the time and keep her company!"

The woman had walked ahead of her father and young brother who were trailing behind with a couple of cows and bulls. Once they caught up I helped them steer the unwilling animals along the path. In an instant the boy and I became friends. He seemed to know a lot about nature and showed me the best places to look for fruits and roots whenever we stopped for a break. Together we stuffed our faces. I put loads in my pockets for my cousins and friends in Kikoma and some more for sharing with my sisters back home.

Rain had fallen not long ago and flooded the valley along the path with glistening puddle pools and shallow ponds. Around these, masses of brightly coloured flowers reached up to the sun, as though competing with the lush green surroundings to attract our attention away from other appeals. For a moment my friend and I stared in silent wonder at the colourful display below, struck by its tranquillity and beauty. Then my friend broke the spell.

"Last one down is a sack full of snails!" he cried out and we sprinted down into the valley, jovially chasing each other.

We soon discovered that the valley was anything but still. It was teeming with life and hidden treasures just waiting to be explored! We saw orange dragonflies with blue metallic wings, aimlessly shooting across the water in an acrobatic frenzy. White heron-like birds stood watching attentively in nearby shrubs and trees. Huge water lilies unfolded their blooms in soft-velvet shades; the pink-purple ones had nice tasting roots that were known for quenching thirst. My friend waded into the water, pulled one up and showed me how to chew the root and suck out the juice. I longed to throw off my clothes and go for a swim but mother would not have allowed that. After all, Sam and I were believed to have fallen ill as a result of swimming in a pond.

While we jumped about at the water's edge, many of the brilliant flowers suddenly came to life, as thousands of butterflies swirled up in the air, their wings dazzling in the sunshine. Yellow, orange, red, purple, blue, black-and-white with batik-like decorations on their wings – some were even larger than my hand! As they circled around us I dashed after the most beautiful ones, round and round as if in some hypnotic dance until I became dizzy and almost fell over. The butterflies quickly got used to us, landing on our skin like multicoloured confetti the moment we stopped moving. We grabbed them by the hand full, squashing several in our fists. A few agile ones flew up high in the air, only to be snapped up by watchful birds in the nearby trees.

Though many years have passed since, I still remember each and every detail, as though these have been permanently etched on my mind. All those wonderful colours, smells and sounds; the happiness I felt that day, culminating in my almost ecstatic dance with butterflies. The experience was so intense. I just wanted it to go on and on, as though I somehow felt that a time like this would never come again.

While the adults rested in the shade, my friend and I played around until we stumbled across the remains of a zebra. It had been savagely killed not long ago – the carcass was still fresh. I felt sympathy for the poor creature, knowing how easily it could have been a beloved cow or calf.

"There might be a lion around," I cried alarmed, as well as a little excited. "Perhaps it is still near!" In childlike ignorance

I showered the undergrowth with sticks and stones to avenge the fallen zebra.

"We better go!" my friend insisted. "Lions tend to walk off when they have devoured their prey but cheetahs and leopards stick around. There could be one in the vicinity.... It may be watching us!"

We hurried back to the group to tell the others and were sternly warned not to stray again.

It was a joyful journey, full of interaction and adventure. Unfortunately our companions needed to increase their pace to get to the market in time, leaving mother and me straggling behind. The distances covered between our breaks became shorter and shorter. Heat and exhaustion began to take its toll on mother, and our milk for drinking along the way was rapidly running out.

My headaches returned and I felt increasingly dizzy. Mother noticed that something was wrong but every time she asked me how I felt I ran off to prove to her how fit and well I 'really' was.

At long last we approached Kikoma. From a tall tree I caught a glimpse of thatched roofs and smoke billowing in the distance.

"Mama, I have just spotted the settlement!" I delightedly called out to mother. "It is to the left of the second hill." Disgruntled she told me to get down.

"No wonder you're feeling poorly, Simeoni! All this running and climbing would make anyone unwell." My return to the ground was clumsy, almost like a fall.

The remainder of our journey we covered in silence. Unlike before I stayed close to mother, subdued and deep in thought. My legs felt strangely weak and I tried to make sense of what was happening to me. Increasingly attentive mother threw an inquisitive glance whenever she saw me stumble. I could no longer muster the strength to just put on a brave face.

However, excitement took hold of me once more, mixed with relief that we were about to reach our destination. I spotted a group of young women searching for a special type of grass that they used for smoking milk and *ghee*. Looking for this grass was a social activity for *Bahima* women, providing them with an opportunity to catch up on each other's family matters and to share ideas, advice and news. They recognised us from a distance and burst into a joyful *Tukutendereza*. Our welcome had begun. Realising that some guests had arrived, children came running from nearby fields, among them several of my cousins. By the time we reached the settlement a small crowd of people had gathered around us even before our arrival had been properly announced!

We were seated inside Aunt Elizabeth's hut and given milk to drink. The exchange of traditional greetings and singing of *Tukutendereza* must have gone on for hours. According to our customs, everyone enquired in great detail after the state of affairs and health of relatives and loved ones. For *Balokole* this also entailed thanking and praising God, something that regained momentum the moment another person entered the hut.

We children, though, had better things to do than staying close to our parents and joining in the singing and greeting. We had to talk and play and impress each other with a bit of wrestling to show how much bigger and stronger we had become. My cousins and friends wanted to know everything about the new place we had moved to. As soon as I had swallowed my last drop of milk we ran off and scattered on the playing fields. There I emptied my purple-stained pockets to distribute all the fruits and roots I had gathered along the way. My sisters would have to do with whatever I could pick for them on our return journey.

Up to this point I had been driven on by adrenaline and a sense of adventure but now the 'illness' got the better of me and I could no longer suppress its symptoms. Shivering with fever I dragged myself back to the hut where my mother and aunt were deeply engrossed in conversation.

"Ruusi, this child has got severe malaria!" Aunt Elizabeth exclaimed, visibly shocked by my appearance. Before we could say a word she ordered for *ombirizi* to be boiled - a fever lowering plant also known as quinine. Abandoning her other guests she hastily prepared a bed for me in a partitioned corner of the hut, away from the hustle and bustle. Leaning against her lap I drank a whole mug of the horridly bitter tasting extract. Still unwilling to give in I asked her to let me know when it was milking time. I had so much looked forward to this last outdoors activity of the day, when together with my cousins and friends I would be fending off the calves and afterwards spend the evening cosily talking and singing in the moonlight. In vain I tried to convince her that an active 'young man' like me should really not stay indoors with the women.

That evening and throughout the night mother attended the fellowship meeting especially convened by the brethren to welcome us. Several times though she had to leave the gathering to come and check on me. I was disorientated and burning with fever, often crying out in my sleep.

"I have never seen a fever as severe as this," mother mumbled half in prayers and half thinking out loud. "If this illness is malaria then it is a type I have never seen before. Lord, what was your purpose for our visit here today? Was it to give Simeoni the chance to say farewell to our relatives and friends? Please, Almighty Father, keep my child alive!" When returning to the fellowship gathering she relayed the news about my worsening condition. It was suggested that anyone wishing to do so could briefly come and greet me. From time to time I would wake up to find someone sitting at my bedside - a child, a relative or one of the brethren.

During the journey I had been bursting with energy; I had climbed trees, jumped about and done all sorts of things but now I could scarcely raise my head or arms to greet the people I had so longed to see. Instead of proudly showing my relatives and friends how much bigger and stronger I had become, I found them quietly looking at me with sympathy and concern.

Our visit was meant to be brief with our return journey planned for the following day. However, that morning my legs could no longer support my weight. I had no grip left in my hands. As mother could not possibly be expected to carry me home one of the brethren offered to accompany us. With sisal strings he tied me onto the back of his bicycle to stop me from falling off. There I sat, slumped like a sack of potatoes. More people volunteered to come along to help me stay upright. In the end we set out on the ten-mile journey escorted by three men with two bicycles.

Mother was clearly spiritually revived and strengthened by the loving welcome and the overnight fellowship meeting. Having overcome her exhaustion and the shock of my sudden collapse, she was full of hope that, with God's help, I was going to pull through.

By now my aches and discomfort had escalated into an excruciating pain. It felt as though every part of my body was being chewed up, as though boiling liquid ran through my veins rather than blood. Still, I could not wait to see my sisters and brothers, especially Sam whom we had left ill at home. I had so much to tell them about the butterflies and all the other amazing things mother and I had encountered on the way to Kikoma. In my mind I was already planning our next visit when I would be better and have another chance of impressing my relatives and friends. Little did I know that this would never be the case. My running days were over.

CHAPTER 3

IN HEAVEN?

"This sickness will not end in death.
No, it is for God's glory
so that God's Son may be glorified through it."

John 11: 4

We reached our settlement safely and were greeted with a joyful *Tukutendereza*. Upon hearing the song, more people emerged from their huts until we found ourselves surrounded by a small crowd of inquisitive friends and neighbours.

"What has happened to Simeoni?"

"Why is he tied to a bicycle?"

"Poor child, has he had an accident?"

Mother explained that I had succumbed to a mysterious illness and that my condition was rapidly getting worse. I was clearly in a terrible state and everyone had an opinion about what this illness might possibly be, ranging from food poisoning to meningitis.

Neighbours took care of our escorts and prepared them a meal while mother put me to bed. Sam seemed to be much better now. He even strolled around a little. Noticing my brother's remarkable improvement I silently wondered whether it would not have been better if I had stayed home too! My condition deteriorated by the hour. Unknown to me people began to fear for my life.

Our escorts had to go back to Kikoma. They would have loved to stay until father returned from the fields, to be of comfort to him, but it was getting late. Before leaving they knelt at my bedside, laid their hands on my head and said a short prayer. They also spoke words of encouragement to mother and all those gathered in our home.

"Things like this happen to test our faith," one of the men proclaimed. "Forces of darkness try and lead us astray but we must always hold onto our Saviour!" Defiantly he broke into an uplifting worship song. *"Whoever is in the arms of the Lord has nothing to fear. Whoever takes refuge in Jesus can be assured of His comforting love."* Everyone around me joined in.

Bonfires were lit to repel the flies at milking time. I could smell the smoke. Soon father would be home with the cows.

When they gave him the worrying news about my state of health he simply refused to believe it.

"Only yesterday morning this boy was running around, fetching firewood and fending off calves," I heard him cry out to mother, "and now you are telling me he can't even get up by himself?" He came over to my bedside and rebuked me as though I were merely scared of feeling pain.

"Come on, son," he demanded. *"Get onto your feet at once!"*

I struggled to raise myself but couldn't. Father pulled me up to try and make me stand but the moment he let go of me I slumped onto the ground. The process of pulling and slumping had to be repeated several times before he was ready to concede that something terrible had happened to me. All of a sudden his promising, strong and active field-boy was lying there helpless like a new-born calf. The illness continued to torment me as if some little monster inside my body was gnawing away at my muscles and bones. My screams could be heard well beyond our hut and neither my family nor our immediate neighbours was able to get any sleep that night.

The following day every recommended herb was tried out on me but none could bring relief. My parents propped me up on a bicycle and somehow managed to cover the seven-mile distance to the nearest rural clinic. I was admitted as an emergency patient and seen by a Dr Patel. It did not take him long to recognise the symptoms.

"This disease is known as poliomyelitis," he pronounced. "It is actually quite rare in Uganda, although lately we are seeing an increasing number of cases. In Asia it is much more common." Concerned by my condition he advised my parents to immediately take me to the larger district hospital in Masaka.

"There is nothing we can do for him here in this clinic," he explained. "We can only try and keep the fever down in order to control the damage." When they told him that my brother was likely to have contracted the same disease, Dr Patel insisted on seeing him as well. After examining Sam a few days later, the doctor confirmed that for him the worst was over. And, indeed, my brother did make a full recovery.

There were no ambulances in the village. My parents had to look for a taxi. This was the first time for me to travel by car. It should have been hugely exciting but I barely noticed it.

At Masaka District Hospital the doctors examined me and confirmed that my illness was polio. They administered painkillers and oxygen which helped to stabilise me a little. However, the hospital did not have the necessary facilities to keep me alive and so they referred me to New Mulago.

New Mulago was the leading national hospital in the capital city of Kampala. Built by the British in 1962 as a gift from Her Majesty's Government when Uganda gained Independence, it was a highly modern hospital, staffed by specialist doctors and nurses, including many expatriates. Although taking me there meant an eighty-mile journey, it was my only chance. The doctors at Masaka offered to provide us with one of their very few ambulances – an old Bedford with basic equipment. They also allowed a nurse to accompany us.

Mother stayed with me but father went home. He had hastily abandoned everything that morning thinking that I would be admitted to the rural clinic. That would have enabled him to look after our household and cattle as well as coming to check on us daily. Besides, he quickly needed to sell a cow. Although my treatment in Mulago would be free, mother needed money to live on whilst staying in Kampala.

"What if things come to the worst and we lose our child?" she quietly asked him, daring to face the dreaded prospect that I might die in hospital. "I would need to hire a special vehicle to bring him home again."

"Try and stay in touch with me," father replied. "I will send you money as soon as I can and join you in Kampala the moment I have sorted things out at home."

There were no telephones in our village; there wasn't even a post office or a postal system. 'Staying in touch' meant that mother would have to pass a message to someone she knew and who happened to be visiting New Mulago. That person would then have to go to the central bus park in Kampala and look out for anybody travelling in the direction of our village who, in turn, could pass the message on to someone planning to visit our home. Any money father sent to mother would be delivered in a similar way, except that he might have to wait for the monthly market before finding an acquaintance intending to travel up to Kampala.

Amidst all the commotion mother stayed prayerful and calm. Now and then she soothingly sang to me one of her favourite songs. *"Those who believe in the Lord are never hopeless; they are indestructible like Zion."*

Her behaviour caught the attention of some members of hospital staff.

"You clearly love your child very much," one of the paramedics observed. "You know he is fighting for his life. Yet you don't seem to be falling apart as we often see happen to parents in your position. Where do you get this strength to pray and even sing to your son? Is it because you are a *Muhima?*"

"It is not me," she replied, "nor is this strength typical of the *Bahima*. I am not better than any other parent. This strength is a gift from the Lord. Instead of letting my emotions take over, I am asking Him to take control. I am putting God in charge of my child. If it is his will he can save him. This boy is also a Christian. He believes this as well. Any of you can have this strength if you place your trust in the Lord."

The man was clearly moved by my mother's faith. He kept talking about it to the nurse while together they tried to get hold of an ambulance. He had reached the end of his shift but instead of going home offered to accompany us to Kampala. Perhaps he thought that the journey might be too much for just a nurse and my mother. Or was he curious to know what would become of me? It was agreed that he would drive home in his own car and be picked up from there by the ambulance.

I was transferred onto a stretcher and laid on the floor of the vehicle with a small foam mattress beneath me for comfort, as the journey was going to take a long time. Mother and the nurse sat on a low bench beside me, gently holding my hands. Every bump in the road made me scream out in pain. Even their touch was painful, as though I was being burnt.

Unfortunately the ambulance driver could not find the paramedic's address. After driving around Masaka for a short while he decided to drive on to Kampala. My condition had become critical. There was no further time to lose. Mother told me later how some twenty miles into the journey she suddenly noticed a car behind us with its headlights flashing. It was the paramedic! When the ambulance failed to turn up at his house he had decided to come after us. After parking his car at a petrol station he boarded the ambulance and we set off together. By now it was getting dark.

I drifted in and out of consciousness, feeling weaker each time I came round. Even my speech was now compromised. The crew did everything they could to make me comfortable but in my mind I begged them to stop touching me, not to wake me up. The unconsciousness gave me somewhere to hide from the incessant, terrible pain. All I wanted was to be left alone and drift off into this fragile, pain-free zone. The last thing I remembered was mother's voice.

"You are God's child. Accept this, whatever is going to happen to you. If you are taken up to heaven, angels will be waiting to welcome you. Father and I will join you later. Don't be scared, my child, stay calm and hopeful. Before too long we shall be together again."

Now and then she interrupted her words of comfort and farewell with a brief prayer. They were like a lullaby to me as I slipped into a coma.

Unaware of what was going on around me I depend on mother's recollection and the stories from medical staff. Several times she tried to describe to me what happened on the rest of our journey, how her hope and faith battled with anguish and despair. At some point the ambulance crew thought they had lost me. The driver slowed down while the nurse and paramedic made frantic attempts to resuscitate me.

"Is it really worth going all the way to Kampala?" they debated amongst each other. "This child could die at any time!" When mother heard this she prayed even more fervently. Shortly afterwards the crew managed to pick up my pulse.

"There is still some life left in the boy," the paramedic announced with visible relief. "Let's drive on."

It was nine o'clock in the evening when the ambulance reached New Mulago.

Four *Muzungu* ('white') doctors were waiting for us. Masaka District Hospital must have informed them that a polio case was on its way. My lungs had collapsed and I was rushed to the Intensive Care Unit. The doctors tried to put mother off from following me, saying that this was a place 'full of electrical machines for saving people who were on the brink of death' but she was not persuaded.

"If those machines can't hurt a person as sick as my son then surely they won't harm me either," she retorted and determinedly stayed put at my side.

I was laid in an iron lung. This is a large cylinder-shaped ventilator with pumps for changing and controlling the air pressure within. Once sealed inside, the constant fluctuations in air pressure caused a patient's lungs to artificially inflate and deflate, thus emulating natural breathing. Mother described the iron lung as a huge metal drum with a stretcher inside. It made lots of noises and tilted so that my legs were sticking up and my upper body faced downward. Only my head was visible. That was all she could see to know whether I was still alive.

"You were almost upside down," she recalled later, "the way a nurse holds a new-born baby by its legs to help it start breathing. Weak as you were, I wondered how on earth you could survive such unusual treatment!" Through an interpreter she put the question to the doctors and nurses who were rushing around with drips and needles, pushing all sorts of tubes into my throat, nose and other parts of my body. A pump drained fluid from my lungs into a glass container. It was such a distressing sight that they asked her to move away. Instead she watched me from a corner.

"I would rather not stand here helplessly," mother muttered to the paramedic who had stayed beside her throughout. "I am better off doing what I know best, which is to bring myself and my troubles to the Lord in prayer." At this the paramedic nodded in agreement.

"In the short time we have spent together you have shown to be a serious Christian," he thoughtfully responded. "Your child is in a deep coma now. To have any chance of surviving he will need all of your prayers and faith." She asked him to join her and together they prayed. Mother prayed very emotionally, pleading with God while thanking him for me, for my life however short, and for making me his child.

"Lord Almighty, our great and wonderful Father. You know how much it tears me apart to say this... but... if it is your will that the life of our dear Simeoni must end then please accept his soul into your kingdom. You know our wishes. You can see the pain in our hearts!. We have already lost three children: our eldest son Karanzi and two others in their infancy. Lord, the power is yours. You can restore Simeoni to us!"

The place was quiet now, except for the bleeping, buzzing and vibrating noises resonating from the machines. Once in a while *Muzungu* doctors congregated around my iron lung, quietly talking amongst each other. Nurses came in to administer medication through the tubes and drips or to empty the bottle of fluid drained from my lungs.

Mother stayed with me in the intensive care unit throughout my time in coma. During the day she watched from a distance and at night she slept in a corner on a small mattress the paramedic had given her. Only much later she told me of her emotions.

"I felt strong and hopeful until I spotted a person lying under a sheet being wheeled out of that room on a trolley, followed by a group of wailing people. When I asked them what had happened they told me that their loved one had passed away. Over time more patients were brought out on trolleys covered up with sheets. That is when I realised that people were actually dying in that place and I truly began to fear for your life. I had to distract myself from despairing by praying more fervently for you as well as for the souls of the departed, asking the Lord to comfort their families."

I was surrounded by radiant light, much brighter than any I had ever seen. The pain had totally gone. Around me images appeared of beings. White people, black people, all dressed in white clothing. They seemed to be looking down at me.

"We will meet in Heaven," echoed mother's voice in my mind. "Don't be frightened, my child, angels are waiting for you."

It was such an amazing, unimaginable sight. The intense brightness, the light, the people! In a state of wonder and anticipation I tried to take in the fact that I had actually died.

"This must be it. This is Heaven – the new life my parents have often told me about!" No sooner had I thought this than my nose detected a horrible smell. Something like chemicals or medicine – so different from the lovely nature scents I was used to. The air was full of it.

Only able to see in a blur I found myself locked in a monstrous, metal box that made odd vibrating and ticking sounds. Struggling to regain my sight I looked around the intensive care room, so brightly lit. Never before had I seen the radiant glare of electric lights.

In a haze I noticed the foreign doctors and nurses gathered around my 'box', dressed in smart, white uniforms. They were the very first *Muzungu* ('white') people I ever set eyes on!

"Your child is trying to open his eyes," the doctors called out to mother. For three days they had kept her at a distance while I lay in a coma. Now they summoned her to come closer and talk to me. It took several hours before I showed further signs of consciousness. Meanwhile mother sat beside my iron lung, singing and speaking softly until I moved my eyes again.

"Simeoni, my child, do you know who I am?" With my impaired speech I tried to say that she was my mama. Mother burst into *'Tukutendereza'*, thanking the Lord while the paramedic translated her words to the *Muzungu* doctors and nurses.

"Oh, Lord, you have spared my child's life, even though he has been swallowed up by this massive machine and all I can see is his head!" At long last my mother broke down. I began to cry too. I tried to wipe the tears from my cheeks but I couldn't. I wasn't even able to raise my head or move my neck. All I could use were my eyes but even my vision was compromised. As consciousness returned so did the excruciating pain. The doctors administered more medication and eventually I dropped off into an uncomfortable, troubled sleep.

The paramedic joked to mother about her crying.

"You seemed so calm when we thought your child was dying and now he has come round you have become all emotional…"

"That doesn't mean anything," she replied. "These tears are what *Balokole* call 'weakness of the flesh'. Today the Lord has wiped the sorrow from my heart!"

He told her that none of the specialists had expected me to pull through and how glad he was to have stayed around to see God do this miracle.

"In the past few days I have discovered something very precious that I do not wish to lose. I want to try and follow your Lord too." They discussed how he could get in touch with other Christians. Mother gave him the names of some *Balokole* living near Masaka District Hospital and we later heard that he had joined their fellowship group. He also managed to convince the nurse, who had travelled with us in the ambulance, to come along with him.

Over time she too became a Christian.

It took several weeks before I could breathe unaided. I was then moved from the intensive care unit to a ward where my treatment continued. Over the next two months the tubes were removed. I regained my speech but not much more than that. I had to be fed like a baby. The doctors told mother that, even though I was out of danger, I needed to stay in hospital for long-term medical care and rehabilitation.

"It might take years," they said, "but there is a chance of significant recovery." Now mother faced a difficult choice. For some three months she had stayed with me in New Mulago, neglecting her home and other children who needed her care too. My youngest sisters Priscilla (whom we called Peace) and Joy were only toddlers. Father had still not come back to see us. It had been too difficult for him to leave our home and cattle unattended, though he had managed to send mother the promised money.

The hospital staff suggested that I be left in their care and discussed with mother how best to prepare me for this. Should she quietly disappear or say 'goodbye' at the risk of upsetting me and destabilising my condition? They decided to test my reactions by pretending that she had gone.

"You know how much I love you," mother said to me one morning while sitting at my bedside. "Even so, I may have to leave you to check on your brothers and sisters. You will have to stay here in hospital where the doctors and nurses will try to make you better. It is for your own good really. The Lord has spared your life and he will also bring us back together again."

While she gathered her few belongings, the *Muzungu* nurses came into action to distract me. Speaking to me with soft, soothing voices they put little toys and magazines on my bed – fascinating things I had never seen before. I was unable to understand what they were saying but could recognise the universal language of kindness and care. I stared at their eyes, captivated by the unusual shades of blue, grey and green. Had I been able to move my arms I would have touched their fair hair and skin! But before long the attraction wore off and I began to ask for my mama. Through an interpreter the nurses broke the news to me.

"Your mama has gone to check on your family. She will be back quite soon. In the meantime we will look after you and when you are strong enough you can go home too." They said many kind and comforting things to me but I was no longer interested. I burst into screams of panic and shock, refusing to stop until I almost passed out. In any case, my lungs were so weak that it took very little for me to run out of breath. Just saying a few words required a huge effort.

Meanwhile mother was standing out of sight near the ward entrance, waiting to see what would happen, praying for wisdom as the sound of my voice faded into merely a moan. When she opened her eyes the matron had joined her, ready to have a word.

"Your son is in quite a bad state after all that screaming and crying. I am optimistic though that we can calm him down and make him get used to your absence. Would you like to go ahead and leave now?"

"It isn't right for me to abandon my son," mother replied. "I feel it deep in my heart." She went over to my bed where I lay breathless and choking, surrounded by a flurry of nurses. After watching me for a moment her mind was made up. She turned round to the matron.

"Now my son has survived a coma I will not let him die here of a broken heart. His father will agree with me. If something were to happen to him now we will always think it was our fault. I must take Simeoni home!"

The decision mother made that day has made a huge impact on my life – emotionally, spiritually and even physically. Before contracting polio I was a happy child, surrounded by a loving family and vibrant *Bahima* community. My upbringing was founded in Christian values and fellowship wrapped in *Bahima* traditions. Being left in the hands of strangers for a prolonged period of time would have suddenly stripped me of that. Later in life I met people with a variety of disabilities who had been abandoned by their parents at a young age, left to the care of institutions. These parents might have had their children's best interests at heart but many grew up feeling rejected and dislocated from their families and culture. To them it was as though the moment they became disabled they were no longer considered good enough to go on living with their loved ones.

By taking me home in this pitiful state and with a very uncertain future my parents showed that they loved me just the way I was. They trusted that God would look after us regardless of what people might think or say.

Their decision not to leave me behind in hospital at such a young and vulnerable age has spared me from ever becoming embittered. I have faced many challenges in the years that followed, including long periods of absence from my family, but at least I was given the opportunity to bond with them and my culture. My parents made me feel loved at a time when it mattered most.

CHAPTER 4

WAY OUT

"When I called, you answered me…"

Ps 138: 3

The doctors at Mulago agreed to discharge me, but only with great reluctance. They would have preferred to keep me in for observation and a prolonged period of physiotherapy and rehabilitation. They knew that we lived in a remote area where medical facilities were basic and not within easy reach. In the circumstances, the best they could do was to give mother instructions for my care.

"Make sure that your child does not lie down all the time," the doctor in charge told her. "Put him on your lap as often as you can, like a baby, and hold him upright with his back stretched between your arms. In that way his spine will get used to taking the weight of his body." He emphasised the importance of continued medical care.

"Without intensive rehabilitation your child's ligaments will contract; his spine may become distorted and he could develop scoliosis. The next seven years will be crucial." Mother enquired whether scoliosis was a life threatening condition.

"Indeed, with lungs as weak as his, scoliosis can shorten his life," the doctor replied, not knowing how wrongly these words would be taken. Somehow between mother and the interpreter it was understood that I was going to die within seven years. As a result, my family and everyone around us were convinced that I would not live beyond my thirteenth birthday. Not until a review appointment several years later did we find out that this was actually not the case.

"If my son takes a turn for the worse I will come straight back to you," mother promised the doctor, "even if it means leaving all my other children in the care of someone else." She was made to sign a declaration that my discharge was her own voluntary decision. The hospital could not be held accountable for any deterioration in my condition, nor be responsible for my death.

"And how do you propose to transport your child home?" the doctor grumbled without being interested in her answer. Mulago hospital did not provide us with an ambulance. Whether this was because of the bad feeling created by my forced discharge or because there was none to spare, I do not know. How I got home was the least of my worries. I was looking forward to going back to my family and friends to be able to show them that I had survived after all! During my stay in New Mulago several patients had died. Although the nurses had tried to hide this from me, the suddenly empty beds and grieving relatives had not escaped my notice. Having overheard mother and the interpreter, it began to dawn on me that I too might not get better and the thought of being left behind to die in hospital was utterly terrifying.

I'll never know how mother managed to carry me out of the hospital complex, together with the small mattress the paramedic had given her and a few other belongings. I was tall for my age, even taller than Sam who was eight years old. With my neck as floppy as that of a newborn baby I was like a dead weight in her arms. Every movement of her body made me cry out in pain. A taxi dropped us off at Kampala Central Bus Park where we made our way through the crowds.

The bus park was packed with people. In those days buses and coaches were the main form of transport in Uganda for anyone travelling long distances. There was only one railway line leading all the way from the Kenyan coastal town Mombassa via Nairobi to Kampala and on to Kasese in the north west of Uganda. The number of buses travelling in any direction depended on the remoteness of their destination. Some places saw a bus only once a week. There were no timetables; a bus simply left when it was full. This normally meant that a stampede of passengers scrambled into the vehicles to claim a space for themselves and their luggage. Buses often carried double their capacity with every inch of floor space taken and passengers sitting on each other's laps. Roof carriers were used for additional luggage, like bicycles, mattresses, baskets with live poultry and sacks of food. Occasionally young men opted to sit there when a bus was overcrowded but that was quite precarious. It was not uncommon for people to fall to their death on those long, high-speed journeys over rough and bumpy roads.

The bus to Bweera was filling up rapidly. The conductor shoved us into the congested vehicle without paying any attention. I felt safe in mother's arms – the best place I could possibly be – until a fellow passenger bumped into her and pushed her over. I looked at mother's face as she stumbled and fell backwards, all the while struggling to protect me.

"Yesu, my child, my child," she cried out. She burst into tears and I instantly joined in.

"Holy Mother Mary," came a shout from a nearby seat. A woman had been watching us and noticed our predicament. She got up and made her way to the conductor to give him a piece of her mind.

"How dare you fail to look after a mother carrying her sick child?" Reluctantly the man halted the queue in order to let us pass, instructing passengers already wedged into their seats to shift.

"I knew you could do it! I knew you would help," mother uttered happily once she had found us a little space. The kind woman overheard her and somehow seemed a little offended.

"How can you praise the conductor when he has treated you so badly?"

"I wasn't talking to him," mother replied. "I am complimenting the Lord in Heaven for taking care of us once again." From experience I knew that this was a good excuse for mother to start talking about God. She always used every opportunity to explain her faith to others. In conclusion mother thanked both the woman and the conductor for the part they had played in God's work.

Once the excitement of boarding the bus had died down I was able to focus on myself. This was the first time in over three months that I had left my hospital bed. The painkillers given to me that morning were beginning to wear off. Tightly squeezed on my mother's lap my body ached all over. I could see it was equally uncomfortable for her. I examined the faces of the passengers sitting around us. Some looked at me with pity; others were clearly ill at ease. Was this a taste of things to come? I had known blind and crippled people but never anyone so totally disabled and helpless as me. Suddenly I could not help imagining what a stir I would cause among the people back home when they saw me in my current condition. How different I must appear from the boy they once knew. I used to be strong and active and now I could not even raise a finger. Besides, the hospital had all the necessary facilities. Whatever I needed was just brought to my bed. Such care and attention would never be possible in our rural home where everyone was required to help out with looking after our household and cattle. How was I ever going to manage...?

The bus was jam-packed and still not moving. I noticed by the expression on my mother's face that she was becoming increasingly troubled. If we failed to reach home before dusk she would have to find a shelter for the night. That would mean knocking on people's doors in an unfamiliar area while carrying me and our luggage.

"O Lord, what shall I do?" I heard her quietly pray. She began listing the names of any *Bahima* acquaintances along the way whom we might be able to approach.

All of a sudden the conductor disrupted her deliberations.

"Out!" he bellowed, "Everybody out! This bus has mechanical problems and will have to be taken off the road." Now there was definitely no chance of us reaching our settlement that very same day. The sudden announcement left mother undecided. Should she look for another bus to take us at least to Masaka or spend the night in Kampala and travel to Bweera the following day? But where could we go? We were unfamiliar with the city and knew hardly anybody there.

The Good Samaritan woman had stayed nearby to make sure that we were all right.

"Why look so troubled?" she called out to mother. "You *Balokole* tend to know the Bible better than we Catholics do. Do not worry! You could not have foreseen that I would be here to support you. I will find you a seat on another bus!"

I interrupted the conversation that followed, choosing the worst possible moment as young children so typically do.

"Mummy, I need a wee. I can't hold it any longer." Now mother's attention was switched to the immediate concern of finding me a toilet. While the kind woman went to talk to the conductor on the next bus destined for Masaka, mother set off to enquire around the bus park with me and her luggage in her arms. As we were manoeuvring through the masses of travellers a voice suddenly rang out behind us.

"Ruusi, Ruusi, thank God you haven't left yet!" Mother turned round only to stare in the face of Mattayo. We had first met Mattayo at New Mulago where he worked as a paramedic and lived with his wife in the staff quarters. They were both *Balokole* and during our time in the hospital had regularly called in on us for worship and prayer, always bringing along some delicious home-cooked food.

Mother was greatly relieved to see her brother-in-Christ. For a brief moment I too forgot all about my discomforts. The two exchanged greetings and mother offloaded her troubles to him; how the bus had broken down and it was getting late and she did not know what to do... Meanwhile Mattayo just smiled.

"I am so glad to have found you," he warmly replied. "When I got to the ward this morning I was told that Simeoni had been discharged and that you were heading for the Central Bus Park. I have got such good news for you!" I could not wait to hear what Mattayo had to tell us, wondering what good news one might expect from Kampala. Certainly it could not be from the hospital!

"We received guests from Sembabule yesterday with a message for you. Your husband is on his way! We are expecting him in Kampala this evening and he will be spending the night at our home."

I could see the relief beaming across mother's face. Father's presence would make our return journey so much easier. She burst into *Tukutendereza*, ignoring the curious glances from people around us. Mattayo hailed a taxi and told her not to worry about the expense; this would be shared between him and father. We could all spend the night at his house. Everything was taken care of.

My mind drifted away from their conversation as I reflected on how important praying really was. Father's imminent arrival was a clear example. In the midst of all the noise and chaos of the bus park the Lord had heard mother's cries for help and shown a way out. At home I had often witnessed events being influenced by prayers, not only in my parents' lives but also in the community around us. Difficult situations were resolved, sick people healed and the bereaved given strength to go on. When my condition was critical mother had never given up praying. Wasn't the very fact that I had survived polio an example of how God heard when we called out to Him? Until this point in life I had largely relied on my parents' faith but there, at the bus park, it began to dawn on me that I too had access to this awesome Authority over circumstances and events. By faith and through prayer I could enjoy an audience with the most powerful God who was able to influence every situation. This realisation was very exciting. I did not have to be an experienced Christian like my parents. Even with my compromised strength I could whisper a prayer and the Lord would hear me. Having seen mother's troubles lifted off her shoulders I told myself to stop worrying about the reactions of people back home or how I was going to manage. I would just look forward to seeing father again and let God sort out everything else.

We were about to board the taxi when mother suddenly turned round and ran back towards the bus park with me still dangling in her arms. She had spotted the kind woman patiently waiting near the entrance to one of the buses.

"You haven't given up yet, have you?" the women called out from a distance. "Is there something wrong with your boy?"

"We will be spending the night in Kampala," mother exclaimed. "I have just heard that my husband is on his way to collect us!" The woman was clearly relieved.

"Well then, it must have been the Lord who stopped the bus!" she responded with a streak of humour. "If there had not been mechanical problems you would have certainly missed him." Mother whole-heartedly agreed. The two went on to exchange words of encouragement and blessings while Mattayo kept an eye on the taxi and the driver impatiently hooted.

Exhausted by the morning's adventure I was glad to be lying down again, this time in the comfort of Mattayo's home. Our hosts did everything possible to make us feel at ease and welcome. Mattayo's wife prepared a bed for me in a small room adjacent to the sitting area and cooked us a lovely lunch. She kindly offered to help mother with looking after me but I made it quite clear that I preferred my mama, so most of my care fell on her. Besides feeding, I needed to be turned over regularly because prolonged lying on one side was painful and restricted my breathing. My arms and legs had to be frequently shifted so as to bring relief, aid circulation and avoid pressure sores. A further dose of medication helped settle me down, giving mother a much-needed break. While I snoozed the adults spent the rest of the afternoon reading the Bible and praying.

Father arrived in the evening, to be welcomed by mother and our host with a jubilant *Tukutendereza*. With the door to my room left ajar I could hear the incredible relief in mother's voice as she greeted him.

"Petero, thank God you have finally come!"

"Where is my boy?" came father's reply. "Is he here with you?"

"Yes, he is resting in the spare room."

"Simeoni, you are alive," father cried out while making his way towards me. Feeling a shout rise up in me, I struggled to push out a sound but my voice was not yet strong enough. How I wished I could run up to him, the way I used to do when I caught sight of him in the fields returning from a long day's work. I was always one of the very first to fall into his arms and welcome him home. Father was still talking when his face appeared in the doorway. I greeted him with a broad, tearful smile.

"My child," he exclaimed, "I have been so fearful for your life. We kept hearing rumours that you had lost consciousness. People told us that you were dying!"

He tightly grabbed my thin, frail body, holding me close to his chest. I instantly felt a sharp pain jolting through my flesh but the joy of seeing father worked better than any pain-relieving drug. I just wanted to remain in his arms as long as possible. For a moment he was lost for words; then he joined mother and our hosts in singing *Tukutendereza* to praise and give thanks to the Lord. Finally he let go of me and gently wiped the tears from my face. He looked at me intensely before turning to mother.

"Ruusi, God has given us our child back. I thought I would never see him alive again!"

It had been very difficult for father to travel up to Kampala. For many weeks he was unable to raise the necessary cash, as the authorities had closed the local cattle market while investigating symptoms of foot and mouth disease. Also Sam had taken long to fully recover. And, of course, father could not just leave our home to the care of our neighbours. They all had their own families and livestock to look after. Every household needed at least one strong adult to guard it against dangerous predators. Only when one of my uncles arrived to stand in was father able to join us.

He poured out the anguish he had felt while being stuck at home. Next mother updated him on what had happened since we parted in Masaka, how close I had been to death.

"Will our son live and get better?" I heard him ask in a low voice.

She told him of the prognosis given by the doctor via the interpreter at the time of my discharge.

"They are giving him only seven years but it may very well be shorter."

Both my parents agreed that, regardless of my condition, God had given me back to them. Whatever the future held in store for us, they would continue to thank the Lord and praise him. They talked well into the night until, drained by the emotion and exhaustion of the day's events, we all dropped off into a fairly uninterrupted sleep.

It seemed years since I had been awoken by song. Listening to my parents and our hosts praying and singing worship songs at the first light of dawn I realised how much I had missed the early morning fellowship. It already felt a bit like coming home.

After breakfast we hurried off to catch a minibus to the centre of town, reaching Kampala Central Bus Park in no time. The chaos there was still overwhelming but this time we were better prepared. Mother knew what to expect.

"We need to catch the attention of the bus conductor and ask him to help us get onto the bus," she said to father. "Yesterday's experience was awful. Simeoni can't go through that again, especially not with such a long journey ahead of us."

Father was a seasoned traveller. We had relatives living all over the country – wherever the environment was conducive for cattle keeping – and he visited them as often as he could. He headed for the conductor who swiftly allocated two seats to mother and me. Now I could lean on her lap rather than being squeezed in her arms, while father stood nearby in the gangway. It was not long before some distant acquaintances spotted us. Deeply touched to find me in this pitiful state they went to great length to show how sorry they felt for my parents.

"How terribly sad this has happened to you!" one of them tearfully exclaimed. "What future can there be for this child? Oh, would it not have been kinder if God had spared you from this suffering and taken him to rest?"

The thought of being better off dead had never occurred to me. Alas, it was something I would often have to hear, throughout the years of my childhood. For now though I was determined not to be disturbed by those insensitive remarks. Nothing was going to distract me from the thrill of the journey. I had never been on a bus before; such an enormous vehicle filled with so many people! We passed fields and forests, valleys and hills. Father had something interesting to tell about everything that caught our eyes.

"That road leads to Nsangi parish where your mother and I went to Bible School and were baptised.

"Your Uncle Daudi's settlement used to be behind those hills. Several of your cousins were born there."

There were so many exciting and wonderful things to be seen. It was an incredible experience for someone who, until recently, had only ever been surrounded by nature. And so we happily retraced that terrible journey mother and I had undertaken by ambulance, just over three months ago.

The bus stopped in a trading centre along the way. Mother raised my head so I could see the vendors swarming the bus, shoving chunks of fried cassava, roasted meat and bottles of juice through the windows to entice the passengers into buying. Some people disembarked and even more boarded. We got off in Masaka, not far from the district hospital where I had briefly been admitted. Masaka was the second largest town in central Uganda where travellers from all over the region mingled on their way to different destinations. Walking around to look for a taxi we met several relatives, friends and brethren from my parents' fellowship group. Everyone went out of their way to express their sympathy and concern. Some tried to hug me but mother was ever so protective.

"Be very careful with Simeoni," she warned. "Even the slightest touch hurts him." One Christian traveller thoughtfully looked at me for a moment.

"If God had wanted to take your son to heaven he would have done so straight away. There is a special reason why his life has been preserved. We must praise the Lord and pray that he will solve all your problems!"

His words were a great encouragement. Slumped in mother's arms I listened to the conversations between my parents and other adults. To my surprise everyone seemed to know a family somewhere with a disabled child (though not necessarily as a result of polio). Perhaps I was not going to be the odd one out after all!

The taxi took us to the small town of Kagologolo where father had left his bicycle when travelling up to Kampala. He bought a large tin washbasin from a street vendor which he tied onto the bicycle carrier. After padding the basin with his coat and some pieces of cloth he propped me up inside, securing my posture with rubber straps.

The final leg of our journey my parents had to cover on foot. The terrain around our settlement was far too rough for vehicles. Even though father manoeuvred the bicycle with the greatest possible care, every hump and bump on the ground made me cry out with pain. Now and then he took me from the washbasin and continued pushing the bicycle with one arm while carrying me in the other.

Although the day was rapidly advancing, it still felt uncomfortably hot. Several times my father and mother needed to rest in the shadow of a tree. Moving away from towns and traffic the pace of life seemed to change as though time itself was slowing down. Every person we met on the way stopped to greet my parents and enquire after their visibly ill child. Even total strangers offered to accompany us and hold our bicycle or luggage so that father could free his hands and carry me for a while.

Throughout our journey mother kept reflecting on the many difficulties we would have encountered without father's presence. So many things could have gone wrong had he not been with us. Another reason for thanking God for his divine wisdom and planning.

Gradually the scenery became more familiar. My excitement increased with every step taken. Although I could not move my head, every so often father turned or changed position, enabling me to cast my eyes in a different direction. I spotted *Bahima* women in traditional clothing looking for a special type of grass. Colourful *Ankole* calves jumped around in the fields. Cattle mooed in the distance. Then, to my delight, an unmistakable glimpse of long, white horns towering among the bushes.

For the past three months I had lived in a strange urban environment. Bright electric lights, discordant noises and the artificial smell of medicines and disinfectants had continually battered my senses. Until that day at the bus park I had never even inhaled vehicle fumes. Now, as we approached our settlement, the beautiful surroundings embraced me with tranquillity and peace. Birdsong filled the air. A revitalising freshness greeted me, treating my nostrils to the wonderful scents of flowers, fruits, animals and soil. As if nature itself went out of its way to welcome me home.

CHAPTER 5

STRANGER

*"...but we also rejoice in our suffering,
because we know that suffering produces perseverance;
perseverance produces character; and
character hope."*

Rom 5: 3-4

Cries of happiness and shock engulfed us as we entered the settlement. There they were, my brothers and sisters together with a large group of relatives, neighbours and friends. The word had passed round that we were on our way and they had all gathered, anxious to see us and find out how I was. It was a heart-warming, emotional welcome, as laughter blended with tears and the reality of my condition began to sink in. I must have been a distressing sight with my neck too weak to support my head, unable to move a limb. My lungs were so compromised that with wide-open mouth I continually gasped for air. People stared at me baffled and dismayed.

"Poor child!" I heard them exclaim. "Look at the state he is in! He is still as sick as ever!" Only mother and I really knew from what depth I had risen. That I had been in a coma and initially could not even breathe without the support of an iron lung. It was common knowledge in Uganda that hospitals sent terminally ill patients home when nothing further could be done for them. Many who saw me that day believed that my condition was still worsening.

"Not even a modern hospital like New Mulago has managed to cure Simeoni," they said to each other. "He still has to be carried. He is weaker than when we last saw him. The *Muzungu* treatment has failed. Petero's son is dying!"

Rumours spread fast. Mother's attempt to explain what the doctor had said upon my discharge wasn't of much help either. It only confirmed that I did not have long to live, as dying within seven years could just as well mean any time soon.

Mother was greatly relieved to be reunited with her family again after three long months in Kampala. She had missed the regular worship with her *Balokole* congregation and was longing to share with them all that the Lord had done, as well as confess her moments of weakness and despair.

Although I had younger siblings I was now the baby in the home, in need of care throughout the day and night. It was no longer possible for my family to attend church services and fellowship meetings together. Everyone was needed around the home to assist mother in caring for me and keep the household running. To provide spiritual support the brethren offered to hold weekly worship meetings at our place. They also helped out in practical ways, as did many of our relatives, friends and neighbours. It was customary that whenever serious illness, injury or death occurred in a family, relatives came and stayed in turns for a length of time to give physical and emotional support. Most days our home was full of people.

My family was deeply affected by my current state of health, though they tried very hard not to show it. One day a close family friend came to visit us with her little daughter. The pretty girl stood at my bedside, staring at me with large, thoughtful eyes. Then she turned to her mother and innocently asked, "Mummy, do you know when Simeoni is going to die?" I could see the pain flash across my sisters' faces.

I had so much looked forward to being home again, but very soon day-to-day life revealed unpleasant realities. In those days we did not have toilets; we used the abundant nature around our settlement instead. I was a very sensitive, proud boy who tended to walk long distances to make sure that no one could see me in my private moments. Now I had to ask someone to carry me out into the fields, watch over me and even give practical assistance. This made me feel terribly uncomfortable and I dreaded each new day. Many hours could pass before I dared confide in mother or one of my sisters, especially when there were guests or neighbours around. Even so, it did not take long before my situation became public knowledge. And, to my great embarrassment, my friends got to know about it too.

How much I had missed my friends! So many things had happened since we were last together. I had not even been able to tell them of my visit to Aunt Elizabeth's settlement, let alone my awesome stories about New Mulago hospital and being looked after by *Muzungu* doctors and nurses. It was good to be with other children again, even though talking to them took a lot of effort.

I was yet to realise how much my life had changed. Every morning, after prayers, my family dispersed to get on with their activities and chores. My older sisters Eseza and Phaibe left for school while Sam and the others took the calves into the fields for grazing. Of course, they could not be expected to stay indoors with me all day! So I lay on my bed, unable to move, staring in the direction my head was placed, waiting for something to come into view. A fly crept up the wall. I followed it with my eyes. It flew off only to land on my face. The itching made me restless. I twitched my eyes to try and chase it away but it was determined to stay put. The sun beamed through the entrance of the hut, casting reflections on the wall. These briefly changed whenever somebody passed by.

"Perhaps one of my friends has come to see me," I would think with a flash of hope and excitement. At last something was going to happen to help me get through those long and boring hours! I could hear children laugh and play in the distance. Soon I became an expert at recognising voices. Those were my friends, noisily chasing each other, a game we often used to play. From what I could hear, they were near the trees behind the neighbours' hut. In my mind I painted a picture and imagined joining in, running with them and laughing, until my dreams were interrupted by a sudden jolt of pain.

Why, I wondered, did they never come to check on me? They used to turn up every morning very early, calling me out to play and take the calves for grazing. Now days could pass without me seeing any of them. Why did they behave like this? I felt like saying sorry to them for not being able to play anymore and letting them down. Perhaps then they would like me again and enjoy being in my presence. I pondered over these things, trying to understand. Who were those friends of mine? What did friendship really mean? Did it only work when people were strong and well? I missed being out there with my friends, but it seemed that now I was no longer like them their friendship had gone away.

I waited for someone to come in and turn me over so I could see what was going on inside the hut. People came and went. My eyes followed them as far as I could. Day after day I lay inside our hut, waiting and watching the world go by. Before contracting polio I would never sit still for one moment. Now I was like a baby helplessly lying in a cot. There was only one huge difference: whereas babies do not know any better I had the faculties of a grown boy. I remembered my life as it was before and I missed all the things I used to be able to do.

The physical pain was relentless too. It consumed every part of my body. I could not even move my limbs or rub myself to try and get relief. I had to wait for someone to come in, hoping that they would have enough time to listen to me and give me a hand, but people were not always near. In those days I wept a lot. Quietly, as I was still too weak to cry out loud. Tears soaked the bedding beneath my face, making my skin all itchy. If one of my sisters came in I would ask her to raise my head and scratch my cheeks. Even such a slight movement worsened the pain and increased my unhappiness about being so totally and utterly dependent on others.

In an attempt to stop me from feeling so miserable my siblings organised play-time with me. It did not take much to cheer me up; I longed for excitement and fun. However, for them it was not easy to know how far they could go. When they made me burst into laughter I often ended up choking, in turn sending them into panic. The opposite was even worse: if left to cry inconsolably, overwhelmed by emotions and pain, I would run out of breath, start shaking all over, roll my eyes and then pass out. Mother did not need to be told whenever this happened. Upon hearing her children scream and cry she would drop her chores, rush inside and try all sorts of things to resuscitate me while my siblings anxiously looked on. Following episodes like these it often took a long time before I had enough strength just to open my eyes and communicate again. It was a tense time for all of us. Our emotions were constantly in turmoil.

Before becoming disabled I could be grumpy all day if a thorn in my foot prevented me from running around in the fields. Now I was in constant pain, only able to watch others as they moved about. I found myself wrapped in a strange, hostile body that could do absolutely nothing for itself. How dramatically my life had changed. I could not run and play in the fields. I could no longer graze calves or fetch firewood or water. I would never be a useful son in the home! On the inside though I felt very much alive. My faculties and feelings were still intact. I was able to listen to people, be a good friend and empathise with those who suffered. I had love; I could appreciate the love of others, and those feelings only seemed to grow stronger. In spite of everything I loved my life and wanted to make the most of it. It was as if God shone his light on the things I was still capable of doing to give me reassurance.

"You are the same child," he was telling me, "Only your body has been affected. Don't lose hope. I have a purpose for you!" Once this became clear I began to look forward to making use of whatever was left of my body, even if it was just my voice or my smile. This attitude filled me with hope and faith that things could only get better. I was not a lesser human being. I too had every right to be happy and loved. Some *Balokole* children even began to enjoy sitting around me, attracted by my zest for life and cheerful response to humour. And so, over time, it became easier for me to accept my situation and let go of everything I had previously taken for granted.

While I slowly learnt to deal with my own feelings and reactions, it turned out to be much harder to come to terms with the attitudes of other people towards me. Everyone could see what had become of Petero's youngest son. How I had to be fed, washed and dressed and could not even wipe my dribbles and tears. For some people it was less difficult to accept this than for others.

"Every person has imperfections, whether visible or invisible," was the Balokole point of view. "In the eyes of the Lord we all need to be made 'whole' again. One day he will restore Simeoni to full health and happiness in his Kingdom."

One of these *Balokole* was my Aunt Mangyeri, a close and loving family friend who never had children of her own. She was very affectionate with large, loving eyes and an ever-joyful smile. Rather than crying over me or treating me in a different way, she took my frail hands into hers and just kept praising God.

"Simeoni, you are still here. You are talking and smiling," she often used to say. "Thank you, *Yesu*, for keeping this child alive." When her beaming smile shone into my face I forgot about all my discomforts and pain. Her cheerfulness was contagious and her attitude an encouragement to us all.

A lot of people, however, no longer knew how to relate to me, especially those who were not Christians. Some kept a distance on purpose, perhaps because they did not know how to handle their own feelings. Others called in on us just to have a peek at this freaky boy with his peculiar condition. When visiting children wanted to go and see me their mothers often held them back. "Stay here!" they might say, "There is nothing left of Simeoni that is worth seeing." Such was the emotional outlook on disability in a society traditionally so intertwined with nature, where health and strength were vital for one's welfare and survival.

Many times I found people at my bedside intensely watching me with expressions of grief on their faces. Like that old family friend who just stood there, struggling with tears while leaning on his stick. When interrupted by mother he lamented, "This boy always used to welcome me by running into my arms."

I enjoyed it when people remembered my past but they always seemed to end with the same hopeless tone. *What future is there for this boy? A decent funeral would have been more bearable than seeing him in this pitiful state!* At that time I did not understand that love could make some people desperate and say such terrible things. To me it looked as if they were wishing me dead. I tried to make sense of this change in them, wondering how well I really knew these people. Had they not become strangers to me as much as I to them? Who still accepted me the way they used to, before I was struck down by polio? Even people with genuine love were behaving differently. They were now constantly tearful and fretting over me. The facial expressions of those around me revealed their unspoken thoughts. Whether sympathetic, over-protective or simply put off, hardly anyone behaved the same towards me. The ease of communication had gone.

Sometimes people turned out surprisingly kind, as was the case with Jovia. She was a girl in the neighbourhood who used to dominate our group of friends before I became disabled. She was a little older and stronger than me but I could run faster, which helped me get out of her way whenever she tried to pick a fight. Among all the children I dreaded seeing her the most. I was sure she would bully and slight me now that I was totally helpless. But despite her tough nature Jovia had tender feelings, something I had not recognised before.

At first she just stood at my bedside, staring at me and watching the adults get on with my care. Then she began to copy them and pull me onto her lap. By the time I was strong enough to be taken outdoors Jovia had more or less adopted me. She took it upon herself to watch over me, fending off snakes and anyone trying to tease me. As a result, other children who would rather have kept away from me were gradually drawn in by her example.

Mother keenly followed the instructions given by the doctors at New Mulago upon my discharge. She showed my aunts and older sisters how to seat me on their laps while keeping me supported in an upright position. Over time, my breathing and talking became easier. Then finally, after months of patience, my upper body began to grow stronger. First I was able to move my head and look in whatever direction I wanted. This gave me the confidence to ask to be taken out in the open. Lying under a tree I could breathe in the fresh air and watch other children play. Sometimes they came over to talk to me or show off with their games. Although I could not physically take part, it made me feel involved, distracting me from pain and any feelings of hopelessness about my current situation.

Things were not always pleasant though. Not everyone in our settlement was *Balokole* or Christian. Some naughty children took advantage of the fact that I was no longer the strong boy they used to look up to. When no one was around they snatched the little toys that had been put beside me for looking at and keeping me entertained. Others threw stones at me or made teasing remarks. Being outdoors also exposed me to curious passers-by who wanted to see a 'dying person'. They came and stared at me, whispering things I could not hear. I dreaded this kind of attention as it was always full of pity. Sometimes I could not bear the negative interest my presence was attracting and had to ask to be taken back indoors.

Then I began to gain movement in my fingers. Not enough yet to hold a cup on my own but to grip something small and light, like a spoon. The muscles in my arms began to tingle. After a while I was able to use my arms a little. That made big difference. Now, whenever someone brought me a small toy I could move it myself rather than having to wait for another child to play with it for my amusement. When we played *nzara*, a traditional 'dice' game with beans, I no longer had to ask others to throw my turn as well as their own and keep the scores on my behalf. If my friends raised my arm I could drop the beans all by myself! Slowly I also learnt to sit again without needing to be held upright on someone's lap. Instead they could prop me up against a tree or the wall of our hut, which was a huge improvement.

After months of patiently waiting, my recovery seemed to be on track. Almost every week there was a sign of progress. Each new movement was received with great excitement, as though I were an infant learning to crawl or take its first steps. On my part though, I had to forget that once I used to run like a deer across the fields and climb the tallest trees. I had to adjust my mind and learn to look forward to the tiniest improvement rather than regret the loss of the boy I once was.

Around that time I caught a nasty bout of flu. Many people in the area got it but I seemed to be affected more than others. I ran a high temperature and rapidly got weaker. My cough developed into a chest infection which left me gasping for air. This brought back memories of the hospital's prognosis of my untimely death. My family feared the worst and rumours swiftly spread about my deteriorating condition.

One evening the local reverend came to our home with a few brethren to say a farewell prayer. It was deeply distressing to hear him administer the special blessing for the dying. I wanted to tell him, "I believe I can fight this. Look, I'm not going to die!" but just drawing breath took such an effort that I had no strength left to speak. My improving health, albeit slow, had given us new hope but in a matter of days that was shattered. Hearing all the fuss and crying around me even I began to wonder, "Perhaps they are right. What if I am really dying?"

Treatment with traditional herbs and modern drugs helped me get through the worst. We realised that my relapse had been no more than a common flu. I had just reacted more severely because I was less strong than other children. I made a full recovery but the sudden deterioration of my health had reminded my family of the fragility of my existence. Even though I felt victorious, having cheated death yet again, it took a long time before they dared hope that I still had some more years of life left ahead of me.

The *Bahima* were constantly surrounded by untamed and hostile nature. Illness, injury and death were never far away. Even so, they were proud of their looks and very particular about physical perfection, the way they perceived it. A *Muhima* could be unwilling to marry someone with a small defect like a deformed fingernail or a missing tooth, let alone somebody who was severely disabled. Despite Christian influences, this attitude was deeply engrained in our culture. Even having an 'odd' or disabled person in the family could compromise the chances of the other siblings marrying well. Whenever a special event took place, like a wedding, funeral or birth, conversations inevitably ended up touching on my misfortunes.

"Poor Simeoni, he will never get married."

"Even if he were to survive, he'll never be a useful person."

Hearing those discouraging words challenged my optimism, making it hard for me not to feel hurt and sad. The *Balokole* in our community did all they could to make me feel loved, encouraging me to focus more on the Lord and to invest my hopes in the life hereafter rather than on people and things here on earth. The closer we lived to him, the less the world could tempt or harm us. This state of spiritual alertness was typical for *Balokole*, who believed that we should try to remain righteous before God at all times so as to be ready for His kingdom. In practice, this meant praying to God the moment dark thoughts entered our minds, before they could turn into sinful ideas and deeds. In my situation, hopeless feelings about people's attitudes towards me and painful thoughts like *'I will never get a girlfriend'* or *'I won't live long enough to see my brothers and sisters get married and have children'* could easily lead to self-pity and lack of gratitude to God. I learnt to share such negative thoughts with the brethren and pray with them. This always brought an immediate relief. It felt like being spiritually renewed – wiped clean, giving me deep peace with God and with other people, including the ones who were hurting my feelings. In time this increased my resilience, helping me cope with the practical inconvenience of being disabled.

The hardest part for me, however, was to surrender my worldly dreams and aspirations and set my mind on God alone. We Christians are meant to live in expectation of His kingdom; we know it could come any day but often feel we have all the time in the world. For me it was urgent to focus on God. I had to be ready to face my Creator, for I was thought to be dying, and every day could be my last.

And so, between the age of six and eleven, I was groomed for life in heaven.

Ever since returning from Mulago I had been suffering from terrible nightmares, especially after a difficult day. All these nightmares had to do with dying or not being able to defend myself from danger. One particular dream kept returning, leaving me terrified and breathless, almost to a point of passing out.

'I am back in Mulago, surrounded by people in white coats. Their faces are partially covered by masks, their large eyes staring at me from behind dark spectacles. They grab me, tear me from my mother's embrace and with extremely long arms lower me into a large, metal box that looks just like a coffin. The box has no bottom. It is just an endless pit. I sink deeper and deeper until even my head is no longer visible. I know why they are doing it. They want to make things easier for my family. When I die I will already be in a pit. There will be no need for anyone to bury me.'

"What about my mama?" I scream. "I want her to see me. Don't leave me here alone. Don't forget about me! Tell mama to come before I totally disappear." I struggle to free myself but have no strength. Stuck in that box I am totally helpless.'

Every night my family had to wake me up and calm me down. While my physical recovery continued, so did my scary dreams.

"God has helped Simeoni through polio and other setbacks," my parents wondered, "but are we really praying enough for him?" Mother came up with the idea of holding nightly vigils for me with some of the brethren, among them my Aunt Mangyeri. Night after night they sat at my bedside, occasionally touching my head, singing hymns and praying until morning.

One night there was a breakthrough. I woke up from a nightmare feeling less terrified. The brethren prayed for me once more and I dropped off again. My next dream was frightening but did not have anything to do with me dying. It was about the end of the world and the return of the Lord. I woke up and told those sitting around my bed about my dream.

"It was scary, yet different from my usual nightmare. I dreamt about the coming of the Lord! *'There was darkness, thunder and lightning. People were running around, screaming and pleading for forgiveness. And then a multitude of angels appeared...'* Thinking that it might have to do with all their talking to me about God's kingdom, they were encouraged by the change in my dreams. The next vigil was held with one specific purpose – to ask the Lord to permanently change my nightmares into Godly dreams. If dreaming about his kingdom symbolised my imminent death, then at least may hope replace my anguish!

That night my nightmare about the metal coffin vanished forever. Instead I dreamt about the coming of the Lord, only this time in a 'fuller' version. I have dreamt this dream many times, also later in life, and it is ever the same, only sometimes I see different people. It is more vivid than any other dream and always comes with this message: *'Listen! Prepare! You can never be ready enough!'*

I always wake up puzzled after this dream, speechless and shattered, the way you feel when you have been crying deeply. I know that my words are inadequate to describe this dream but I will try.

'The world is covered in deep darkness. The earth quakes. People tremble with fear. There is great tremor everywhere, from outside and within!

Then a breath-taking spectacle begins to unfold before my eyes. Amazing heavenly beings appear. The skies are filled with angels, emerging from the left and from the right. In the middle is an enormous, illuminated cloud and through it shines the dazzling light of the Lord. It is almost blinding, yet so fascinating that I want to keep looking at it. From the cloud the image of the Lord emerges – a huge body of light... I can't quite make it out.

The image takes on a more humanlike shape as it gradually draws nearer; nonetheless it remains spectacular. Above and beyond the image extends a magnificent sky, glowing like a diamond blue sea. On its right is a giant living being that looks a bit like a lamb. The air is filled with wondrous music and song.

There does not seem to be a particular instrument or tune. The sound is crystal clear and deeply moving, bouncing off the soul even before it reaches the ears.

On the left the earth remains unusually dark. Here the dead rise up and come to life, preparing to hear their judgement. I gaze at them, hoping to recognise someone I know. Many are restless, weeping bitterly. Still, there is a sense of anticipation. Angels of the Lord tell them to calm down, the way you soothe a child when it is frightened.

"Be still, just wait for the outcome. The Lord knows you. He can forgive you."

On the right, in the far distance, I see more dead people. Their appearance is faint, yet bright, and they don't seem to be too fazed by what is happening. They are more jubilant than the living, their voices echoing the ones of the angels. Some of the living move into their direction.

On the far left beyond the horizon lies a dreaded place, a danger zone. One instinctively begs and prays never to be taken there.

In the middle, near the horizon, is a mass of water like a wide river. I stand with the living in front of the water. There is great commotion among us – a mayhem of lamentation, anxiety and fear, mixed with excitement and elation. The young ones, like me, seem less terrified than the adults. Everyone, though, has the same reflection, "What is my fate? Have I done enough?" Some praise God with shaky voices, their worship full of pleading. Others try to run away. There is time for people to interact with each other.

"This is awesome!"

"It must be true!"

"This is the Coming of the Lord."

The living also talk to the dead but these don't seem interested. Their attention is solely focussed on the Lord. Eventually to put our minds at rest they answer back.

"Yes, we know you. There is nothing we can do for you now. You must look up to the Lord. Only he can save you!"

We are overwhelmed by emotions as our whole lives are laid out before us and we wait for the Lord to pass judgement. His presence *is awesome. Power and glory surround him. Yet he radiates great mercy and calm. I feel no terror, even though I am trembling with fear. Spectacular things keep unfolding while he speaks. There is deep peace in every word he utters but the people before him remain anxious as they await his verdict. His words do not enter through the ears but radiate deep into the heart, as though the soul knows before the ears can hear. The closer the Lord comes, the greater the tremor within me.'*

Then I wake up.

Spending my days lying under a tree I had plenty of time to observe the splendour of God's creation, as far as my eyes could stretch. It gave me great joy to imagine how anything beautiful here on earth would be even more glorious in heaven. No longer could the word 'dying' fill me with fear. Whenever people talked about it, which happened frequently, I began to think of it as an adventure – something exciting rather than shocking. I loved to hear Bible verses about God's kingdom.

"Tell me about it. Where does it say that there will be no suffering and pain?" "How will this make up for my life as it is now?"

Often I had deeply interesting conversations with other Christians about heaven, wishing these to go on and on. Over time I learnt to avert sadness by seeking closeness to the Lord. He was my one and only consolation. He helped me rise above my disability, the prejudice and pain – even find happiness! I often thanked him that no one else in my family was in my position. The thought of my little sister Peace or any of my other siblings suffering the way I did was just unbearable. As long as my relationship with God was good he would comfort me with his peace and reassurance. I could always count on his love and it was there in abundance. I feel privileged to have been given the chance to discover this at such a very young age.

CHAPTER 6

A CHARCOAL LANDSCAPE

"When you walk through the fire
you will not be burned;
the flames will not set you ablaze.
For I am the Lord, your God,
the Holy One of Israel, your Saviour."

Isaiah 43: 2b-3a

Two seasons came and went without rain and the effect of this on the land was evident. The once lush, green pastures were brown and dry; the hills lay bald under the scorching sun. Huge clouds of dust whirled up in the air, driven on by a searing, blustery wind.

We had moved to Izinga several months ago as it was one of the last places with sufficient grazing land and water. Now even here the wells had become small, muddy puddles. We had to dig deep to find any groundwater from which we could drink. There was not enough water to sustain our herds. Our beautiful *Ankole* cattle – our livelihood, our pride! Weakened by hunger and disease they collapsed one by one under the weight of their horns. It broke our hearts whenever yet another cow succumbed to some trivial illness that could otherwise so easily have been treated. Peasant tribes in the area suffered too. Their crops were dying, plantations withering. There was very little food to go round and, worst of all for us *Bahima*, hardly any milk.

Over the past year a large number of *Bahima* had settled in Izinga to flee from the drought. On a positive note, this had been wonderful for social life. Under normal circumstances, families of the same clan used to live together in one settlement and *Bahima* settlements were quite dispersed. According to our customs men were not allowed to marry from within their own clan. They had to travel far to look for a bride. In Izinga people from many clans were brought together, creating a large community that flourished and buzzed with activity. Old family contacts were revived, youngsters made new friends and numerous marriages took place locally. For my parents and other *Balokole* Izinga provided a wonderful opportunity to further advance the word of God. Christian fellowship groups sprung up all over the area with many more people accepting the Lord.

But there was a downside to such concentrated living. It placed a huge demand on the area's resources, with people, cattle and wildlife all competing for the last remaining grass and water. Our council of elders played an important role, not only in solving domestic problems and disputes but also in deciding how to deal with the shortages. They determined which herd could graze where and rationed the water so that cows were allowed to drink only once a day in spite of the terrible heat. True to our Bahima traditions and customs we helped each other out, sharing the cows and milk we had with anyone in need. Had we not been so united in facing the challenges together, the situation would have reached breaking point.

Then fires began to break out. Every time one was extinguished another ignited elsewhere. For more than a week we saw flames shooting up on the horizon, lighting up the night sky with a bright orange glow. To us children it was a spectacular sight.

"Wow, just look at that light," we cried out in excitement. "That fire must be huge!"

"That one wasn't there before. It is moving in our direction!"

We could easily have watched all night had our parents not urged us to come indoors. The grown-ups were only too well aware of the dangers, although they tried very hard not to show this. Every night we went to bed without knowing how much further the fires would spread. Of course I could not walk around our settlement to see what was going on but there were plenty of rumours.

"Women and children have arrived from western Izinga. Their homes are destroyed. Some men have been killed while fighting the blaze!" With shock I realised that this was only a few hills from where we lived.

"Have you heard? Mr Matovu was burnt to death when trying to save his plantation. Thank God, the rest of the family has managed to escape!" Mr Matovu was one of the local banana plantation owners with whom we used to barter milk for food. Seeing the anxiety grow on the faces of the adults, my excitement turned into fear.

A large bush went up in flames near the other end of our settlement, fortunately away from the wind. But on our side a forest was burning. Although still in the distance the fires were moving visibly closer, posing an imminent risk. Defying the intense heat and smoke, father and every other strong man rushed out of the settlement with freshly cut branches to beat down the flames. Meanwhile women and older children ran to the wells to fetch water, filling up every container they could find, even our milk pots for drinking. This was to be used as the last resort, in case our homes were to be engulfed.

For a whole day and night the men fought the blaze, just about managing to keep it at bay, but by the following morning the fires were advancing again. Away from the wind a large stretch of forest had been destroyed overnight, leaving all of nature in turmoil. Birds circled above the smoke as their nests went up in flames, snapping up the insects fleeing from the heat. Wild animals ran around restlessly. I had never seen them so close to our home! Then the wind began to turn, blowing burning particles right up to the enclosure. A few terrified cows and goats escaped, only to be trapped in the flames and perish. Even though the adults were deeply alarmed they tried to spare their younger children from these gruesome details, knowing that we would not be able to handle the shock and fear. Still, we had some idea of what was going on. We could see a wall of fire closing in on us from all directions.

From time to time one of the men came running back to the settlement to check on us and give the latest update.

"It is overwhelming. So-and-so has just succumbed to the smoke. We've had to carry him home!" All day long the men fought the fires; we had not seen father for hours. Around the settlement zebras, monkeys, pigs, antelopes and other wild animals emerged from the undergrowth to flee for their lives. When it comes to the awesome force of bush fires, all living creatures are equally vulnerable and insignificant. For three terrifying days and nights people and animals faced the same enemy – a raging, smoking inferno. At night an orange glow pierced the darkness while during the day our sight was clouded by thick, black smoke. We were hardly able to breathe.

On the third morning the fires had reached the enclosure at the other end of the settlement. I saw women run around in panic, their small children crying with fear. Upon hearing the commotion a couple of men rushed back from the fields to come to their aid. Next, one of the huts caught light. This time teenagers and women joined in to fight the flames. At this point our community faced a difficult decision. Should we abandon the settlement or stay put to try and save our homes and possessions? The men managed to make a firebreak around our settlement and a corridor for us to move through in case we were forced to leave. From then on they put all their efforts into keeping these areas safe.

That evening we were told to prepare for evacuation. My brothers and sisters gathered whatever belongings they could carry and everyone assembled in the centre of the settlement. Among us were the women and children who had recently fled from western Izinga. I was small enough to be carried on the back on an adult but stretchers were needed for the older sick and the elderly, and these had to be made from sticks and poles. But where could we go with our cattle? I listened to the debates going on all around us.

"Leave this settlement only to be killed by wild animals? At least the enclosure gives us some protection at night."

"The little calves will run off in panic and die! Yet, if we don't take them with us, they won't survive either!"

"If only we had left earlier…, when the fires were further away!"

How could we ever make our way through that furnace? If we found ourselves surrounded by fire, the sick, elderly and very young could never be expected to run through the flames. We would all be burnt alive! Once more the decision to evacuate was put off. Every free moment the believers among us came together to pray and sing worship songs, but some non-Christians were bitterly cursing.

"Why bother talking to that God of yours," they argued. "Don't you see that he is destroying us?"

Everyone was coughing badly. For days we had hardly eaten or drunk; only prayers kept us going. Mother watched over us as well as she could. Now and then she called all her children together to encourage and comfort us. *"Yesu is seeing all this. He will show a way out!"* Then, in the early hours of the fourth day, an utterly exhausted father came to tell us that the fires had been brought under control. Thank God, we had survived. Sadly, many wild animals had not been so fortunate. Already crowded together in a relatively small area because of the drought, they had proven an easy prey for the flames. The air was filled with smoke and the stench of burnt flesh.

For once we were allowed to have a lie in, but father and mother were up earlier than ever to consider our immediate future.

"There are no pastures left for our cows. The longer we stay here, the weaker they'll get. We won't survive unless we leave now!" In huts all over the settlement similar discussions took place. "There is not a moment to lose. If we stay we will die!"

The fires had not just destroyed grazing land and natural habitat. Almost overnight our large, thriving *Bahima* community disintegrated, as households had no other option but to fend for themselves and go their own way. We had grown so close to each other, with families bonding through friendship and marriage. Everyone had reaped the benefits, with the men working together and the women helping each other out. We children were never short of playmates. It had been a happy time in spite of the hardships and drought.

Nevertheless, many families were reluctant to build another large settlement elsewhere. We had learnt how detrimental it could be for so many people to live in a confined space, placing an overwhelming demand on already limited resources. Not that there would have been much prospect of finding an area that could sustain everyone. The search for green pastures would take people on desperately long journeys, crossing with their cows into Tanzania or walking hundreds of miles to north-eastern Uganda, as far as Karamoja. Some went to remote parts of the country where tribes lived with alien, hostile customs, such as cattle rustling, witchcraft and human sacrifice.

And so, after the traumatic experience of bush fires came the added grief of having to split up. No one ever looked forward to the drudgery of breaking up a settlement but much greater than this was the sense of loss and regret.

Almost overnight the social fabric of our community had been torn to pieces. Saying goodbye to all our friends and neighbours was emotional and painful.

"Children, it's time for morning worship. Soon I'll be off to find out whether there are any pastures left for our cattle... or whatever is left of them," father woke us up, his tired voice summarising the crisis. Getting out of our hut we were instantly struck by the sight of sheer devastation. No longer the fertile hills and valleys as we knew them. Instead a vast charcoal landscape stretched out before us and, within it, the smouldering carcasses of countless zebras, monkeys and deer. The tall trees, once home to many nesting birds, now charred and bare. The wind blew over the blackened fields. Ash clouds blinded our eyes. I felt so sorry for all those creatures that had lost their lives in the flames.

Miraculously, a stretch of land near one side of the enclosure had been left untouched by the fires. I saw rabbits, snakes and birds clinging onto the withered bushes. Here we could leave our cows to feed on the dusty, dry grass for a day or two while father went to look for new pastures. In the distance a few more isolated patches had escaped the blaze. It did not need an adult to realise that, had we decided to flee the previous night, our survival would have been very doubtful.

Father did not even wait for a morning drink. Starting the search he set off on his bicycle, but not without leaving us with clear instructions.

"Get ready to start packing. If I am not successful in finding grazing land nearby we will have to break up our home and move!"

A few hours later uncle Yokana arrived with worrying news. Although he lived three miles away from us their area had also been burnt! From mother's remarks I knew that this was one of the places where father had hoped to settle. Uncle Yokana confirmed that father had been informed of the situation but had decided to cycle on and look further afield.

Reluctantly mother began to put some milk pots together and organise the packing. Still she clung onto the hope that father might be successful. If only he would find some grazing land not too far away. Then she could wait with me in our hut while father and the rest of the family moved our cows and belongings to the new location and build a settlement there. That would spare me from the considerable risks involved in spending nights out in the open without the relative safety of a proper shelter and enclosure. Uncle Yokana tried to reason with her.

"Do you really think you can protect yourself and your son in a deserted settlement? Are you as brave as Mrs Karugaba?"

Everyone knew the story of Mrs Karugaba. She was the wife of a drunkard who tended to spend all their money on drinks. Often he returned in the dead of night, exuberantly singing and shouting. On one of these nights, as he was making his way home, a lion had besieged their settlement. From within their hut Mrs Karugaba could hear her husband's distant voice gradually getting closer. She anxiously turned to prayer – if only she could warn him before it was too late! But the lion did not wait. It jumped over the enclosure landing on top of the couple's hut, causing the roof to almost cave in. Without further thought, Mrs Karugaba grabbed her husband's spear. Calling out "*Yesu*" she thrust it upwards through the roof, right into the lion's chest. With the spear still wedged in its body the animal leapt to the ground in front of the hut. There neighbours came to her aid and finished it off. A little while later Mr Karugaba arrived, jovially singing, blissfully unaware of how his wife had just saved his life through an extraordinarily brave deed.

No night went by without us hearing lions roar in the distance. It was common knowledge that once lions had tasted human blood they always came back for more. Of course Uncle Yokana was right.

Darkness fell but no one was in the mood for our usual time of singing and story telling. Mother called us all together in our hut to lead us in evening prayer. At this point my uncle became furious, ready to storm out in protest.

"I am not going to take part in this meaningless worship of yours," he yelled with great indignation. "Your God! Only a couple of days ago he tried to roast us and our cattle alive!" My uncle was not a Christian.

"Yokana," mother calmly replied. "If, as you say, the bushfires were started by God's power, then that same power can also rescue us from our current situation."

Soon afterwards everyone went to bed, exhausted by the turmoil of emotions, insecurity and many sleepless nights.

While we anxiously waited for father to return, Uncle Yokana stayed around to assist in the running of our home. By now our cows were mooing unhappily from hunger and producing only a few drops of milk. As time passed we realised that father must have gone much further than anticipated. The last person to meet him told us that he had seen him heading for Uncle Daudi's area, some fifteen miles away. I spent the days in front of our hut, staring at the blackened hills and whirling ash clouds, my eyes wandering where once my feet used to run. Without any trees and shrubs I could see further than ever before.

It took four days for father to return. From a far distance I recognised him by the way he walked beside his bicycle, a skill I had mastered ever since becoming confined to one place. A few youngsters ran out to greet him. As he drew nearer I looked up to his frowned face covered in dust and sweat, telling the story of an unsuccessful mission. Yet, God had to be praised. Mother burst into *Tukutendereza* to welcome her worn-out husband home.

He sat down and drank a bit of milk as we anxiously gathered around him.

"Looking at your faces I wish I could give you better news," he sighed, "but things are even worse than expected.

Last night I met up with Uncle Daudi who was actually getting ready to come this way and see us. His problems are even more pressing than ours. His village has been swarmed by tsetse flies that are heading this way as we speak."

Tsetse flies were known to cause a terrible illness, turning strong and healthy people and cattle into unproductive, sickly creatures, eventually leading to an untimely death.

"*Yesu*", mother exclaimed as she carefully poured father a little more milk. The list of misfortunes seemed to be growing and growing. Drought, diseases, fires and now pests. To *Bahima* people this could mean only one thing: the death of our beloved cows and consequently an end to our unique way of life and traditions. Until that moment mother had stubbornly clung onto her faith, as though our problems were only small trials and rescue would fall from heaven any time.

"There is only one thing left to do, dear people," father concluded. "We have no time to waste. We must be on our way and find a safe place before the tsetse flies reach this village. By tomorrow Uncle Daudi will be here with his cows. Then we will start our expedition together." For the first time I could see that mother's faith had taken a pounding.

"If we are not going towards Daudi's area you must be thinking about the River Katonga," she cried out with some despair. "But that is almost forty miles away from here! Simeoni is too frail for such a long and arduous journey. He'll never make it!" She glanced at me full of love and concern as I meditated on what was to become of us.

Uncle Yokana and father began to break down the hut while mother put the calabashes and wooden milk pots together. It wasn't long though before father came rushing back inside.

"I have just realised something that can make life so much easier for us all," he exclaimed. "Remember the healer in the market place? Ever since I told him about Simeoni's illness he has been nagging me about bringing our child to him."

"Surely you don't mean that you want to take Simeoni to a traditional healer?" mother opposed. "What if his practices are not compatible with our Christian faith? What would the brethren say?" But father defended the idea.

"We can share our plan with them and pray for it together. I think they will consent. After all, the man uses herbal medicine, not witchcraft!"

It made sense to leave me in a safe place, as this would enable my family to walk the long distance, build up a new settlement and come back for me when everything was habitable and ready. Our own relatives were either on the move themselves or lived too far away. The healer's place seemed a perfect solution.

"Let's pray for your idea then and bring it into the Light," mother sighed. "Our brethren have to know what we are getting ourselves into. I don't want anyone to turn round later and say that we have done something ungodly."

Father did not waste a minute. He was back again on his bicycle, only to return a little while later with the vicar and a few of our Christian friends. After praying together everyone agreed that, in the absence of a suitable alternative, it would be right to entrust me to the care of the traditional healer.

And so a whole new experience began to unfold. I was to live in an unknown place with people I had never met before. Even worse, I was to go all on my own, without my family, not even my mother who had always stayed by my side ever since I had become disabled.

Now the decision was made, there was no turning back. All of a sudden everything moved very fast. Father put me on his bicycle carrier, tightening the leather straps that were used to keep me from falling. I burst into tears and so did my brothers and sisters, distressed by the unexpected decision to take me away. Putting on a brave face mother grumbled at them while father told me off as I inconsolably sobbed. And off we went.

CHAPTER 7

THE CORNFIELD

"Do not be anxious about anything,
but in every situation,
by prayer and petition,
with thanksgiving,
present your requests to God.
And the peace of God,
which transcends all understanding,
will guard your hearts and mind
in Christ Jesus"

Phil. 4: 6-7

As father cycled on I soon found myself distracted by the dramatic scenery around us. Tied onto the back of his bicycle I had a rare opportunity of being raised to the height of a standing person, giving me a much better view of the devastation caused by the fires. The area affected was enormous!

We passed roads where I once used to walk with my father before contracting polio, on the way to church, to the market or to visit relatives. Once familiar places, now barely recognisable and charred. How happy those memories were. So different from my current situation. Now father was about to dump me in a strange place with people who belonged to another tribe with very different customs! Whereas we *Bahima* were cattle keepers those people were peasants and hunters.

We met a few relatives and brethren along the way who asked us where we were heading. Father explained what had brought him to this desperate decision of entrusting me to the care of strangers. It wasn't hard for him to convince them. They appreciated the difficulty of his position but glanced at me with such sympathy and concern that it did not take long before I burst into tears again.

Father stopped and announced that we had almost reached our destination.

"Before turning off the main path we should have a short prayer."

He began to pray. For the first time I realised that he was struggling with words, often pausing to take deep breaths.

"Heavenly Father... We commit Simeoni... into your caring hands." I could not resist the temptation to open my eyes and have a quick peep at his face. His features were worn by anxiety, burdened by the enormous responsibility of having to move our family and herd to an unknown location.

"*Yesu,* may you bring our search for new pastures to a quick and successful conclusion. May we soon be reunited again with our beloved child...

"May your presence comfort him in our absence."

I looked at father again. His face was calm now, radiating trust and hope as though a huge load had been lifted off his shoulders. My spirit was boosted as well. I began to feel that I might just get through this whole experience.

"Come on, my little field warrior, let us not be seen by these strangers with tears streaming down our cheeks," father continued more cheerfully. "We have prayed to the Lord and he has heard us. You will see."

He negotiated the bicycle through a cornfield. The path was narrow. We often had to dodge the leaves to prevent them from slapping into our faces. Eventually he got off the bicycle and pushed it along, until we emerged into the open.

Two young children of about four and five stared at us with runny noses. Flies swarmed round their stuffy eyes. Closely nearby were some female goats with their kids. In the background stood three small thatched *Banyankole* huts, the smallest one for storing crops and the other two for housing people and livestock. Opposite the cornfield, behind the huts, was a banana plantation.

Father lifted me off the bicycle while the children looked on, giggling cheekily. The traditional healer and his wife welcomed us courteously and reassured father that there was no need to worry about me. I would remain in safe hands. Father gave them a little money and the presents we had brought along as a token of gratitude for being prepared to look after me: a pot of milk and some *ghee*. He would come back to check on me later and pay the remainder as the treatment progressed. Although feeling terrified I put up a brave face. A seven-year old does not want to be seen crying, especially not in front of those strange children!

Father carried me into one of the huts. The interior was terribly messy. A shabby dog raised its head. Its ears were covered with sores and flies; it had wounds all over its body. Within minutes I felt the nip of a flea bite. The dog was blamed and chased outside.

"Knowing you, my child, you'll be able to put up with this, won't you? Having come this far, you would not want to turn back now?" father swayed me into agreeing. He had to hurry back to help with the breaking up of our home.

"Yes, father, I'll be all right." I could see from his face that he really did not want me to stay here, but we both knew that the alternative would be much worse. Being left with mother in a deserted settlement was infinitely more dangerous. I asked him to take me outside so I could see him leave the way we had come – through the cornfield. Thankfully he agreed, not knowing how often the memory of his disappearing image, his final wave and our farewell *Tukuntendereza* would replay in my mind, every time bringing tears to my eyes.

"Little man, you are going to make yourself ill," the healer attempted to calm me. "How long are you going to keep up this crying? Until your father comes back to collect you? Soon our son will be home. Possiano is only a few years older than you. He is learning to hunt and has taken the goats for grazing."

My ears picked up the rustling of the wind through cornstalks, the same sound as father and I had made when approaching the healer's home. I felt a flash of hope. Perhaps father had changed his mind. He had seen my distress and decided that he did not want to leave me behind after all in this stranger's home in the middle of nowhere! And so I sat there the rest of the day, just listening and waiting.

It was evening when the son of the healer arrived home. He was a boy of about nine or ten with a small spear in one hand. In the other he carried a *panga* – a large machete used as working tool, and piece of bloody game. His share of the hunting catch. The pride on his parents' faces was obvious as his father introduced me to Possiano. The boy threw his spear nose down into the ground and stretched out his bloodstained hand to greet me. From a young age I had been taught to fear *pangas*, as well as the people who carried them. I stared at him, frozen with terror. Then it struck me that if I were to survive in this strange environment I had better be friendly and on my best behaviour. Reluctantly I grabbed hold of his bloody hand.

I was helped into the little hut where the healer's wife had begun roasting the game on a fire. Traditionally we *Bahima* were very particular about what we ate and drank. Our staple diet consisted of dairy products. When it came to meat we only ate beef. Eating game wasn't just against our customs, it was considered undignified, even scandalous. Christianity and education had begun to loosen those tight rules. There was now some allowance for eating the meat from chicken and goats but not yet from hunted creatures.

"*Yesu*, please help me not to eat this," I quietly prayed. How I wished that father had explained our customs to the healer but that was too late now. Possiano looked on proudly as his mother turned the roast. The younger ones watched, their mouths watering. If only they knew my anguish! I decided to be polite. I would say that I wasn't feeling well. That my tummy was hurting. Perhaps next time I would feel confident enough to tell them what I could and could not eat. Fortunately the healer's wife also cooked a lovely dish of *matoke*, sweet potatoes and vegetables mixed with the *ghee* father had given, and that saved my day. But how was I to relate to these people? I didn't know them. Their customs were so alien. A sense of loneliness welled up in my heart, which over time would grow into a deep smouldering sadness.

Emotionally exhausted I longed to lie down and rest. At home it would be bedtime now. Time for story telling... My brothers and sisters playing and giggling in bed... My parents' muffled voices reflecting on the day's events. With a sudden jolt of fear I remembered the machetes carried by the healer and his son. I was at the mercy of these people, and *nothing*, not my father's encouraging prayer nor the soothing remarks from the healer was going to stop me from being petrified!

Noticing how tired I was, the healer's wife prepared me a place to sleep. The hut had a small extension where they normally stored food. That night it also housed the goats that had recently given birth and needed to be kept a close eye on. My bed was made up in that corner – a heap of grass, a woven mat, a goat's hide and the little sheet my parents had given me for cover. A few sacks of potatoes separated my bed from the goats and their kids. I lay down determined to pass out. By the time I woke up it would be light again. Then they could take me to the spot where father had disappeared, under the tree near the edge of the cornfield.

The fire, our only source of light inside the little hut, was put out. Everyone retired to their sleeping places, leaving me haunted by fear in the darkness of the night. I rubbed my eyes and closed them tightly. My body yearned for sleep but my goat neighbours were restless, seemingly determined to keep me awake. It did not take long before I realised that I did not just have goats for company.

"Ouch," I cried out. The healer called my name, thinking I was having a nightmare.

"Something has bitten me. We've been invaded by safari ants!" He told me not to worry. I felt more bites between my shoulder blades. This time I was determined to find out what kind of creatures were having a go at my skin. Struggling to reach my back I managed to catch one and squash it. From the sudden gas-like smell I immediately recognised what they were. Bedbugs. Their bites left a burning sensation, quite similar to nettle stings. Unlike safari ants that tended to attack and move on, I knew these nasty bugs were there to stay. As the night progressed and my bed warmed up, more and more emerged from their hiding places. The bites became countless. On my back, my bottom and any part of my body that touched the bed or bedding. However much I longed to sleep it was safer to stay awake. Maybe then I could squash a few more bugs before they got the better of me.

Wide-awake now my mind ran wild. What if father or Uncle Yokana suddenly realised that they could no longer endure my absence, just as I was lost without their presence. What if they were coming back for me? Perhaps they had worked out an alternative plan? I waited for the cocks to announce the new day. This usually happened at around four o'clock but it was still very early. There were many more hours to go. The relentless biting together with the stench of the goats and squashed bedbugs was unbearable. How I wished this to be my last night in this strange and horrible place.

Cocks crowed and birdsong filled the air. A glimpse of light pierced through the thatched roof of the hut. I must have dropped off towards morning, exhausted from a sleepless night. Fortunately my fears of being murdered by machetes had not materialised. The adults and Possiano had already left to cultivate the fields. Most of the heavy work was done before the sun became too hot, leaving the lighter tasks such as weeding, pruning and sowing for later in the day. When it was time for the goats to be taken out for grazing, the boy emerged from the plantation with a handful of leafy plants. He laid these out to dry in the yard, away from the entrance to the hut.

"Don't you dare to go near these or father will be cross!' he instructed the younger children. The curious five-year-old quizzed him what the green plants were for. Realising that I might be listening Possiano lowered his voice as though he did not want me to know that my treatment was about to begin.

"This is medicine for the crippled boy who has come to stay with us."

It was nicely warm in the shade and Possiano offered to help me get out of the hut. How I wished to enjoy the daylight I had been yearning for all night, but I dreaded being carried by this young stranger. What if he lost his grip? With my helpless limbs I would not be able to support the fall.

"It is much better to be out in the open," he kindly insisted. "The children are going back with me to the fields. You'll be left here all on your own." I gave in but, rather than being lifted, we agreed that I would sit on a hide, holding on tightly while he pulled me along, just as my brothers and sisters used to do back home. Before leaving, Possiano showed me how to use his catapult, a handy tool for hunting small animals and game. *Bahima* were not familiar with it.

We practised archery and spear throwing, and then only for sport or to defend ourselves, never for hunting purposes. His kindness was reassuring, diluting my fearful perception of him and his tribe.

It was a beautiful morning. Nature was generous as ever with its cool breeze and orchestra of exuberant birds. From time to time the cornstalks rustled, instantly triggering memories of my arrival and father's departure. I had plenty of time to meditate on what might be happening to my family. What sort of night they would have had compared to mine. Had they broken up our home by now? If they had, they would be sleeping out in the open, lying under cowhides in small temporary grass shelters to shield themselves from wind or rain. Life was very dangerous without the protection of strong permanent huts and fences for our cattle, especially in unknown terrain. I had heard numerous stories of people and cows being snatched by lions, leopards, cheetahs or hyenas while moving between settlements. Besides, there would be snakes, poisonous insects and an increased risk of falling ill from fever caused by mosquitoes! At least I was not exposed to all that, nor did I have to be carried along on a stretcher and watch others herd the animals and carry our belongings in the heat of the day. Although I missed my family very much I decided to be philosophical about the whole experience. I was better off with the healer. After all, I had survived my first night.

Around noon the healer and his wife returned from the fields with their youngest children, interrupting my contemplations. They enquired after my night as though anticipating a compliment. Not brave enough to tell them how dreadful it had been I gathered strength and pulled up my shirt, revealing numerous bite marks.

"I'll hang out your bedding," the healer's wife murmured a little embarrassed. "That should do the trick." But I knew very well that it would do no good. Once bedbugs had infested a place they just kept reappearing at night, attracted by the warmth of a body. The healer looked at the plants Possiano had laid out in the sun to dry. They were getting soft and floppy. After examining them closely he decided it was time to break the news to me.

"We better get you something to eat, young man. This is going to be the first day of your treatment." I did not fully appreciate what this treatment entailed, although I had heard that some of it could be painful. The word 'treatment' was exciting. It meant something was going to happen, something to keep me occupied rather than just sitting, worrying and waiting. Although a little apprehensive, I looked forward to my treatment.

The meal was my favourite: *ntura* (garden eggs) cooked with potatoes and cassava. After we had eaten, the healer called his wife to bring the large banana leaves they had brought from the plantation. A place was allocated behind the hut, a part of the compound I had not seen before. The leaves were spread out in layers, roughly woven into a mat. This was normally done when a small animal was being slaughtered to protect the meat from getting soiled. I curiously looked on.

Then he picked me up, carried me in his arms and stretched me out on the banana leaves. Glancing round I spotted a small bonfire with several red-hot glowing iron tools. The healer began to undress me. Gripped by panic I started trembling all over. I tried to stop him, to fight him off. But how could I? I was still so weak from polio. I screamed, crying out for my parents, breathlessly pleading with the healer not to hurt me.

"Don't worry, child," he just said. "These tools are going to make you better. Soon you'll be walking again!" But there I was, lying face down on the banana leaves, stripped naked, out in the open... the tools in the fire, and no one, no familiar face, no loved one to hold my hand and watch over me.

He pulled one of the burning tools from the fire. Petrified I closed my eyes. There was nothing else I could do. At the first contact with my skin I screamed at the top of my voice as though my life depended on it. I managed to swing one of my hands backward to stop the tool from hurting me. Instead it burnt my palm. The healer beckoned his wife to come closer and lend him a hand. Not that my resistance would have stopped him but they needed to pin me down so he could position the burning elements precisely on the spots he was targeting. Apart from my raging mouth I was totally overpowered. He burnt me several times around the base of my spine and my hips. Then they turned me over onto my back and pressed different burning hot tools onto my pelvis and knees. Later the healer explained to me the purpose of this treatment. It was meant to 'kick-start' my muscles and nerves, to more or less try and shock them into waking up and functioning again.

Suddenly I felt myself overcome by anger and blame – all the emotions I had been trying to reason away. My family had rejected me. I had been betrayed. How could my parents have left me here? Why had they not told me more about the treatment? Had I known I certainly would not have dwelled on missing them and fearing for their lives. I would have focussed on my own predicaments instead.

The herbs Possiano had left to dry in the sun were pounded in a calabash and rubbed into the wounds to hasten the process of healing. Thus the first phase of my treatment was concluded. It left me feeling so terribly weak, in a much worse state than before! And so the nature of my treatment unfolded. It certainly wasn't the sipping of plant extract or the gentle rubbing of herbal ointment on my skin. It was going to be a much more elaborate undertaking. The healer did not seem fazed by the pain his treatment had caused me.

"If it gets too bad I'll give you some *Tonto*," he casually remarked while carrying me back into the hut and placing me in my little corner. *Tonto* was a traditional wine made from fermented sweet bananas and sorghum. I could never accept this kind of drink! We never used alcohol at home. It was against our *Balokole* discipline. The healer's wife began to cook our evening meal. The fire was lit, filling the little hut with smoke. Soon it would be night again.

"Is the crippled boy not feeling well?" Possiano asked his mother when returning from the fields.

"Keep your voice down," she silenced him. "He is having a little rest." I had covered my eyes and nose to try and hide from the smoke. Somehow I longed to relate my experience to Possiano, hoping that he might have a little empathy with my situation. Dinner was ready but I had no appetite. Besides, every movement was so painful that I decided to give it a miss. I tried not to think about my family as this only brought waves of anger and sadness, which, in turn, made me feel very sorry for myself. Instead I concentrated on making myself as comfortable as possible, wriggling to wrap my sheet tighter around me so that no bedbugs or other insects could get to my flesh. Actually, I did not really dread the bedbugs so much anymore. The discomfort of their bites was nothing compared to the agony caused by the burning of my flesh. Having gone through the treatment I felt quite ready to take those tiny creatures on! Exhausted by crying, fear and lack of rest from the previous night I dropped off into a troubled sleep. It did not last long. The burns were sticking to the bedding and each attempt to turn caused them to crack open again.

The cocks crowed, waking us up to another day. Soon it would be dawn again. The day started just as the previous one. The couple and Possiano left as early as possible to cultivate the fields while the younger children stayed home to look after the goats. Upon his return a few hours later Possiano helped me get out of the hut. He noticed how delicate my movements were and that from time to time I stopped him from pulling the hide. This made him curious. After settling me in the shadow he asked me how I felt. I showed him the burns and he cried out in shock. This small gesture of compassion meant a lot to me. A sign of friendship in the making!

Something of a pattern began to emerge. Each day Possiano came home early. He helped me to get out of the hut and gave me something to drink, a small calabash with *eshande* – banana juice that had not yet fermented into alcohol. Then he got out his kit: a machete, a spear, quite often a stick and set off to graze the goats. When it was time to prepare lunch his parents came back from the fields. Later in the day the boy joined up with a team of adults for his hunting apprenticeship. At dusk he returned home, often with a piece of game.

Days passed. Many times I looked at the wounds around my pelvis and knees to see how they were healing, longing to see my smooth skin again. I wondered what was still awaiting me. Would father come back before the treatment continued? Whenever I saw someone with a handful of herbs I became terribly anxious. Were they meant for me or for some other use? What were the healer and his wife doing? Did I smell the smoke of a bonfire at the back of the hut?

In the meantime my recovery from polio that had started well before I came to the healer continued. My muscles gradually became stronger. I could stretch my arms a little further and put a bit more weight on them. Eventually I was able to shift myself on my bottom and crawl a short distance on my hands while dragging my legs along. Now, without depending on Possiano, I could reach the edge of the cornfield where father had disappeared. There I could sit and watch and wait for the day when he would come to take me home.

My newly acquired mobility and independence were only short-lived. The healer decided that my condition had not improved enough. Further treatment was needed. My attempts to show off with my crawling had not done the trick. It was time for the healer and his wife to prepare the second phase of my treatment, one that would turn out to be even more painful than the first. The couple pounded some special plants, mixed these with water and smeared parts of my body with the thick, green solution. Fortunately there was no bonfire in sight. Ignoring my curious questions they worked in silence. Once again banana leaves were spread out on the ground and I was laid down to dry in the sunshine. It wasn't bad at all, I thought. Nothing compared with the burning of last time. The only discomfort was that my skin became very dry, almost to the point of cracking.

The healer summoned his wife. I could see her hesitating briefly when he instructed her to get hold of me and pin my arms and upper body firmly down to the ground.

"Hold him properly," he insisted, "or else it will be much more painful!" It was then that I realised that they had not yet finished with me. Once again the couple were going to use some painful objects. They may have tried to avoid alarming me by concealing the nature of my treatment, but now I erupted into rage and panic. I screamed for my mother and father. If only someone from my family could see what they were doing to me, albeit in the name of healing! But there was no one to sympathise with me, no one to my rescue. I was on my own, entirely at their mercy.

"This will be over before you know it, young man," the healer said soothingly. "I have to make sure your body is properly dry so the skin will crack easily when it is touched by the blade. You really won't feel much of the cutting."

His words were not reassuring. I remembered the terrible pain his previous treatment had caused me and could tell from the wife's face that she dreaded what was coming. Swiftly the healer reached into his pocked, pulled out a piece of paper, unwrapped a razorblade and set upon me, starting with my hips. I tried to free myself, helplessly struggling and screaming, almost choking on my saliva. I became so breathless and overcome by panic that momentarily they halted the cutting. The wife released one of my hands to rearrange the banana leaves beneath me. I used the opportunity to try and touch the parts of my body the healer had just cut.

"Child! If you brush your hand against this blade it will slice off your fingers!" the healer reprimanded me, but I had to find out how badly I was bleeding. I pulled back my hand. My fingers were covered in blood. I saw streams of blood running down the banana leaves and almost passed out. But my hips were not the only areas earmarked for treatment. The healer had also smudged my legs, knees and back with the herbal solution. At that point I began to fear for my life. I felt guilty for not having prayed enough. If I had, maybe father would have arrived in the midst of this and come to my aid. Instead of screaming for my mother and father I began to cry out to God, asking him to help me, to stop them from hurting me.

This was not well received by the couple. When they heard me exclaim the name of God they thought that I was casting a curse upon them.

"You'd better pray for us rather than swearing," the healer snapped at me. "This is for your own good! We are trying to make you well again." They turned me onto my stomach and continued the cutting around my back and along my waist towards my bottom. Once that was done they pulled me up and rubbed a different kind of herbal solution into the wounds. It stung terribly but more or less instantly stopped the bleeding. Then they made me lie down again and continued cutting my legs and knees. By this time not only my whole body hurt but also my head from all my screaming. It felt as though my brains were about to explode. Finally the healer carried me back into the hut, still naked and dripping with ointment and blood.

Night fell. The healer and his family were sitting cosily around the fireplace while I lay on my bed with bedbugs and pain for my usual companions. I refused the food they offered me, partly because I felt feverish and partly from unhappiness with the people who had put me through all this without showing any care or emotion. My head ached badly. My ears were blocked from all my screaming and crying. Eventually I fell asleep, only to replace pain and discomfort by vividly reliving the whole experience, this time in my dreams. *'A woman grabs hold of my head and pushes it to the ground. A sharp blade flashes in her hand. She is going to cut my throat!'* I managed to shake off the nightmare and come back to reality. The pain was unbearable. Unable to drop off again I waited for the first light of dawn.

To my relief I lived to see another day. This time I decided to stay indoors. I did not want anybody to touch or move me, not even one inch. I had to accept that a miracle was not forthcoming. Despite my prayers father was not going to suddenly reappear and take me away. Strange as it may seem, I felt consoled by the thought that I had probably seen the end of the treatment. The worst was over. All I now had to do was get better. Mercifully, I did not know then how wrong I was. The burning and cutting would be repeated several times on various parts of my body. What could I do? I was too weak to resist. Even if I had been stronger I did not want to risk making the healer dislike me. After all, my life was in his hands.

Throughout my stay at the healer's I lived in fear, never knowing what would happen next. Often he examined my limbs and pulled me up to try and make me stand, but I showed no sign of being able to move my legs, let alone walk.

"The worst part of the treatment is now over," he eventually reassured me. "From today I will only rub your skin with plants and herbal solutions." I was not sure whether to believe him or not. What if he changed his mind?

The cuts took much longer to heal than the burns. The ones on my knees were rubbed open by sand, causing them to become infected and preventing me from crawling. But in time these healed too and I was able to go outside again, play with Possiano and get back to my little spot under the tree in front of the huts. From there I could keep an eye on the path through the cornfield.

The healer and his wife often had visitors. Besides practising traditional medicine they brewed *Tonto* and other alcoholic drinks which they sold from home. A rustle in the cornfield announced each new arrival. The sound always hit me with a flash of anticipation, but it was always a stranger, an animal, or just the wind. Never father. The couple also sold their brew on the monthly market. Everybody looked forward to market days, though probably no one as much as I did. After all, father had said that circumstances permitting he was likely to come and see me on a market day.

He did not turn up on that occasion, nor in the few months that followed. Spending my days at the edge of the cornfield I counted my scars and sores. How many burns and cuts did I have altogether? How many were still oozing with pus? Over and over I recollected what had happened to me, longing to tell my family the whole story. Their silence made me miserable and impatient. Why did they not send a message, at least to say that they had not forgotten me? I imagined my brothers and sisters enjoying themselves in the new settlement, playing and discovering new places. Were they actually still remembering me? Dark thoughts crept into my mind. Maybe they did not want me back. Maybe the daily care for me had caused them too much trouble. In those days *Bahima* were totally reliant on cattle which meant we had to keep moving in search of green pastures. Care homes for the disabled did not exist. It was therefore not uncommon for *Bahima* to permanently leave their disabled relatives behind with people from other, non-nomadic tribes. I heard visitors talk about it to the healer.

"Don't you realise that this child has been dumped here?" they said. "His parents have moved on. Why are you still bothered with him?" Occasionally a visitor knew my family and had seen father in the market place. I received such news with mixed feelings. At least he was still alive. He had not been eaten by a lion. But why did he not come back to check on me? My parents were Christians and I totally trusted that they loved me. Yet, I could not reconcile their conduct with what I was going through.

As time passed, my hope and expectations faded, only to be replaced by anxiety and fear. Frustrated by my lack of improvement and father's long absence the healer and his wife grew weary of me. As my presence in their home became a nuisance their care and attention diminished. Possiano, who until then had been praised by his father for helping me so cleverly, was quick to read his parents' mood and began to withdraw as well.

One thing gave me particular trouble while staying at the healer's. My crawling in the dusty compound exposed me to *jiggers* – tiny flea-like parasites that thrived in warm, sandy soil. The adult female insects reproduce by burrowing under the skin of human beings and other mammals. There they expand to the size of a pea and squirt out tiny white eggs, which causes swellings, severe itching and fever. Cow dung was a very effective repellent, so at home we never had *jiggers*.

Initially the healer's wife had taken the trouble to remove them from my hands but now she was no longer bothered. Before long I had numerous *jiggers*, especially in my knees, the palms of my hands and under my finger nails. The swellings were very uncomfortable, making it difficult for me to move about. Not that anyone cared though. Whenever I fell ill with fever they just left me indoors, in my little corner.

The family used to bathe by the well and bring back a bucket of water so I could wash myself. Now they stopped doing this and I became very dirty. Days could pass without me having a proper wash. The couple also no longer felt compelled to return at lunchtime to cook a meal for themselves and for me. Instead they took food into the field and worked till late afternoon or into the early evening. So it often happened that I went without anything to eat and drink for a whole day. Sometimes even for two days if the evening meal consisted of game that I did not feel free to eat. I became very thin and frail. Drained by emotions and troubled by hunger and thirst I spent many days alone either in bed or at the edge of the cornfield, waiting for my father. I had much time to think about my life, what it used to be like before being struck by polio, and everything that had happened since. Perhaps this was how it was always going to be: away from my family, at the mercy of strangers. The thought made me so sad and fearful for the future that I did not dare think any further.

Then, one day, I remembered something I had learnt when still a very young child. In all circumstances, however difficult, my parents used to *pray.* Whether faced with illness, bereavement, the loss of a cow (our only source of income!) or any other kind of trouble, they always turned to prayer. Tired of crying, fed up with all the things that made my head ache and unable to find anything else to hang my hopes on, I closed my eyes and began to pray. Not just the short prayers I normally said at bedtime but pouring out all my troubles before the Lord, crying out for him to intervene whilst reminding him of previous experiences he had helped me through. Like the time at the bus park in Kampala when mother and I were on our way home.

The relief was almost instant. I could see clearly again, hear the birds, breathe in the air as though a hood over my head had been lifted. From that day on, whenever struck by an attack of anxiety or heartache, I turned to the Lord in prayer. Only this could take me through the wall of despair. I also sang the hymns we used to sing at home and recited any

Bible verses I could remember. Often my prayers ended in tears as they reminded me of our family worship. However, gradually my fear and anger diminished. In time I even dared to feel hopeful that one day I might see my family again. Talking to the Lord became something I enjoyed doing rather than only resorting to when all other means of trying to feel better had been exhausted. Although prayer did not take away the physical pain and discomfort, it gave me peace and reassurance. Instead of dreading the long and lonely days I began to look forward to having uninterrupted time with my Lord. Prayer and worship became my companions, replacing those overwhelming emotions of sadness, pining and fear.

Once again I ran a high temperature. Thinking I was suffering from malaria the healer gave me quinine to drink. It did not really help. Worn out and severely weakened by hunger and neglect I prepared myself for the possibility of dying without ever seeing my family again. I tried to console myself with the knowledge that we would be reunited in heaven but the thought of my life ending in this way was so depressing that I soon stopped talking to people altogether.

One day I managed to drag myself out of the hut into the sunshine, shivering with fever. The healer's wife found me there crying and had a closer look at the swellings on my knees. Realising that *jiggers* might well be the cause of my fever she set upon digging them out with a safety pin. It left my knees so raw and sore that I could not crawl about. So I stayed indoors, feeling depressed and nursing my *jigger* wounds. I was lying in my little corner, staring miserably through the entrance of the hut when all of a sudden the figure of a man emerged from the cornfield. He wore a hat and put his bicycle against the tree, the very tree where I normally spent my days. Curious to see this visitor I looked at the shadows, waiting for him to appear. Then I heard a familiar voice.

"*Hodi, hodi, muriyo?*" – "*Hello, hello, is anyone there?*"

The visitor stooped in the doorway. He took off his hat, thus revealing that dear face I had seen in my dreams almost every night. Even during the day I had so often imagined seeing father that I wasn't sure whether this was a dream or not. Only when the healer's wife welcomed him it began to sink in. It was true. Father had finally come back for me!

I burst into tears of joy and relief, unable to stop myself. He took me in his arms and comforted me. It was difficult for him not to show the couple how shocked he was to find me so distressed, thin and dirty. He told me how much they were missing me back home, how unhappy everyone felt about my long absence.

"We have had so many problems in our new settlement," he said. "Lots of things have happened. Actually, your mother and I were expecting the healer to send us a message notifying us of your recovery, but this never came!"

As he spoke, my anger and disappointment melted away. I could see him, feel him, smell him as he embraced me, and I knew that it was real. The healer and his wife looked on slightly embarrassed. Seeking to know my father's intentions the man politely suggested that, if father preferred to leave me behind, he could perhaps do some further treatment. I wanted to scream, *"Father, I know that I am just as disabled as when you first brought me here. I still cannot walk but please don't leave me behind!"* But the Lord spared me from any further anguish.

"If the treatment hasn't worked by now then keeping my child here longer won't make a difference," father resolved while handing the healer the outstanding payment. Clearly relieved the couple agreed with his decision. And so I was 'discharged'.

"We must travel back immediately," father spoke with a sense of urgency. I could not wait to get away, even though I wanted to tell him my story and show him my scars. I longed to see myself back on the path that had brought us, through the cornfield and beyond. Father folded away my filthy bed sheet, stiffened by dried blood and pus.

"How have you been, my boy?" he asked me, struggling with his emotions. The little sheet and the state I was in spoke more than words could say. I just wept. Amidst my sobs I could hear him murmur with a hushed, disgruntled voice.

"We thought we were sparing you from the threat of wild animals and vultures, only to surrender you to beastly treatment by fellow human beings!"

Father wrapped me in his coat and carried me outside. The couple and their younger children watched in silence as he tied me onto the bicycle carrier. He mounted and we said goodbye. Glancing to my left I spotted Possiano in the distance, emerging from the undergrowth with his spear and bow and arrows. Noticing father, he stopped in his tracks, his eyes transfixed on me as though he could not believe what was happening.

"That is Possiano!" I called out. Father did not look up or slow down. That name meant nothing to him. I remembered how emotional we used to be at home when parting company with friends. Possiano was the only person who had been there for me at the healer's place, though towards the end his attitude had changed. I smiled and waved at him. He seemed unsure whether to stay put or come running towards us, probably because he was unable to gauge the manner in which we had parted from his parents. As he disappeared from my sight I decided not to dwell on his recent disinterested behaviour. I would rather remember him for the friendliness and care he had shown.

And so I left triumphantly, not crawling through the dust but head up high, elevated on the back of my father's bicycle. Slowly we made our way along the winding path through the cornfield – the cobs now ripe and yellow. Once again tears streamed down my cheeks. Only this time tears of utter relief and joy as I realised that the moment had finally come. After months of yearning and praying I would soon be back with my beloved family again.

CHAPTER 8

A PERMANENT HOME

"If you say, 'The Lord is my refuge,'
and you make the Most High your dwelling,
no harm will overtake you, no disaster will come near your tent.
For he will command his angels concerning you
to guard you in all your ways;
they will lift you up in their hands,
so that you will not strike your foot against a stone.
You will tread upon the lion and the cobra;
you will trample the great lion and the serpent."

Psalm 91: 9-13

Some of the corn had already been harvested. The stalks lay felled across the path, making it rough and bumpy. The path itself seemed much longer than I remembered. I could not wait to reach the end, to leave behind the healer's home and everything associated with it. What if father changed his mind...? I breathed a sigh of relief when at last we cleared the cornfield.

Out in the open the impact of the bushfires became a reality again. Bits of charred wood snapped beneath the bicycle wheels. Yet I could see signs of new life all around us – lush, fresh green bursting from the bare and blackened earth. I inhaled the fresh air and soon began to bombard father with all kinds of questions.

"Is everyone well? How did the move go? What does our new settlement look like?"

"It has been quite an undertaking," he gasped while straining himself to keep going over the rough terrain. The bicycle squeaked, his body swayed back and forth at every push on the pedals. "Your brothers and sisters will have a lot to tell. Don't worry. We'll make sure that you are safe... Uncle Daudi may come and stay with us for a while." His tone was calm and comforting as though to reassure me.

Uncle Daudi was father's elder brother. Also known as *"Rutagandara"* ("The one who never dithers") he was a strong and fearless giant, unrivalled in traditional stick fighting, fencing and wrestling. Troublemakers in the marketplace hastily dispersed when he approached. Drunkards stayed at a safe distance. Although he used his courage and strength to oppose injustice and defend the weak, he readily picked his own fights, like an elephant bull out to mark his territory and dominate the herd. Father, though less imposing, used to be a tough and agile wrestler too before he became a Christian. He, Uncle Daudi and a third brother were a formidable force to be reckoned with, well-known in the community as "The *Basasira* Brothers", named after their clan. With both father and Uncle Daudi around we would surely be well protected, but I had noticed the evasiveness in father's voice. Was he keeping something from me? I dared ask no further until at last curiosity got the better of me.

"Have we joined up with any of our old neighbours?"

"The only neighbours in the area are the *Mwigirane* and *Kiramujanye*," father replied, "and they may not be with us much longer."

I did not know those names. Could these be local tribes I had never heard of?

"I am not even sure whether we ourselves will be able to stay there," father continued, leaving me mystified and a little troubled.

We passed homes and plantations, churches and schools. Children came running after us, calling out while pointing at my dangling, skinny legs, "What has happened to that boy?"

Father took a short break to deliberate on what route to take and brace himself for the journey ahead. Moving on, the scenery around us became increasingly inhospitable and overgrown until we were completely surrounded by wilderness. I could see no trace of any human life at all. It struck me how difficult it must have been for my family to walk through this vast, desolate terrain while herding our cattle and carrying our belongings.

"This is only a shortcut," father panted. He was cycling at a vigorous pace. "The route we took was much, much worse!" Often the path disappeared altogether, forcing him to get off his bicycle and push it along. I noticed his wariness and how he observed every sound and movement in the bushes. Sometimes he stopped to listen, only to quickly jump back on the saddle again and cycle on as fast as he could. Despite the heat of the day he took no moment to rest.

"We must clear this place before nightfall," I heard him mutter. He pulled his long *Bahima* stick from the bicycle frame and put it over his shoulder, poised to use it should the need arise. It was frightening to see father, my infallible hero, so apprehensive and alert.

"You will have to be strong," he spoke again, his voice sounding calm and stern. "Don't panic if you get startled. I am with you. God is with us."

"I am not scared, father," I replied. That was the least I could do to support him. Seeing he wasn't up for a conversation I added merely in my mind, "But what is it that you are fearing?" His eyes scanned the area. Mine followed. I even kept looking behind, in case 'it' was stalking us.

"This is where the poor souls perished," he unwittingly spoke.

"What souls, father?" I could not help asking. "What has happened here?"

"You will find out in time."

He was still speaking when I spotted bones lying in a field around us. They looked like animal bones which put my mind at rest a little.

"They are not only after animals," father said at last as though he had been reading my mind. "They have claimed many of the *Mwigirane* and *Kiramujanye*." Again those peculiar names. I kept looking up to father in anticipation of a further explanation but he spoke no more. I fell silent too, gripped by a sense of imminent danger.

We entered a large forest stretching out over several hills and valleys. Now our path was reduced to a narrow track leading through dense undergrowth. Normally places like these were only braved by groups of people accompanied by strong men, ready to defend their families and livestock. But father and I were all on our own in this dark, forsaken forest. With heightened senses my nose detected all kinds of scents of animals and plants. All around us noises from different creatures, some louder than others. Hissing, whistling, rustling and crashing – the forest was teeming with life. With the earplugs of innocence removed I kept anxiously gazing in the direction of every sound.

"This area is ruled by vicious beasts like none we have ever seen," father said at last. "Just look at that poor creature there. It is clearly in distress."

A kob whizzed by, putting us on high alert. Father got off the bicycle and stared intensely in the direction from where the animal had emerged. My mind ran wild, "What if father had to fight a lion or a leopard? I would be totally helpless, tied to the carrier of a bicycle. If only Uncle Daudi were with us..." For a while we waited with bated breath, peering around us, wondering how safe it would be to proceed. Mercifully nothing further happened, and eventually we moved on.

"Thank you, *Yesu*, for keeping us safe so far," father prayed out loud. I could tell that he went on to pray for protection, but quietly so as not to alarm me. I totally trusted my father. Yet in the back of my mind I wondered how he, who knew so much about the dangers of nature, could brave such a wild and lonely place. Did he get his confidence from the Lord?

Father kept up the strenuous pace, desperate to clear the forest. Despite our precarious situation I could not help noticing the trees and shrubs in the shadows, dripping with delicious fruits.

"My brothers and sisters must have had a wonderful time with these. If only I could pick some…" The fruits seemed to be hanging there like bait, trying to lure us from the relative safety of a moving bicycle. We had not eaten and drunk all day. Father grabbed a handful of berries and I quickly gobbled them up. For a moment not only my thirst was quenched but also my hankering for those days when I used to track wild fruits, before I got polio.

Every now and again we were startled by sounds. A screech, a cry, a wild rustling of leaves very close to the path. All of a sudden an impala jumped in front of us. More followed, running in disarray.

"These animals are being chased," father observed with obvious apprehension, "I do hope we have not come between a predator and its prey!"

There was a skirmish in a nearby bush. Father stopped dead in his tracks, ready to drop the bicycle but changing his mind when realising how vulnerable this would leave me. With the saddle against his hip he stood there motionless, stick raised should he need to use it. He spotted a lioness only a stone's throw away, busy wrestling down her prey.

"Oh no, that poor creature is being killed," I cried at the sound of growling and groaning. My heart was throbbing in my ears. Then the commotion died down.

"She has got what she was after," father decided, "We need not fear this one anymore." But his attention was focussed in the opposite direction where more impala came running our way. "There must be a second lion around. These ones are also being pursued!"

A few impala crossed in front of us. If a lion were to come after them we would be right in its path! Unable to move forward we could only wait and pray. I wished God would do a miracle, heal my legs so I could fight alongside father. All sorts of Biblical stories ran through my mind, igniting my imagination. I would be strong like Samson, or brave like David when he faced Goliath. For a moment I drifted away from reality, mixing fantasy with prayer.

Another lion emerged behind the impala that came fleeing our way. She spotted us and, distracted by our presence, slowed down from her chase. Now father and I had become the sole focus of her hunt. Stealthily the vicious beast drew nearer until we were merely separated by a shrub. At that very moment something inexplicable happened. Rather than continuing in their flight, the impala halted abruptly as though startled by something that stood in their way. Father and I could not make out what it was. We saw nothing unusual. Next they twirled round and began to dart back *towards* the lion, actually leaping right in front of her nose before disappearing in the undergrowth. For a moment the lion hesitated. Then she slowly turned round and followed suit.

The hold-up, however unpleasant, had given father a much-needed break. After praying and thanking the Lord he was able to resume our journey with vigour. Even so it took us two hours to clear this terrifying, yet amazingly beautiful forest. At times the terrain was so rough that the only way of moving forward was for father to put me on his shoulders and carry the bike against his chest.

Finally we reached the savannah: open plains under a clear blue sky with flocks of birds swelling and swerving. In the distance numerous zebra and antelope peacefully grazed alongside each other. The wider view brought us a moment of relief. If there were any predators here, then at least we would be able to see them approach!

"Wow, look at that," I cried out in amazement, " I have never seen one so nearby!" As if nature wanted to make up for all the nastiness it had thrown at us, a giraffe emerged from behind a clump of trees. Father slowed down, giving me a chance to watch the majestic animal, gracefully feeding on the thorny branches.

Slowly a most wonderful landscape unfolded. All around us lush, green pastures, flowery shrubs and trees laden with fruits. Streams of fresh water seemed to spring up from the earth. Although at times still densely overgrown, it looked like paradise. What a contrast with Izinga, that drought stricken area from where our family had fled.

"We are nearly there," father announced, pointing at the horizon. "Look Simeoni, there is our settlement!" Smoke billowed from huts in the distance. I counted only seven. In our previous settlement we used to live with lots of families. Further away more plumes of smoke. Clearly we were not the only people in the area.

We still had to cover several valleys and hills before reaching our new home. The sun began to set, bathing the world in an orange glow. Every creature seemed to try and make its presence known, either to see off the day or to announce their nightshift with a loud chorus of buzzing, chirping and croaking. Never before had I experienced nature so bursting with life.

Down in the settlement my family was waiting for father. What news would he bring? After several months without contact with me no one knew what to expect.

"There they are! Petero has returned. He has brought Simeoni with him!" A loud cheer went up the moment we were spotted. Everyone dropped their chores and came running towards us. Although it was dark I recognised Phaibe, Miriam, Eseza, Sam and a few of my cousins. And there were my mother and Aunt Esther, calling out with arms in the air.

"Child, are you well? Thank God, he has brought you safely back to us!" A jubilant *Tukutendereza* erupted. The bonfire in the kraal flared up, illuminating their faces as they congregated round the bicycle. How I had longed to see them. Arms reached out to embrace me, only to be hastily retracted amidst cries of disbelief.

"*Yesu*, what has happened to him?"

"Look at the state he is in!"

Father dispersed the little ones. He untied me from the bicycle and carried me into one of the huts where a cowhide padded with rags had been prepared for me to sit on. Now, in the glow of the fireplace we could see each other more clearly. I noted my family's expressions of shock and dismay. After the excitement of the journey I had almost forgotten my time at the traditional healer's. One look at them brought it all back to me. Mother summoned my sisters to quickly prepare warm water. Everyone offered to do something – fetch milk, wash my clothes, anything to transform that filthy, emaciated boy in front of them. I was washed and my skin gently rubbed with cream. At the very first daylight herbs would be gathered so they could treat my sores.

They observed me in silence as I drank the milk. I told them my story and together we cried. My siblings were keen to have a look at my scars but mother hastily stopped them.

"Keep those bones covered, my child!" she almost burst out. "They look as if they are about to pierce through your skin!"

As father watched and listened to me he suddenly rose up in anger. "I certainly did not pay all that money for my son to be harmed. Look what we have got back in return!" He was disappointed that the traditional treatment had failed. Indeed, they all were. It seemed that everyone had hoped to find me miraculously transformed and back on my feet again.

Telling my story affected my family more than me. I was just relieved to be able to share it with them. Whereas for me it was the beginning of emotional healing, they still had to come to terms with what had happened to me. My troubled emotions lifted. Theirs were stirred. I could read the anger, regret and remorse in their faces.

"Poor Simeoni, what have we done to you?" one after the other uttered. Yet every apology was followed by a similar, helpless remark. "But we could not have kept you with us. You would never have survived the journey we went through!"

There was not much time for talking and reflecting. Soon everyone hastened to finish their chores before retiring inside the hut for the night. Our cows were unusually restless. I could hear them sniff the air. Instead of spending the evening cosily talking, singing and telling stories, there were intervals of silence as people listened to noises nearby and afar. The atmosphere was strangely tense.

"What was that?"

"Shush, try not to worry Simeoni." Their attempts to protect me only aroused my curiosity.

"So tell me, how are things here?" I insisted, "How have you been?" In the end my siblings let me in on their secret.

"There are many leopards, cheetahs and lions in this area. We have already lost several cows. Everybody has been affected!" In the distance a lion roared. Hyenas howled as though competing with each other. The closer the sounds the greater the sense of apprehension around me.

Although we lived within a settlement we were not well protected. The enclosure was not yet solid and strong. Even our huts were still in the making. The men had been too busy guarding their families and cattle, while the women could not move about freely in search of the type of grass used for thatching the roofs. In those days *Bahima* huts were only made of woven sticks and grass. They did not even have doors. The only entrance had to be kept open at all times to enable us stay in close touch with our cattle. In this way father could dash out unhindered at the very first signs of distress. Locking yourselves in while your cows were defenceless out in the open was considered just as scandalous as fleeing from danger and leaving your children behind. Besides, our huts were extremely inflammable and doors would pose an obstacle in the event of a fire. We were particularly vulnerable to cheetahs and leopards as these could climb over the highest enclosure or sneak through tiny gaps. They were known to snatch young goats and calves from the pen and enter huts to attack small children. Hyenas also crept in at night to look for an easy prey. These cowardly creatures could tear the flesh or a limb from vulnerable livestock, even from human beings when they lay sound asleep.

It rained that night, as it often did in the area. Water leaked through the roof. To keep dry we covered ourselves with cowhides on our large traditional *Bahima* bed. Miriam, Peace and Joy on one end, Sam and I on the other, whispering and giggling.

"Stop pulling the blanket, you are making me cold."

"If the mosquitoes bite me it will be your fault." Deeply content I listened to the familiar chatter of my siblings as it mingled with my parents' prayers softly murmured in the background.

"Oh *Yesu*, we thank you for Simeoni's life. You have always stood by him, whatever he has gone through. In all our troubles you have always helped us out. As once again we are surrounded by danger, we put our trust in you." Soon I dropped off, lulled by the soothing sound of dripping water and my parents' reassuring voices.

There was no need for anyone to tell me about the difficulties our settlement was facing. The following day I could see it for myself.

It was around mid-morning. The herders were out with our cattle when all of a sudden alarm cries resounded from the other side of the hill. Next a stampede of cows came thundering towards us. The calves in the nearby fields scattered in disarray. Everyone seemed to know what to expect and what to do. Women rounded up their youngest children, quickly counting them before retreating inside the huts. Teenagers chased after the panic-stricken calves. Meanwhile the men rushed out of the settlement armed with sticks and spears. Some ran towards the herders who clearly were in trouble. Others tried to stop the cows from dispersing, steering them back towards the kraal. Two women hastily grabbed me by the arms and legs and dragged me indoors, their faces wrought with terror.

"A pack of lions is approaching!"

Huddled together inside our hut we listened to the continual alarm cries of the herders, echoed by the men who came hurrying to their aid. Outside our cows were mooing, their long horns clattering, their hooves trampling the earth. Usually lions did not attack a settlement during the day. However, when failing to catch a cow they could turn their frustration on human beings. Many youngsters and women were still out in the fields to cut grass, gather firewood or fetch water. The tiny calves in the pen would be an easy prey too. From the entrance to their huts mothers fearfully peered in the distance, calling out the names of loved ones and exchanging announcements with each other.

"I think I can see your son!" A boy came racing from the valley, shedding a bunch of firewood along the way.

"Have you seen Eseza?"

"She must be right behind me. I saw her running this way!" Not until every missing person was accounted for did the anxious calling die down. Now we were able to turn our thoughts to ourselves.

"Quickly, block the entrance with firewood and logs," mother instructed, "Anything you can find!" I was pushed with the little ones towards the back of the hut where we peered through small gaps in the wall and listened to the worried exchanges.

"What if the lions break through from behind?"

"Put more wood on the fire. That may help to deter them!" Meanwhile father and the others were out in the fields, facing grave danger with nothing but sticks and spears. The whole experience reminded me so much of that terrible time of the bush fires.

To our relief the men were able to fight off the lions and chase them away as far as they could. The next few hours were spent calming the cattle before leading them to different pastures. During most attacks we lost several animals. On this occasion one of our cows had a large chunk of flesh ripped from her back. Although they managed to pull her alive from the claws of her assailant she died from her injuries a few days later.

"The *Mwigirane* and *Kiramujanye* are unharmed too," one of the herdsmen informed us. "Sadly, they have lost a few of their cows!"

This time I could not rest until I had found out who these mysterious people were.

The *Mwigirane* and *Kiramujanye* were the nicknames given to Tutsi settlers who had fled from Rwanda in 1959 after a Hutu revolt had toppled their king. Many Tutsis were killed. Hundreds of thousands escaped to neighbouring countries, including Uganda. Following a period in refugee camps they gradually dispersed with their herds of cattle in search of grazing lands. Unfortunately they were unfamiliar with the Ugandan terrain and ill-prepared for its inherent dangers. Their traditional settlements were insufficiently reinforced and their fences far too low, which left them vulnerable and exposed to predators. Whenever under attack by a pride of lions they would call out in their language, "*Mwigirane*" which translates as, "Cling together!" If there was enough time they swiftly formed a circle. The strongest men on the outside armed with sticks and spears. The women, children and other vulnerable people huddling in the middle. Far too often an attack was followed by a cry of lament. *"Kiramujanye!" "He (or she) has been snatched!"* Before long the Tutsis in Uganda were nicknamed the *Mwigirane* and *Kiramujanye* after those sad and desperate cries.

The *Bahima* never mentioned those names without sympathy and respect. We understood far too well the suffering of that community. After all, we had a lot in common. Both the Tutsis and Bahima descended from the *Chwezi* who many centuries ago had travelled down along the Nile to establish kingdoms in Western Uganda, Rwanda and Burundi. We regarded the Tutsis as our pastoralist cousins. Even their cattle, the Nyambo, were very similar to our Ankole cattle.

One group of Tutsis had set up camp only a few hills away from us. They were having such a rough time. So that was what father meant on our way home from the healer when he said, "They may not be there for long..." That is why he was thinking of us moving too. Now I understood just why he had taken so long to come and collect me. I began to realise what could have happened to me had I stayed with my family during the move to this new location. How for tens of miles they had had to fight their way through this hostile nature, spending nights in makeshift grass huts with no protection other than bonfires, sticks and spears. My vulnerability would not only have made me an easy target but also endangered others as they tried to keep me out of harm's way.

Yet, the area was so fertile. I could see those ripe, juicy berries dangling in the trees beyond our enclosure. The more I looked at them the more I wished to eat some! The adults knew how restricted their children were in tracking and other field activities. Often they brought home fruits, nuts, roots and large pieces of honeycomb extracted from termite mounts or hollow trees. Nonetheless, this could never match the adventure of picking our own. Danger or not, we ourselves had to find a way of getting out there.

One day, when no one was looking, my friends and I decided to invade a bush not far from the enclosure. With sticks clenched in our fists we made our way to the entrance. Well, to be precise, the other boys walked while dragging me along on a cowhide. For a moment we waited motionless, intensely observing the vegetation for movements, listening to every sound. When all seemed clear we dashed out into the forbidden woods. A few boys climbed trees to be on the lookout. Others grabbed as many fruits as they could possibly carry. Meanwhile I directed everyone from my position on the ground. Once we had gathered enough we hastily retreated within the settlement and divided our loot. In time I would become the mastermind behind many such daring adventures, organising and leading 'my troops' in terribly risky, yet wonderfully exciting fruit picking raids.

For many days we had been expecting Uncle Daudi's arrival. At last he did turn up, as usual at the least expected time, in the pitch-dark and all alone! In fact, he had first followed the wrong track and strayed to the Tutsi settlement. There he was given a firsthand account of human casualties and cattle being lost to predators. He found Mrs Gatete nursing her husband whose arm and collarbone had been torn off by a lion. Also in their hut lay the body of their son, twenty years old and just recently married. The lion had first attacked Mr Gatete. When the son came to his father's rescue he was himself overpowered and killed.

By the time he reached our settlement Uncle Daudi was fuming. He was well aware that previously other *Bahima* had failed to settle in our location. Several of them had perished. He was also deeply moved by the suffering of the Tutsis.

"How could you decide to live in such a notorious area after everything you have already gone through?" he chided father. "However fertile and green, this is not a place to set up home. You are with far too few experienced men to conquer this nature."

That night we slept peacefully, ignoring the noises outside the settlement, lulled by a greater sense of security – whether true or false – now both father and Uncle Daudi were with us.

The following morning my uncle and father called together all the men of our settlement.

"I have not joined you here to become food for wild beasts," Uncle Daudi asserted. "If we don't deal with those lions now they will force you to leave this place!" Everyone agreed that something had to be done. There was no time to waste. Uncle Daudi went back to the Tutsi settlement to gather more men together. Those unable to fight surrendered their spears, including Mr Gatete.

"It won't be of any use to me now," the poor man groaned as his wife handed over his weapon. To console the grieving couple my uncle made this solemn promise: *This spear will be the first to hit the lion that has claimed the life of your son!*"

The men were split into groups to guard the two settlements and stage a vigil out in the fields. As the Tutsis had suffered most, their camp was surrounded with bonfires. This, it was hoped, would repel the man-eating lions and steer them in our direction. Outside our settlement the strongest group lay in waiting, led by Uncle Daudi and father. Along the path a huge chunk of meat was put down as bait.

Night fell. Milking time had just ended when we heard howling and growling noises swiftly drawing closer. As expected, leopards and hyenas were moving in on us for their nightly hunt. Before long a lion roared frightfully nearby. Uncle Daudi grabbed a rope and sticks and spears, as many as he could carry. Armed with these he ran out of the settlement.

"Don't be a hero," father shouted after him, "Do you think you can just tie up a lion the way you do with a bull? These beasts have claimed the lives of many people!"

"Just be on standby and listen out for my cries," Uncle Daudi called back over his shoulder. "And when you approach with the others, make sure to aim your spears!"

Unknown to father, my uncle had surveyed the area during the day and found the track that the lions tended to follow. He climbed one of the trees adjacent to this track, using the rope to make a base among the highest branches. There he sat and waited.

Some people claim he deliberately cut his hand to lure the lions towards him, using the scent of his blood. Others say that he got injured in the ensuing fight. Inside the hut we prayed and listened, keeping our eyes peeled throughout the night. Mother told us to stay near the back of the hut. We widened a small gap in the woven grass wall to try and catch a glimpse of my uncle. Branches swayed in the glare of the moon. There was no trace of him.

From his hideout Uncle Daudi spotted two fully grown lions slinking up on our settlement. When reaching the piece of meat on the ground they totally ignored it – a sign that they were not after just any food but looking for human prey! They reached the tree where my uncle lay in waiting. He shouted and hurled sticks at them to provoke them and assess their ferocity. The animals pounced on the tree and wildly stormed up and down between my uncle and the group of men guarding our settlement, growling and stirring up dust. Now it was beyond doubt that these were the lions hunting after people.

Father and his group briefly retreated within the enclosure to calm our terrified cattle. After checking on us they hurried back to lure the lions out in the open where they would be an easier target for their spears. Uncle Daudi climbed down to the lower branches to use himself as bait. One of the lions leapt at him, narrowly missing his legs. Again she jumped up. Again and again. As her torso soared in mid-air my uncle launched a spear. It was the one from Mr Gatete. The weapon slammed into the animal's chest. More spears, sticks and stones rained down upon the wounded creature. Still she kept on raging.

Now both lions turned to the men on the ground. Uncle Daudi came down to help them. Together they overpowered the injured beast but the other retreated, only to re-emerge a moment later and attack one of our neighbours. He was mauled so badly that his guts came spilling out. They hastily carried him home and we children were told not to look. The next day he was taken to a faraway hospital. As far as I heard he survived.

Over and over the men speared the second lion. She ran off and they had to pursue her. For several hours they were out there in the dark, looking for the wounded animal, fearing to be pounced on. We heard a loud screaming. Was it horror or jubilation? We were unable to make it out. Finally some people recognised the Tutsi victory song. The good news swiftly spread.

"The killer lions must be dead!"

At the very first glimpse of daylight everyone wanted to go and see the dead man-eating lion. I begged to be taken out too. A cousin carried me in his arms and raised me up above the tall grass. There she lay, terrifying even in death. Pieces of broken spear sticking out of her body. Her half-open eyes staring straight at me, as though at any time she could rise up and strike again.

This event brought the two communities closer together. We began to regularly visit each other. Our men showed the Tutsis how to build impenetrable enclosures around their huts and kraals while they helped us finish the building of our settlement. We exchanged traditional survival skills and methods of looking after cattle. We also grazed our herds in the same areas so we could defend each other. The union provided mother and her fellow *Balokole* with a great opportunity to further spread the Gospel. The two communities held Bible study and prayer meetings together and many people, young and old, accepted the Lord. God really did an amazing work out there in the wilderness.

I thought we had seen the best of Uncle Daudi until a few weeks later. The adults were relaxing in the sunshine after their early morning tasks when we heard a loud commotion from within our own neighbourhood.

"Help, he is killing me!" It was a woman's cry, followed by the screams of children. "Help, mummy is being hurt!"

Several men jumped up. What was this alarm all about? A woman came running towards us, desperately trying to get away from her raging husband. He was known as a quiet man but very strong and jealously protective, especially when drunk.

"Get back to the house," he savagely yelled. Beating his wife right in front of our eyes he began to drag her away.

It had been Uncle Daudi's turn to keep guard during the last hours of the night and he had gone for a rest. Realising that there was trouble he got up, only to find people from a distance reasoning with the husband, pleading for restraint. Increasingly angry the man was having none of it. His wife stood nearby, bent over and crying with her arms wrapped around her stomach.

"How dare you beat up a woman? How dare you humiliate her in front of her children?" my uncle confronted the man, walking straight up to him. "You even have no qualms to disregard your fellow men to whom she has turned for help!"

"If you feel sorry for her," the man retorted, "then you better take her place. Come on and I'll put you both on one heap!"

"That's an invitation I gladly accept," my uncle readily replied as though he had been waiting for this moment. "If you really want to fight, you better fight a man!"

He ordered the woman to take her children home. He did not want them to see their father being beaten and disgraced. He and the angry husband stormed out of the settlement to an open stretch of land.

"Those two are going to hurt each other!" several people exclaimed. A few went after them, ready to intervene. We children were also sent home but secretly crawled up to the enclosure to peep through a gap, excited at the prospect of a long, thrilling contest. I saw the man charge up to Uncle Daudi, crashing into him like an angry bull. Their arms locked. A brief scuffle followed. Next my uncle tossed him high up in the air. He fell to the ground with a thud. There he remained, groaning in agony.

"Get up and fight!" my uncle demanded. "I won't beat you while you're down, the way you did to your wife."

At that very moment father returned from the fields.

"Daudi, what are you doing?" he called out deeply dismayed. "Have you forgotten that you are a guest here in this settlement?" He swiftly stopped the fight and arranged for the man to be carried home, fearful of what he might do to our family once my uncle had departed. It took many days before the injured man was able to leave his hut. When he finally reappeared my uncle strode up to him with a disarming smile.

"I have been meaning to call on you before returning home. I hold no grudges against you, nor do I wish to end my stay here without us making up. Why don't we have a drink together?" Reluctantly the man agreed. My uncle walked several miles to the nearest village brewer, only to return a few hours later with a huge calabash full of *Tonto*. The two men shook hands, sat down together and, while bragging to each other about how brave they had been in all kinds of extraordinary situations, they merrily shared the lot.

That evening the man slaughtered a young bull and invited the whole neighbourhood for a field roast. We had a cosy time singing and listening to stories. Meanwhile the teenagers and young adults held wrestling matches, inspired to show off their skills to Uncle Daudi and the elders. Shortly after this event my mother visited the wife to see if she could help. She talked to the couple about the Lord and they allowed her to pray with them. The wife became a committed *Balokole* and joined the fellowship group. Although initially apprehensive the husband also began to attend our Sunday worship meetings. Over time he refrained from drinking and stopped being violent.

At some point in his life my uncle had been baptised, hence his Christian name 'Daudi', the *Orunyankore* word for 'David'. Nevertheless, he was fiercely resentful of Christianity and in particular of anything to do with the Revival.

"Wherever I go I find this relentless testifying and preaching about turning away from sin," he used to grumble to my mother. "If it wasn't for fear of our creator *Kazoba* I would have sorted you crazy *Balokole* out long ago."

Soon after his stay in our settlement God's grace caught up with him too and he accepted the Lord. My Uncle Daudi, the one who rubbed shoulders with royals, who was renowned for his bravery as one of the great defenders of the realm. From the moment he was converted he never fought people again, not even for a good cause. This fearless gladiator became the one to back off when someone tried to pick a fight. He 'turned the other cheek' as our Lord Jesus had commanded. Many years he spent revisiting the communities and homes where he had caused havoc in the past, only not with a spear in the hand but with the Holy Bible. His mission was to ask for forgiveness and preach the Good News about Jesus. He did not need many words to testify to God's saving power. Everyone who knew him was intrigued by the huge transformation.

"If this Jesus can change Daudi," people said, "then he can do anything!"

The death of the man-eating lions brought us some respite but it was not the end of our troubles. The area was infested with other dangerous animals like leopards, cheetahs, hyenas and wild dogs. There were more lions, though these had not yet discovered a taste for human blood. Pythons and poisonous snakes were hiding in almost every bush and hollow. Even our cows were occasionally bitten. Sometimes huge swarms of African bees clouded the skies, attracted by the lush vegetation. If they swooped down on a settlement their stings would often prove deadly. The wells and marshes provided a breeding ground for mosquitoes and other insects, causing many people to succumb to malaria and other water-borne diseases. In the meantime, modern medical facilities were far away and hard to reach. The land may have provided us with abundance but all creatures seemed to conspire against us living in that location, as though to prove that this was their territory and we were there at their mercy.

Eventually the settlers had to concede that they were fighting a losing battle. It was time to move back to a less hostile place, even if this meant sharing grazing land and water with many other people (which of course could put a strain on these precious resources and lead to scarcity again). Uncle Daudi agreed to take care of our home while my parents looked out for a new location, this time with one thing foremost on their minds. Following the string of past events – pests, droughts and fires leading to my stay at the healer's, as well as the more recent challenges and dangers – our new home had to be in a secure environment where I could grow up safely and they could care for me. Perhaps even a place where we might settle for good!

By now many *Bahima* were abandoning their semi-nomadic lifestyle. Rather than living in remote, traditional settlements where everyone was exposed to hardship and danger, they began to buy pieces of land and build permanent homes. There the women could live with their children and other vulnerable dependants in the vicinity of clinics, schools and churches while the men took their cattle for grazing on rural public lands, at night camping in temporary shelters.

Once again the brethren came into action, this time helping in the search. Among them were Aunt Miriam and Uncle Ezekiel who had already bought a few acres of farming land in Bweyale, Sembabule district. With the help of local

Balokole a place was found only a few miles from where they lived. When my parents went to survey the area, they met a *Bahima* woman with a disabled child. She told them how much her child had benefited from living in a stable environment. Her testimony helped settle the matter. Father sold a large number of cows, using the money to secure us our very first permanent home.

Our new home was a spectacular place. A large traditional family hut set in four acres of well-tended agricultural land. The fields were crammed with pineapples, cassava, millet, sugar cane and sorghum. Smaller plots had neat rows of beans, carrots, tomatoes, onions, aubergines, cabbages and groundnuts as well as bamboo for building. Wherever there was soil we found something useful growing. It seemed the previous owners had not left any crop untried.

I pointed at a large strange shrub with masses of white flowers glistening in the sunshine, wondering what delicious fruits such magical plants would produce.

"That is cotton," father said dryly, instantly switching off my adventurous appetite. The banana plantation was huge and interspersed with avocado trees and rows of coffee bushes. Monkeys were feasting on the bananas, leaving half eaten bunches hanging on the trees. They noisily scattered as soon as we approached. The sweet scent of ripened fruits greeted our noses. We counted at least seven species of bananas: *matoke* for cooking and others for roasting, brewing or just eating ripe. The compound around the house was littered with mango, orange and papaya trees. Such a wealth of crops right on our doorstep! Surely from now on buying and bartering food would be a thing of the past. We even had our own cornfield, though the sight of it rekindled memories that were better left undisturbed.

The hut itself was built in the traditional *Baganda* style, with mud walls up to shoulder level and a large thatched roof. Unlike our own *Bahima* huts it even had the added safety of a door. It was a relief to find a readymade home waiting for us without first having to camp in temporary grass shelters while a settlement was being constructed. I wondered why anyone would have wanted to sell such a wonderful place. My parents explained that sometimes the *Baganda* developed land in order to sell it for profit. They might also relocate to a smaller plot when a family member had died. We later discovered several graves in the banana plantation. It seemed likely that the previous owner had sold this farm as a result of bereavement.

Father gathered us all together in front of our new home and pointed in every direction.

"This is where most of our herd has gone!" He spoke with deep emotion, reciting the names of all the cows he had had to sell in order to buy this place, *"Bugondo, Choozi, Ngabo, Gaaju...* ('Spotty one, Black one, White-band, Pale-brown')...". The list went on and on. The reality of his words hit hard and dampened our excitement. Over recent years we had already lost many cows. Cattle ownership was our wealth and pride. With so few left, the very respectability and status of our family was at stake!

"We must take good care of what has come into our possession," father warned us grimly. "From now on we will have to depend largely on growing crops."

It would prove to be quite a challenge. As semi-nomadic pastoralists we were unfamiliar with agriculture. We did not even know the purpose of some of the plants, let alone how to cultivate such a huge variety. We had to learn everything as we went along, including how to prune, weed and harvest, and what crops to sow in which season.

When I was discharged from Mulago the doctors had advised my parents that a healthy, balanced diet would be vital for my development and growth. Now that at last we had the necessary resources, the adults went out of their way to feed me up. Rapidly gaining weight I became strong and energetic. Soon it was no longer necessary for anyone to help me move about. I was crawling all over the place like a caged animal set free. The farm had plenty of natural materials for children to play with and my creativity knew no bounds. I made catapults the way Possiano had taught me. Armed with these I learnt to shoot down fruits from the trees. I wove sisal nets to carry my loot to a little den where I sat down and ate them. My footballs made from banana fibre became very popular with the other children.

"Has anyone seen Simeoni?" became a common cry each morning at the crack of dawn. Often I was in the plantation busy constructing a cart from felled banana trees. With a *panga* I trimmed the stems and tied these together with sisal to form a base to sit on. I sculptured slices of banana trunk into perfectly round wheels, making axles from sticks to which a rope was attached for steering. The side of a large termite mount provided a perfect launch pad. After clearing and smoothening the soil I drenched it with water to make a slippery surface. Sometimes I used wee if we were short of water. I dragged my cart to the top of the slope, got in and raced down with a terrific speed. I spent whole days in the banana plantation perfecting my vehicle. Often other children had a go as well, which was nice as they could help me push my cart back up the ramp.

After a couple of months I began to lose interest in our immediate surroundings. I wanted to be with my brothers and sisters who often went further afield. Together we devised a way for me to move at a faster pace than crawling. If someone walked behind me and lifted my legs off the ground I could actually run on my arms! Our only puzzle was how to stop me from getting thorns in my hands. A pair of old sandals, locally made from car tyres, was the perfect solution. With those on my hands we could go anywhere we wanted, even as far as Aunt Miriam's home a couple of miles away.

Initially my parents and big sisters were wary about my adventures. Only when nothing more serious occurred than the odd cuts and bruises did they become less protective and stop fretting over me. I think they actually welcomed my absence. Being very active and cheeky I had become quite a handful in and around our home.

As I got fitter and healthier, the general sympathy towards me began to wear off. Soon I found myself drawn into squabbles with other children. Miriam and a few cousins were the first ones to dare me, and the others followed suit. Initially I told mother every time someone was teasing me, which must have been quite tiresome to her. After a while I felt strong enough to stand up for myself. When it came to physical scuffles the others always had an advantage. Towering over me they could easily pull my ears or slap my face. I, on the other hand, would grab their feet and bite their ankles. Whereas they were able to run off after kicking or punching me, I always had missiles close at hand, like sand and stones for hurling at them. Otherwise I just bided my time – until they were sitting down and I had them within easy reach.

What I could not do with my hands and teeth I learnt to do with words. Other children picked up English expressions at school that made wonderful swearwords. My favourite one was 'come on' which we thought meant 'dog', as it was what *Muzungu* people were known to say to their dogs. If anyone said 'come on' to you, he was being very offensive and could be assured of a fight. Also words like 'baboon' and 'silly' were interpreted as terrible swearwords, like telling someone that he had no brains. Of course *Balokole* parents did not approve of their children quarrelling and fighting. If caught by mother she disciplined us by making us apologise to each other and then to *Yesu* in prayer. By the time we had finished doing so all anger and upset would be gone. Only if we had been very mischievous would father get involved. His punishment could range from a serious telling-off to doubling our chores or having a go at our bottoms.

One night safari ants invaded our home. By the time we noticed their presence they were already all over our bodies – inside our clothes, in our hair and even in our ears and nostrils. Safari ants move in huge numbers and usually in columns. They are unstoppable, attacking anything in their way. Their bites are nasty and painful. We woke up in mayhem, children crying, adults yelling. Everyone was jumping up and down to try and shake them off.

The conventional way of repelling these insects was using smoke and fire. By brushing lightly over them with a bunch of burning grass one could disorganise their advance, destroying many in the process. One of my sisters grabbed a handful of grass. She lit it in the fireplace and frantically set upon fighting the ants. Yet, more and more kept coming. On the floor lay a pile of hay covered with a cowhide to make a comfy seat. It caught fire and the flames rapidly spread. Now our attention was diverted from fighting the ants to tackling the blaze. We tried to put it out with hides and blankets, throwing sand at it and every drop of fluid we could find. When it became clear that our efforts were futile we children were dragged to safety. Moments later the adults scrambled outside with anything they could salvage. From a distance we watched our beautiful house burn down to the ground. Thank God, at least we were unscathed! The rest of the night we spent out in the open beside the smouldering remains of our home.

The quality of our lives had improved so much in the few months in this permanent location that my parents refused to be deterred by this setback. Regardless of the costs involved they decided to replace our traditional *Baganda* style hut with a proper house. It was to be a 'modern' one, not made of bamboo, mud and grass, but with *karatusi* poles, dug foundations and walls plastered with a mixture of clay and sand. Just like the church in Kikoma they had helped to build several decades ago. Once again father had to sell more cows, and the *Balokole* community rallied round with prayer and practical assistance. Whilst we sheltered in a temporary hut our new home was erected. It had a corrugated iron roof and windows with wooden shutters, making it much warmer, lighter, airier and stronger than any of our previous dwellings. After moving in we turned our temporary shelter into an outdoor kitchen. Now there was no longer a need for an indoor fireplace which meant that our home was free of smoke. At night we lit paraffin lamps and candles. It was yet another giant leap away from our traditional lifestyle.

One day mother left for the Maternity Clinic. When she came back she had a baby brother in her arms. The birth of another boy was an exciting event in our family. It was a consolation too. My parents had not been lucky with sons. They had lost their eldest, Karanzi, two years before I was born. Two more sons had died in infancy and their youngest was a disabled. Now God had given them another healthy boy. They named him Enock *Mwesigye* which means 'Trust in the Lord.'

Enock's presence bridged a gap in my personal life too. Whenever I did not feel strong enough to join the others outside, I stayed at home and played with him. It took away the boredom of waiting for the others to come home from the fields. It also freed up mother to get on with her chores. I loved my baby brother. He was so dependent and restricted in his movements, reminding me of the time I was recovering from polio. We bonded and developed a mysterious way of communicating whereby I seemed to understand his cries and could anticipate his needs.

Little Enock was always very happy and excited to see me but one day he fell ill. He cried a whole day and night. Poor mother could not get a minute's sleep. Unable to console him my parents rushed him to the local clinic. All sorts of remedies were tried out, modern and traditional. Nothing seemed to help. The baby just kept on crying. He was no longer able to eat and drink and soon became so weak that he stopped responding altogether. His breathing was very shallow. Whenever he did come round he would only feebly cry. Fearing for his life we anxiously prayed to the Lord, begging him to spare the child.

I felt desperately sorry for this little boy, so helplessly trapped in a hurting body, so incapable of expressing what was troubling him. Had I not been in a similar position not so many years ago? I prayed for him and suddenly felt that I ought to be doing something. This in itself was strange, as mothers know much better than young boys what to do with crying babies. Besides, everyone else had tried to comfort Enock by cuddling, rocking and walking around with him, all to no avail.

"Please, mama, can I hold my brother?" I asked.

"Your back is not yet strong enough," she hesitated, "you may topple over and drop him."

"Let him have a go," father intervened. He sounded resigned, almost bitter. "If this son must die like the others, at least Simeoni should have a chance to say goodbye to him."

Mother put the baby in my arms. He was fearfully pale and thin, his eyes half-closed, his little heart racing.

"O *Yesu*, don't let my baby brother die," I just kept on praying. "You have given me back my life so please help Enock too." All of a sudden I felt a huge wave of affection glowing through me and flowing into Enock's body as though someone was wrapping the two of us in a soft, warm blanket. Enock stopped crying. Instead he began to groan. Holding him close to my chest my tears dropped onto his little face. I raised his head to wipe them off, only to find myself looking into the clearest, brightest eyes I had ever seen.

"He is gone," people cried around us, shocked by the sudden silence. Meanwhile Enock and I stared at each other, his eyes interacting with mine and following my movements. His little hands reached out for my face.

"Look, he is alright!" someone shouted. Everyone started laughing from sheer puzzlement and relief. Mother took him from my arms and waited for him to start crying again.

"You better stay near," she said to me, but little Enock was fine. And when he did cry again a few days later, it was just a normal cry, like that of any other baby.

CHAPTER 9

PROPHECY

*"God chose the weak things of the world to shame the strong.
God chose the lowly things of this world and the despised things
- and the things that are not - to nullify the things that are,
so that no one may boast before him."*

1 Cor. 1: 27b-29

I was nine or thereabouts and my life was as near to normal as it could ever be. I played with other children, even joined them in the fields. Just like all my brothers and sisters I got common childhood diseases like measles, chickenpox and whooping cough from which I recovered without further complications. By now the doctors' prognosis that I would die within seven years of contracting polio had almost been forgotten. I was strong and agile but unlike the other children I moved around on hands and knees. There was no further recovery to be expected nor any progress to look forward to.

Then news reached our village about new treatments for people with crippling diseases that were said to be successful. These treatments varied from taking herbal remedies and bathing in hot springs to operations by *Muzungu* doctors. At first my parents were very sceptical. They had not yet forgotten my previous stay in Kampala without getting cured, followed by my disastrous time at the traditional healer's. Most people felt that I had come back from those treatments in a much worse state than before.

My parents ignored the rumours until a family friend told them about an acquaintance who had greatly benefited from modern medical care in New Mulago hospital in Kampala.

"I know a child who used to crawl like Simeoni," he told us. "She was operated on and is now walking again with callipers and crutches!" In those days operations were rather uncommon and generally very much feared. Survival rates were low, as many hospitals lacked essential equipment and medication. Besides, they did not use sophisticated anaesthetics but chloroform which caused terrible side effects. Everyone had heard stories about people succumbing on the operating table.

"If a normal person can die from an operation what about our Simeoni who has already been to the grave and back?" my family wondered. The decision was not easily taken but my parents did not really have a choice. Unless something further was done for me I was destined to crawl in the dust for the rest of my life.

As usual, whenever my family faced an important decision, the Christian community was involved. My parents met with the brethren who listened to their dilemma and prayed with them for blessings. Only after doing so did they feel ready to go ahead and take me to Kampala. No sooner were the plans announced than a serious debate broke out within the wider family. Opinions were deeply divided. For some people modern treatments were something of a miracle and therefore very appealing. They believed *Muzungus* to be 'the arms of God' when it came to dealing with African diseases. They were able to prove this with an example.

"If Simeoni had not been put in an iron lung he would never have come out of his coma. Surely the best place for him to be is with the *Muzungus*!" Others doubted the wisdom and godliness of my parents' decision.

"Aren't we being ungrateful to the Lord who has blessed us with Simeoni's recovery? Is it fair to put this child through dangerous operations when his life is no longer at risk?" The thought of operations also rekindled old fears. After all, we still believed that I was going to die within seven years, and this period was not yet over.

"What if he won't survive?" people worried. "He is such a lively presence in the home, so full of energy and laughter, a joy to have around!"

Some relatives were quite resigned, especially those who were not Christian. "This boy is as good as gone," they argued, "Why try and patch him up? Let him stay home these last few years of his life and die there in peace. No good can come from modern treatments."

There was also the issue of practicality. The treatment was likely to take months. No adult could be expected to abandon the home for such a long time to look after me in the city.

As I overheard others debating my future I began to feel increasingly troubled. I was happy with my life the way it was. I did not want this to be disrupted. The possibility of leaving home made me anxious. I knew father and mother would not be able to stay with me in Kampala while I was being treated. It brought back traumatic memories of being left with the traditional healer. Once again, so it seemed, my life was at stake. *Why me? Why always that feeling that one day I will be abandoned?* The thought made me fearful and sad.

While people weighed up the pros and cons, it was up to father to make the final decision. There were financial implications too. Although treatment in public hospitals was free in those days, he would have to pay for our journey. Then we received the unsettling news that foot and mouth disease had broken out in a nearby county. As a result, quarantine was put in place and the cattle markets closed. If the disease spread to our area it would be impossible for father to sell a cow or dairy products! Now he had no choice but to act without delay, thus putting a stop to any further deliberations. I was not given a say in the matter. Only when the decision was made did they ask me how I felt about it. I tried to see things from the positive side. Perhaps one day I might walk again! Wasn't it exciting to get out of the village? Travelling by car and bus was an adventure. It would be an opportunity to meet other children like me and find out how they managed. If only it could be of short duration though... If only someone would stay with me!

Fortunately the authorities closed our local cattle market too even before father could sell a cow. Quietly I breathed a sigh of relief, not knowing that my parents were sharing their disappointment with the brethren who had supported them in their plan. These brethren rallied together and raised lots of money, enough for father to take me to Kampala. One day they came to our home to break this 'wonderful' news. Everyone burst into *Tukutendereza*, thanking and praising the Lord. Only my heart was very heavy. Yet again I had to brace myself for a very uncertain future. There was no way out. Soon we began to prepare for our journey.

Goodbyes were said and tears flowed as father tied me onto the back of his bicycle. This time we set off for Nkonge railway station quite a long distance away. From there we would take the steam train to Kampala. In those days trains ran only a few times a week. Father cycled as fast as he could over the hilly *murram* roads, arriving at the station just as the train was approaching. When we boarded the carriage he looked drained, almost ill. Our compartment was crammed with people. Fortunately they offered me a tiny space to sit but father had to stand throughout the night long journey. Our fellow travellers stared at me with pity. Once again I had to hear those usual well meant, yet insensitive remarks.

"Poor child, how could God have allowed this to happen?"

"If he were one of mine I would have wished the Lord had taken him to rest."

"You better take him to a witch doctor," someone suggested to father. "I can give you the name of a good one. He should be able to undo the curse that is upon your child."

By the time we reached Kampala father was so exhausted that he almost passed out. He lifted me off the train and put me down on the platform. Then he rushed back to gather our luggage and set off once more to collect his bicycle. It was not safe to leave our belongings unattended. There were many thieves and muggers in Kampala, especially in busy public places. Father put me on his back, the bicycle on his shoulders and, clasping our bags to his chest, staggered through the station and up a long, steep flight of stairs. I could feel the beating of his heart. His body was shaking all over. Any moment I expected him to collapse from sheer exhaustion and strain which would have sent both of us tumbling down the steps. We had only gone halfway when an imposing figure appeared at the top of the stairs as though he had been waiting for us. It was a Muslim man, a *hajji*, dressed in a white kanzu.

"Take courage, Sir," he called out to father from a distance. "Help is at hand!" With outstretched arms he forged his way down through the mass of people. His eyes locked onto mine.

"When I left home this morning I felt that God was going to show me something special!" he exclaimed. "Now I know what it is. God is great!" All the while he stared at me intensely.

"Don't worry. I mean well. You can trust me," he grinned while taking the bicycle and luggage from father. With his large, well-fed body he shielded us from the jostling crowd as we made our way up the stairs.

"Sometimes," he continued, "we receive blessings that we perceive as burdens." By now father had sufficiently recovered to respond.

"How come you speak like a *Balokole* and yet you are a Muslim?" As we moved through the station the two talked about God and how he speaks to us in mysterious ways, no matter our differences in background or tribe. In those days Christians and Muslims lived in harmony in most parts of Uganda. They were both God-fearing communities. Any religious differences were defused by shared customs and values, such as hospitality, charity, dignity and respect.

The *hajji* spoke calmly to father but he emphasised every word.

"I want you to hear this from me because I know something that you may not be aware of," he said. "God has a special purpose for this boy. You should love him even more than any of your healthy children. God willing you shall witness how the love and care you give him now will yield a much greater return in the future. Now you struggle under his weight but through his life you will be carried!"

I wondered what he meant. Would I get better and walk again? Would someone else carry father because of the love he had been showing to me?

The *hajji* was happy and clearly relieved to have discovered the mission that God had intended for him that day. He walked off and returned with something to drink – a Fanta for father and a Cola for me. I had never had a fizzy drink before and almost spat it out on the woman standing beside us. After getting me some fruit juice instead, he sat down with us. I could see from father's face that he was recovering by the minute as he and the *hajji* continued to talk.

Father always remembered this event. He kept pondering over the *hajji's* words, spoken at a time when he was in very low spirits.

"God's message can come from an unexpected source, my child," he quite often said to me. "I have no doubt that the Lord has a special purpose for you." He always ended such conversations with a thoughtful remark based on something he had read in the Bible.

"When we keep quiet and cease to praise Him, surely the stones will cry out!" (Luke 19:40).

Father and the *hajji* debated how we could best reach New Mulago. The main roads were risky for someone unfamiliar with cycling in the city and it was not easy to take a bicycle on the local buses. The alternative would have been to hire a taxi but father had brought his bicycle along in the hope of saving some money. In the end the *hajji* showed us the safest route and we parted with smiles and handshakes.

"Goodbye, son," he said while placing his large hand on my shoulder. "May the blessings of Allah rain upon you both."

"And may *Yesu* bless you with salvation!" replied father.

We got lost a few times but eventually managed to reach the hospital complex. The road leading up to it was very steep. Even cars and buses struggled to get all the way to the top. Now and then father had to walk beside the bicycle and push it along.

Halfway up the hill stood the tallest building I had ever seen. Built by the British and officially opened by the Duke and Duchess of Kent in 1962, New Mulago was one of the most impressive and modern buildings in Uganda. Many regarded it as the best teaching hospital in East and Central Africa, with highly sophisticated equipment and lots of *Muzungu* staff. The original hospital, dating back to colonial times, was now called Old Mulago. Made up of a large network of one-storied buildings it lay scattered over the brow of the hill. Adjoining Old Mulago and slightly further downhill was a bus stage with on the opposite side of the busy road a thriving market place and trading centre. I had been in Mulago once before when critically ill but I had not seen much of it. In fact, I could not even remember what part of the hospital I had stayed in.

The Polio Clinic was situated in the Old Mulago complex. Its official name was Round Table Polio Clinic, as the Kampala Round Table Club had been involved in the funding. The clinic was set in several acres of green with large exotic trees from Europe. Through the fence I spotted a number of children and adults crawling around or limping with crutches. They all looked relaxed and cheerful. No one showed any sign of fear or distress. I had heard many a story about scary operations but my worries and resistance evaporated at the sight of this lively place. Father and I looked at each other, seemingly thinking the same. Surely, it had been a good decision to bring me to this place. We entered the compound and were shown the way to the clinic reception. An eager Ugandan clerk awaited to take my details.

"Name of the patient?" he asked us.

"Simeoni Ninsiima," replied father. For a moment the clerk looked thoughtful. Then his face lit up.

"That will be Simon Ninsiima," he said, writing that name on my file. Looking at father's puzzled face he asserted, "The English version of your son's name is Simon. We keep all our records here in English!" He must have been unfamiliar with the Biblical name Simeon given to me when being christened. Not knowing any better father and I went along with this man who seemed to be an expert on anything *Muzungu*. So from that day on I became Simon Ninsiima in my medical records and consequently in all other formal documentation.

Attached to the clinic was the Polio Hostel where people stayed while being assessed, awaiting the availability of theatres and wards in New Mulago and for subsequent rehabilitation and treatment. No one seemed critically ill. In fact, patients moved around quite freely. They were even allowed to go to the nearby shops and canteens, depending on their age and strength. The hostel housed disabled people of all ages who had all suffered from polio. Some were in a poor condition, only able to lie on their beds. Others crawled around the compound with a tremendous speed. Everywhere I spotted little people, full of mischief, playing hide-and-seek under the beds, giggling and laughing. I could hardly believe my eyes. Back in the settlement I used to be the odd one out but here in the polio hostel I was surrounded by my own 'species'. It felt like coming home.

Father talked to patients and carers while waiting for my turn to be seen. Everyone was eager to share their experiences with us, though they might not have expressed themselves in polished, medical jargon.

"The doctors knocked me out and cut me up before putting me in this plaster," a disabled young man explained. He was now learning to walk again with callipers and crutches. Those words were terribly shocking. Yet, I longed to be part of these people. Soon we found ourselves surrounded by a group of curious children who were asking father all kinds of questions.

"How old is he? Where does he come from? Is he staying here? Are they going to cut him too?" Proudly they showed off their scars, like little veterans of war. One boy had his bones broken and kneecap removed to straighten his leg. Looking at the scars I remembered the unbearable pain I had felt when cut by the traditional healer. How would I ever survive an operation like that? Although I had heard people talk about chloroform I did not understand what it was. No one had ever explained to me the purpose and effects of anaesthetics.

Later I met people at the polio hostel who were scarred much worse than me. Their wounds had also been inflicted in the name of traditional healing. A young man told me how a healer had rubbed him with a mixture of *ghee* and herbs before pressing scorching hot stones all over his body. It had left him with enormous scars. A girl with one arm weakened by polio had been burnt with hot metal all the way up to her shoulder. Another small child was totally disfigured. I felt so grateful that father had taken me away from the healer's place before my treatment could escalate into something so much worse.

Once or twice a week the consultants and doctors made their rounds through the hostel with a group of medical students in their wake. The leading specialist was Professor Huckstep who had come all the way from Australia. We were cleaned up and nicely dressed for the occasion. Off the floor, on the edge of our beds and on our best behaviour, as though a president was about to inspect his guard of honour.

The doctors' round was always anticipated with excitement, but also with dread. Whereas some patients looked forward to being discharged, others nervously waited to be told the nature of their treatment. I closely watched the people in white coats as they walked from bed to bed. One of them pulled what looked like a hammer from a very deep pocket. He reached for the legs of a young girl and started knocking on her knees and ankles. His actions confirmed my worst suspicions and fears. What else was he hiding in those pockets? Perhaps the knives that were used for operations! I held my breath as the doctors drew nearer, praying that they would not cut me right away. Straightening up as much as I could I put on my sweetest face and most disarming smile. What else could I do to avert the approaching danger? A thorough examination revealed that most of my ligaments had severely contracted, especially my hips, knees and feet.

"Your son requires drastic surgery followed by long-term rehabilitation," a doctor explained to father via an interpreter. "It will take several more assessments before we can proceed with the appropriate treatment. In the meantime he will have to be admitted."

Nearly all patients at the hostel had a close relative staying with them, especially the young ones. Only a few older children were left in the care of the hostel. A staff member told father that my treatment was likely to take months, if not years. It would therefore be acceptable for him to go home now and come back to see me some time later.

"Are you happy for me to leave you, my child?" father asked me. "I need to raise more money and find someone able to stay with you in Kampala."

I wanted to remain in the hostel and explore this exciting place, full of people like myself, but the thought of going through scary treatments on my own was too hard for me to bear. Sick with fear I burst into tears, silently hoping that showing father my emotions might convince him to delay his departure!.

"It really won't be long," he tried to comfort me. "Soon somebody will come to look after you." He had to leave; his presence was needed at home. We made our way to the fence, father and I, followed by a group of crawling children. Their parents had reassured father that it was all right for him to leave me behind. They would happily keep an eye on me. Besides, there were plenty of staff members at the hostel so I would be well looked after.

I could not escort my father all the way to the bus stage as this would have meant crawling along the busy street. Near the entrance of the compound he and I said goodbye, exchanging our usual farewell blessing.

"May the Lord's grace and peace be with you," father began. Seeing that I was about to cry again he decided to keep it brief.

"You know how much we love you, my son. God willing, someone will come and join you soon." Then he walked off.

My new friends showed me a place near the fence where I could clearly see the road and bus stage with all the buses and taxis arriving and departing. Sometimes they sat there in the shadow of the special trees, hoping to spot someone they knew. I saw father walk beside his bicycle. He looked back and waved. Next I caught a glimpse of him cycling through the busy traffic. One last wave and he was gone. I did not actually see him board a vehicle. Perhaps he had decided to go to the central bus park and take a bus with a roof carrier for the bicycle. After our horrendous journey to Kampala he probably did not feel like going by train again. There was no way of knowing how he was getting on or whether he would reach home safely. I missed him even before he was out of sight and wondered how long he would be thinking of me.

The bus stage at Mulago was noisy and busy – a jumble of traffic, people, colours and sounds, but inside my head it was strangely still. As I looked around, everything seemed cold and distant. Nothing appealed to me anymore, not even the company of my new, crawling friends. Remembering how long it had taken us to travel up to Mulago I realised how far away I was from home. Father's presence had boosted my confidence to enjoy my new surroundings. He had given me a sense of protection. Without him I felt extremely vulnerable and insecure. Once again a deep sense of abandonment befell me. Suddenly I could see beyond the crowd of cheerfully crawling and limping children. They might have been disabled just like me but they were total strangers.

Unlike previous times when I had been away from home, I was to find myself among Ugandans from many different tribes, as well as Europeans and people from all over the East and Central African region. With most of them I could not even communicate. I did not understand English and Swahili, the international language commonly used in East Africa. The languages spoken in the north and east of Uganda were totally alien to me. All these people had different ethics and ways of interacting. It was terribly intimidating for a child brought up with Christian values and discipline, within the confinements of our rural *Bahima* culture. For sure, we patients had something in common. We had all suffered from the same disease and were attending this clinic for treatment. Yet, it was a place so different from anywhere I had ever been.

My new friends asked me to come and play with them but dispersed one by one when I ignored them. I stayed near the fence, trying to keep the picture of my disappearing father vivid on my mind. Somehow I hoped he would come back, perhaps with a flat tyre or to give a last minute instruction. It would not be nice for him to turn up again only to find me gone!

The day was advancing. A bell rang to announce that it was dinnertime. As father and I had already eaten I decided to skip the meal. I waited near the fence until darkness fell and a caretaker called me indoors. Having been brought up in a rural environment I would not have minded staying outside all night. However, life was different in this new place. Reluctantly I crawled after the caretaker back to the hostel.

Many children in the polio hostel had been there for months. I discovered that the boys played in 'gangs' that competed with each other. Each 'gang' tried to convince me to join them by showing off with all the things that they could do, like arm wrestling and racing on crutches, or sneaking out to the canteens and shops.

"Are you really allowed to leave this place?" I asked them in awe. "How do you manage to cross that busy road with all those cars and buses?"

"Oh, that's easy!" they cheekily responded. "When we crawl across, the traffic will have to stop!"

As a well brought up *Balokole* child I wondered how proper it would be to belong to a group of children that was rivalling another. I had no experience of this type of friendship and never been in a position to make such a choice. Before long some of the more streetwise boys started picking on me, calling me names like *Mulalo*, the *Luganda* word for 'shepherd'. In their eyes I was a backward child who knew nothing beyond cattle keeping! That made it easier for me to make up my mind and team up with a group of boys who were a little more receptive.

The hostel had lots of non-medical staff. There were managers, administrators, cleaners and people serving food, but it was the task of relatives and carers to deal with the patients' personal laundry. Noticing that I did not have anyone to care for me an older patient showed me how to wash my clothes in a bucket of water. I could not even reach the taps and soon started looking quite shabby. Someone else's carer helped me out until I devised my own style of cleaning my clothes. I just washed them while sitting under the shower.

After a few days I began to venture out and explore the vast compound around Old Mulago. My new friends took me on a tour along all the interesting places: the outpatient clinics, canteens and wards, some of which had been empty ever since facilities and services were moved to New Mulago. This was the first time for me to see a wheelchair. Large and heavy, it was almost entirely made of wood but softly cushioned and very attractive. Occasionally I was allowed to have a go in one. This gave us the opportunity to explore more distant places, like across the busy road and bus stage, all the way up to New Mulago. Our most exhilarating pursuit was racing down Mulago Hill. It was not easy to control and steer a wheelchair while speeding down a slope. When you gripped the rim to try and stop it, you got friction burns all over your hands! Countless times we toppled over, ending up covered in cuts and bruises but that was all part of the fun.

One day we managed to get to the top of the hill: me in the wheelchair pushed by a friend with a limp and flanked by two others on crutches. With the three of them clinging onto my chair we began to race down the steep, bumpy road.

"Beep, Beep! Vroom, vroom," we yelled, exuberantly laughing and waiving. Pedestrians jumped aside with obvious concern on their faces. Faster and faster we went. As the chair gathered momentum it began to shed its human load. I could hear my friends cry out behind me as I struggled to stay in control. At last the wheelchair veered into the verge where it overturned and landed in a ditch, leaving me trapped underneath. This time we were really hurt and unable to offer a plausible excuse to the hostel staff for the damage caused to ourselves and the wheelchair. We were seriously told off and from that day on the use of wheelchairs was restricted to within the hostel premises.

If any rivalry did exist among the groups of children, then it was easily forgotten. When it came to adventures and special events we all shared in the excitement and fun. The hostel received regular visits from 'friends of the polio clinic and hostel' which could be individuals as well as organisations. Kind Asian ladies came round with scrumptious sweets and spicy snacks. People from the Rotary Club and Lions Club gave us boxes full of toys and treats. They even took groups of children on outings. Professor Huckstep's pioneering work with polio patients attracted interest at national and international level. Visitors from many different countries came to see us, including celebrities and other important people. We were often photographed and in 1966 a film called 'Polio in Uganda' was made about the polio clinic and hostel.

The meals were often a highlight too. Our food was cooked in the huge kitchens based at New Mulago and brought over in heavy metal trolleys, transported by a dilapidated Bedford. I quickly learnt from my friends the latest 'rule for survival': *"The ambulances with doors carry patients but a tatty old one without doors brings our food. When it approaches you must get to the ward as quickly as you can or else you'll miss your dinner!"*

Each morning we had porridge for breakfast and at ten o'clock a mug of milky tea with a soft, freshly baked white bread roll that smelt and tasted gorgeous. There were 'rice days', 'meat days' and 'bread days'. On those days we made sure not to stray far from the hostel, as we did not want to skip a good meal. Less popular were the 'boiled potato with cabbage days'. We were not used to the way this food was cooked. The nasty, unfamiliar smell hit our noses even before the trolleys were offloaded from the vehicle.

There were always events to look forward to at the polio hostel but also things to dread. With my assessment almost completed, the time for my treatment drew near. At one end of the ward I could see children and adults lying on bed with their legs in traction. These were metal frames clamped onto the beds, like scaffolding with strings and pulleys attached to keep their legs suspended while at the same time being pulled down by weights. I was told that this was done to treat contracted knees and hips. The weights were only allowed to come off when a physiotherapist came round. For months those patients had to lie there with their legs up in the air, needing help with everything, from washing to the use of bedpans. I wondered what would happen to me if I were put in traction. How would I be able to cope without any close relative around to care for me?

As the weeks passed and no one came I grew increasingly worried. Every day, after every breakfast, I crawled to the place where I had last seen father disappear among the traffic. There, under a large shady tree I watched the buses and taxis, hoping to see him or any other familiar person emerge from the crowd of passengers. Oh, I missed my family so much!

Yet, something made my stay at the polio hostel really worthwhile. It was exciting to be around children who had responded well to operations and were learning to walk again with special appliances. It sent my imagination wild to think that I could be just like them. Perhaps I might even totally recover...! I would be so popular back home. Every child in the village would want to be my friend.

"Through his life you will be carried," the Muslim man had said to father. Could there be any truth in those words? How thrilling it would be to find myself walking again one day. Perhaps even be so strong that I could carry my own father...

CHAPTER 10

NEW MULAGO

"For I am convinced that neither death nor life, ...
neither height nor depth,
nor anything else in all creation,
will be able to separate us from the love of God
that is in Christ Jesus our Lord."

Rom. 8: 38a, 39

None of us spoke English but the more experienced 'inmates' knew what words to listen out for. "When Professor Huckstep or any of the other doctors, say, *'This chap ....taken down...,'* that means operation. Then you know it is your turn. There will be no escape. Down you will go until you face the knife!"

When at last I heard those dreaded words it felt as though my world was coming to an end. At home I had seen animals being slaughtered and I never got used to the helpless, petrified look in their eyes. In my fearful imagination I saw myself in their place. Was I not just like those poor creatures to be slaughtered at the hands of knife-bearers, whether butchers or surgeons? And so the day came for me to be taken by ambulance (one with doors!) to New Mulago. Everything I had been told about this hospital was true. It was massive and modern, full of amazing machines and equipment, with miles and miles of corridors, all brightly lit. Almost everywhere I passed I could hear peculiar, humming sounds. The whole building seemed charged as though running on an engine. A strange, unpleasant smell reminded me of my time in the intensive care unit several years ago. It brought it home to me that this was a place for people who were really very ill. The hostel smelt much nicer.

"Have you ever been in a lift before?" asked the nurse who was pushing my wheelchair. "It takes you up without having to climb stairs." I had climbed trees but never stairs, except when father carried me on his shoulders through Kampala railway station. Nor had I ever been in a building where floors were on top of each other. The motion of the lift left me breathless. It churned my stomach the way the bus had done when clearing a steep hill – that day when father and mother were taking me home from Mulago.

The corridors were bustling with people – patients, visitors and medical staff, the latter in uniform, looking very important and busy. I was taken up to the Orthopaedic Section and allocated a bed in Ward 3B. It had a little lamp that I could switch on by myself, something I had never done before. A plastic radio earphone protruded from the wall.

The nurses were kind but could not extinguish my fear. *What if I was going to be cut up straight away?* By now I had seen and heard quite enough to wish I could escape from the building and run for my life!

Ward 3B was huge with dozens of beds, many hidden out of sight by partitions. There was so much to take in. Very early in the morning cooked meals arrived in large metal containers with shelves from which serving trays were pulled. These containers were plugged into the wall, something that seemed to be done with every piece of hospital equipment. Throughout the days nurses scuttled up and down with trolleys laden with medication, bandages and bedpans. Occasionally an altogether different trolley passed our beds, one that looked far more appealing. Largely made of glass it was stocked with special things like sweets, cakes, snacks, bottles of drink and various toiletries. This trolley stopped at some of the beds but never at mine. I wondered which lucky patients would be entitled to such treats. It took me quite a while to realise that those things were actually for sale and therefore only given to people with money!

In my ward were patients with different conditions and in various states of health, either recovering from an operation or awaiting one, like me. Now I was able to witness with my own eyes what surgery did to people, how they responded to the chloroform and pain. To me it seemed as though you first needed to be taken to the brink of death before you could receive any benefit from an operation. As the chloroform wore off, patients were sick and confused and remained in that state for hours. Vomiting terribly, some rolled off their beds, needing to be restrained like drunkards! Children moaned and screamed for their parents. Even adults were crying and yelling. When a patient took long to come round, the members of staff got terribly busy. In turn this sent my imagination wild. *What if that poor person is dying?*

There were other children on the ward awaiting surgery. Together we watched the occasional scenes of mayhem and shared our worries and fears. Then, one by one, they too were taken away and brought back in a dreadful state. An older boy who had already been operated on noticed my anxiety.

"Really, it will be over before you know it," he kindly reassured me. "You'll have one nasty day and the next you're on the mend. Maybe by then your family will be here with you!" But I was not so sure. There was a time when I did not fear death. I was even ready to welcome it! That was when the prospects for my health and future were bleak. In those days I had surrendered my childlike hopes and aspirations. I had learned to look forward to the consolation of a new and better life in the kingdom of God. Although still clinging onto this faith and longing to be close to my Lord, I had since experienced the sweet taste of survival. I had accepted the limits of my disability and discovered new abilities and strengths. Now I wanted to hold onto my life and get the most out of it. To me operations and chloroform were synonymous with dying and I was not ready for this. I loved life and was no longer prepared to give it up.

Whatever treatment awaited me, it soon became apparent that there would be quite a wait. Every so often doctors stopped at my bed to discuss my case and refer me for an x-ray or test. To my surprise most days were rather boring, so the moment I had settled in I decided to look for adventure. Not yet confined to my bed, I did not want to miss out on this chance of a lifetime to explore my fascinating new surroundings. What was happening at the end of the corridors? Where did all those people go to? In the weeks that followed, the hospital became my newfound territory and uncovering its mysteries my mission.

New Mulago was one of the few tall buildings in Kampala at that time. It consisted of three six-story wings, connected by long, open corridors that looked a bit like bridges. In whatever direction I faced – above, below or sideways, there were always people hastily walking along those 'bridges'. The hospital even had a helicopter pad in the compound for very important patients. Whenever a helicopter approached, those of us able to get off their beds, dashed for the nearest window. A perfect excuse for us children to race each other in our wheelchairs through the corridors to try and get a better view!

One of the boys in my ward had fallen from a tree and broken his leg. He wore a plaster cast all the way from the thigh to the ankle where two metal rods protruded. The plaster was stained red with blood that seemed to well up from within. This boy also moved around in a wheelchair and was just as curious as I. Together we set about exploring the hospital building further. Our favourite place was the sixth floor where prominent people were treated and where children were not allowed. If we kept very quiet and stuck to the corridors the nurses might just ignore us. The wards on that floor were beautiful and posh, but the greatest thrill was the view from the bridge – as if we were on top of the world!

Whenever a high politician or military officer had been admitted this section of the hospital was cordoned off and put under guard. Of course, this made it all the more tempting. On such occasions we could find no rest until we had treated ourselves to a rare glimpse of all the armed bodyguards and soldiers.

The people working at New Mulago wore different colour uniforms with all sorts of caps, bands and stripes. This was just as intriguing as the building itself and I had to find out what these meant. The way I used to track small animals in the wild I now set upon trailing people in uniform to discover where they were going and what kind of work they did. This led me to all kinds of interesting places, like the radiography department, maternity wards, hospital kitchens and maintenance workshops as well as the much-dreaded operating theatres, Intensive Care Unit and mortuary.

Without family around to cheer me up I set about making friends with whoever I met, whether patients, visitors or staff. Being an open, inquisitive child, people seemed to find it easy to chat and joke with me. I began to pick up words in Acholi and Langi, languages spoken in the north of Uganda, and English and Swahili, which I practised on my new friends. Greeting them in their own language always brought a smile to their faces. In turn a kind remark or gesture from them helped reduce my loneliness and fill the void in my heart.

New Mulago was a fascinating place but nothing more so than the hospital lifts. These were small silver-metal rooms without windows that could take you almost anywhere you wanted by simply pressing a button! When the doors closed, you remained sealed inside, cut off from the outside world and eerily alone. The thrill of using these lifts did not always come without a snag. Once a boy and I got trapped inside and the lights went out, leaving us screaming with panic in the pitch-dark. Fortunately that boy was a bit older and bigger than me and he eventually managed to find the emergency bell. Another time, when I could not get hold of a wheelchair and there was no one around to give me a hand, I had crawled into a lift that was apparently known for getting stuck. It never levelled with the floor. When the doors opened you could peer through a gap into a seemingly bottomless shaft. All of a sudden this lift stopped moving but the buttons were far too high for me to reach. When at last the doors slightly opened I quickly wedged my hands in-between to keep them from closing again, unaware that the protective strip around the edges had been damaged. As the doors rammed open and shut, the sharp metal sliced through my hand. I was bleeding badly and could see a bit of the bone. That day I lost a fingernail and needed stitches. Much worse though was the shock of being cut. It reminded me of why I was in hospital... A taste of things to come...!

The nurse tending to my wound told me not to wander off again without the use of a wheelchair but I did not mind that at all. For now I had lost my appetite for adventure and would rather stay close to the ward.

Countless times I got stuck in a hospital lift, either alone or with others. Many years later I still dreamt about this: lifts shooting up with great speed or endlessly falling, with me locked inside in the dark.

I loved looking at the clouds through the windows of the corridors and wards. They reminded me of the sky back home. I imagined my family looking at them at the very same moment as I. Caged within this glass and concrete world I became overwhelmed with an urge to venture outside. I desperately needed to breathe in fresh air and crawl through soft, green grass. Someone told me that you could get out of the building via the casualty department or the canteen but I did not know where these were. Eventually I found a hectic place on the ground floor with numerous people sitting in wheelchairs or lying on trolleys. Some were moaning in agony, their clothes soaked in blood. Others looked limp and lifeless even though they had no visible wounds. I saw doctors and nurses rushing from patient to patient, pushing oxygen masks over the mouths of the very sick ones and summoning each other for help. Next of kin hung around with anxious faces. Cleaners trudged through the chaos to mop up the puddles of blood. After a while I plucked up courage to have a closer look at this unusual place – so scary and at the same time so very intriguing. I had never seen anything like that at home.

In the corridor was a quiet place where I parked my wheelchair and watched. On the wall beside me were telephone booths that patients were allowed to use. I tried to make a phone call too by imitating others. Having never used those things before, I wondered how they worked.

"All you need to do is put in a coin," a fellow patient showed me. "And even if you don't have any money you can still make a call. Just dial 100 and speak to an operator."

Lifting the large black receiver I dialled the required number. Nothing but buzzing and clicking noises. I was still trying to make sense of these when a male voice blurted into my ear.

"Good afternoon, New Mulago... How can I help you?"

Oh no, what had I done? At once I dropped the receiver, spun around with my wheelchair and raced back all the way to the safety of my ward. Away from this spooky man, in case he came after me!

The casualty department became a place I visited quite often. Although shocking and awful, there was always some sort of commotion and I could never get bored. I watched ambulances arrive, forever bringing more sick and injured people. Then, for a brief moment, the main doors opened to reveal a glimpse of the outside world I so much longed to reach. However, throughout my stay in the hospital I never dared to cross that gruesome, hectic place.

After one of my expeditions to the casualty department I ventured into a lift to look for some fun, to try and forget the horrible sights I had just witnessed. As the doors were about to close, a man entered with a trolley that was larger than usual and covered with a hood.

"When you see a trolley with a hood you must get away as fast as you can," other children had often warned me, adding in an ominous whisper, *"There could be a dead body inside!"*

I hastily tried to get out of the lift but the trolley was blocking the exit. With a growl the man stretched out his hand and reached for the buttons above me. Making myself as small and insignificant as possible, I tightly closed my eyes. He shifted the trolley towards me. I could hear his feet come closer. Fearing what he might do next I prepared to launch the loudest scream ever to be heard in New Mulago. Mercifully the lift stopped at the very next floor where he got out with the body. Much later I found out that 'body pushers' were generally viewed with superstition and treated like outcasts. Perhaps that was why they were always so unkind and grumpy.

From that day on I never again used the lifts on my own. If I wanted to go anywhere I waited for someone else to enter. When that person got out I got out too, even if I had not yet reached my floor. Lifts could come and go but unless there was at least one other passenger I did not dare to board. I also never dared to stray towards the mortuary again. When next visiting the casualty department I was much more aware of the suffering of the people in that place. I quietly whispered a *'Thank You'* to God. At least I only had polio. I was not so badly hurt and bleeding as many of those patients.

Slowly my zest for exploration cooled. I had accumulated enough experiences and impressions to keep my mind occupied, in my frantic search for a buzz to elevate my spirit and keep me afloat. I had tried to make sense of my situation but nothing could give me the answer I craved for. Besides, the time for my operation was drawing near and I preferred the relative safety of my bed.

Once a week a hospital chaplain made his rounds of the wards. I had not noticed him before, probably because I never stayed long enough in the same place. He carried a Bible and a songbook, reminding me of the clergy who often came to visit my parents. The sight of him made me realise how much I had missed the regular worship and close fellowship with Christians back home. Standing in the pathway the chaplain read a few verses from the Bible and explained to us their meaning.

"Nothing can separate us from the love of God, no matter where we are or what situation we find ourselves in.

"The Lord gives us hope and comfort but also expects us to do his will and put our trust in him."

Somehow these words seemed to reach for the turmoil within me and bring calm to my emotions and thoughts. Opening his hymnbook the chaplain began to sing a tune I recognised from home. Other Christians in the ward joined in. Shyly I hummed along too. Before leaving he prayed with us and gave us a blessing. When he passed my bed I told him that I was *Balokole* and he stayed for a brief chat.

The visit of this man was precious and timely. Besides lifting my spirit by giving me a taste of home it strengthened my feeble faith. It challenged me to dare hope that God had the best intentions for me regardless of what was going to happen.

In the bed on my right was an Asian boy who often got visitors, including his younger sister. They were always quarrelling and teasing each other. Their parents spent most of the visiting hour trying to keep them apart. Yet, the girl seemed to enjoy her brother's presence and he was clearly sad when it was time for her to go home. Watching their games and scuffles I became totally engrossed in trying to make out what they were up to. Catching my eyes their mother shrugged her shoulders. She pointed at her children, saying something in English that I could not understand. Yet I knew exactly what she meant and we both burst into laughter.

After the boy was discharged, a young woman was given the bed next to his. Her name was Merab and she was very kind and pretty. She looked like a *Muhima* but only spoke *Luganda*. Realising that I never had visitors and did not like to take treats from strangers, she instructed her younger sister to offer me a *mandazi*. She was not to move from my bedside until I had accepted. Merab was frail and mostly bed-bound but I never asked what was wrong with her for fear of being intrusive.

She must have noticed me kneeling and praying underneath my blanket. Every morning and evening I asked *Yesu* to protect my family and bring someone to stay with me. Then I would also tell him how scared I was of the forthcoming operation.

"It is good to see you pray, my child," she said to me one day. "That is what I do too. It helps me when I am troubled."

She was such a comforting, motherly figure who instinctively knew how I felt, always asking the right questions as though she could read my mind.

"Are you missing your family, my dear? Are you dreading your operation?" Then I moved closer to her bed and we talked about my feelings. To stop me from worrying she told me stories that reminded me of home. She seemed to know everything about the *Bahima* way of life and was ever ready to listen. In time I began to love and respect her as if she were one of my aunts.

One morning Merab was taken away for her operation. I did not see her for several days. When at last they brought her back the nurses removed the empty bed between us and replaced it with two screens, one around Merab's bed and the other closer to mine. She no longer talked to me but I could hear her groan. None of her relatives were allowed to come nearer. Only doctors and nurses kept disappearing behind the partitions. Once Merab's younger sister had a quick peep. When I asked her how my friend was she could barely speak for tears.

"O, she is in such a bad way. No one wants to tell us what is going on!"

A few days later there was a sudden burst of activity around Merab's bed. A nurse accidentally shifted one of the screens. Through the gap I caught a glimpse of my sweet, loving friend as she lay there surrounded by medics. They were doing all kinds of things to her, like banging on her chest. Then one of them said, "She is gone."

Merab's relatives burst into crying. Her sister ran out into the corridor, screaming with shock and grief. The doctors walked off, leaving it up to the nurses to wash and wrap the body. No one seemed to spot the opening between the screens. Meanwhile I sat there watching, fixated by what they were doing.

"Time to go and play outside the ward!" the matron instructed all the children who were able to get out of bed. A little while later a boy spotted one of the dreaded trolleys with a hood. When I next returned to the ward my special friend was gone.

Back home I had known family friends who died but never anyone so close. With the passing away of Merab the veil of my youthful innocence lifted. The world wasn't one huge playground after all! I began to realise how vulnerable life really was and that nothing could be taken for granted. People could be here one day and next be gone forever. All their love and kindness suddenly ceased to exist, leaving only memories behind. This new awareness made me feel very exposed, like being without clothes on a cold, rainy day.

Aged nine I was the youngest patient on the ward who did not have a carer and never got visitors. When the nurses found out about this, several became extra attentive. I often heard them say to each other what a charming, affectionate boy I was, with such receptive eyes and an infectious smile. As for me, I just loved looking at them sitting on the edge of my bed, crisp and clean in their blue and pink dresses with white collars, belts and bands around the sleeves. Their small, white caps had little folds in the middle, like a paper fan.

One nurse called Nabatanzi was especially kind to me, even making a point of coming to see me on her days off. She affectionately called me '*Baze*', meaning 'little husband' in *Luganda*. This was a traditional way of saying, 'You are a promising man in the making.' Sometimes she brought a few friends along. Together they would pretend to argue about which of them was going to 'win' me. Of course I knew that this was done with humour but it made me feel very important. Also a bit burdened though, as I wanted to keep each one of them happy. Their kindness and attention helped dilute my sense of abandonment, taking my mind off the ever-present fear.

As the day of my operation drew nearer, the pining for my family increased. Each visiting hour I gazed expectantly at the door of the ward, observing everyone walking through it. At times I was so convinced that someone from my family was going to come that I stayed in the corridor from morning till evening and refused to line up for food. What if they turned up and were unable to find me in this massive building? I had to make sure to be in a place where they were likely to pass. Still, no one came and the whole exercise only left me disappointed and hungry.

"Operations are really not so dreadful," the nurses tried to comfort me but I was out of spirits. I had seen how other patients benefited from the care and presence of a loved one when recovering from chloroform and pain. Whatever they said, I was alone. I had nobody staying with me.

In the bed opposite mine was a young girl called Akiki. She was probably two or three years younger than me and had also suffered from polio. Her breathing was irregular and shallow. She almost constantly needed the aid of an oxygen machine. Akiki had beautiful, large eyes, the sweetest I had ever seen and a gorgeous smile. Her face was peaceful and innocent, though a little worn from suffering. Seeing her reminded me of the time when I used to be so fragile and weak. Knowing what she was going through I felt so much for her. Most of the time she was too breathless to speak but her mother, who day and night stayed at her bedside, always instinctively knew what she wanted. Akiki was also waiting for an operation. Her mother told me that without it her daughter's life would be even more at risk. Often she commented on how precarious Akiki's condition was.

Only one hour a day Akiki was allowed off the oxygen machine. During that hour I positioned my wheelchair close to her bed. As she could only move her fingers we weren't able to play, but I discovered several ways of keeping her amused. While her mother sat in a chair, dozing or doing a bit of knitting, I chucked balls of crumpled paper at the ceiling and tried to catch them. I did clumsy headers and pretended to be falling over or made funny faces, told stories and did magic tricks with little things hidden in her blanket. In the meantime Akiki lay there staring at me with her large, sweet eyes. Sometimes she looked around the ward but became restless the moment I stopped playing. Seeing a smile light up her face was always very rewarding and certainly worth labouring for!

Akiki and her mother received many visitors – a chain of relatives and friends who brought home-cooked meals that filled the ward with a delicious smell. They were from Toro in Western Uganda and their language was a quite similar to mine, which meant that I could understand what they were saying. Often they commented on how sorry they felt that no one ever came to see me.

My operation was expected to take place any time now and I was not feeling well. Actually, I was sick with fear and hoped that by staying in my bed, well hidden under the blanket, the doctors might forget about me. Akiki must have noticed how I felt, the way I looked through the window, earphone in the ear, staring at the sky. The moment she was allowed off the oxygen machine her mother took her across to my bed where she sat in her little wheelchair. She was unable to speak but in her dreamish eyes I saw a lot of affection. She stayed at my bedside, expectantly staring at me. Although I was not in the mood for making her laugh I eventually gave in and did a few tricks. She broke into a lovely smile which instantly made me feel better.

A date for Akiki's operation had already been set but mine was to take place before hers.

"Haven't you been taken down yet?" the nurses asked as they passed me, throwing a quick glance at the chart at the foot of my bed. I was only allowed a few sips of water – no breakfast or mid-morning snack. Having watched other patients I knew that your time was up the moment they stopped you from eating. I could not help thinking about my late friend Merab and the dead body in the lift and all those other patients who had come back from their operations so terribly sick from the chloroform.

Seeing the nurses preparing to wash me and change me into theatre clothes, Akiki indicated that she wanted to be taken to my bed. At that very moment a monstrous man approached in a blue, sloppy suit with a cap on his head and a mask with little strings round his neck. He kept on talking, fast and quite detached.

"We are going to get you there. You know the name of your doctor, don't you?" How I wished him to shut up! The nurses lifted me onto a long, narrow trolley and covered me with a sheet.

"Akiki is upset," the little girl's mother conveyed. "She wants to say goodbye to you." My trolley was pushed towards Akiki's bed. Her eyes were filled with tears and so were mine. Was she crying because she somehow sensed that I was going to die? The thought made me ever so fearful and sad. The mother raised her daughter's hand and waved with it. Meanwhile the hideous man wheeled me off the ward accompanied by several nurses. Down in the lift we went and through endless corridors. Upon approaching the theatre doors, the man in blue covered his face with the mask. By now I was actually crying.

"You are a brave boy," the nurses kept saying. "We will stay with you until it's all over." Till the very last minute I hoped that father would turn up, just as he had done when mother and I were stuck at the bus park in Kampala. He could stop them from hurting me. Surely he would not fail to do so if he found me helplessly lying on this trolley!

As we entered the wing I noticed several doors leading to operating theatres. An overwhelming stench of chloroform filled the air. I recognised it from the patients who had undergone surgery, and from the smell of their vomit. The people with masks seemed to multiply now. "They must be wearing those masks to stop them from inhaling this horrible smell," I thought, and looked forward to be given mine. In a corner lay a lifeless man on a bed with bottles of fluid mounted above him. No one had bothered to put a mask on his face which I found extremely unfair. Were these the last things I would ever see here on earth? I remembered my family. So many memories came flooding back in a very short time. Would they be thinking of me? They did not even know that I was in danger! Why weren't they at my side when I needed them most?

I was laid on a green bed, huge lamps in a circle above me. The light was so bright and blinding that I suspected them to be part of the tools used for knocking people out. All the more reason for me to keep looking aside! Lots of people gathered around me in baggy suits with aprons and gloves – nothing like the pretty nurses' dresses or smart white coats usually worn by doctors. I could just about recognise Professor Huckstep's forehead and voice. The theatre room was full of unfamiliar looking machines. Turning my head I spotted a table with tools. In a flash I was back with the traditional healer as he stretched me out on banana leaves and prepared to treat me with cuts and burns. Once again I had no choice but to surrender. My situation was entirely in other people's hands.

"This will be over quickly, little boy," one of the female attendants soothed me. "How far can you count in English?" Something was put over my face with that familiar disgusting smell. They kept on chatting while I tried to show them how well I could count.

"One, two, three, four ... fifteen, sixteen" I mumbled. Then I disappeared into nowhere.

My nurse-friend Nabatanzi was at my bedside the moment I came round. I did not even know that she was there. I felt violently sick, as if about to throw up my whole stomach and not merely its contents. With every breath I smelled chloroform, only it now seemed to well up from within me.

"Mama, *Yesu*," I cried, "They are killing me!" Those nasty doctors had given me pain that I did not have before. Half awake I noticed bloodstains on my sheet. Were they still operating on me? Nabatanzi covered me with a blanket. I tried to fight her off, my brains tumbling inside my skull. I just did not know what I was doing.

From what I later understood, my operation involved several incisions around my hips, thighs, knees and ankles to cut contracted tendons and force the release of tightened joints. To me it felt as though all the bones in my legs had been broken. At some point I was transferred to a ward, not my usual one but a recovery section. I did not see anyone I knew and stayed there for several days. Then I was moved back to my original ward, close to the nurses' desk and not opposite Akiki. The ward was so large that I could not see her bed. I looked out for her mother, hoping that she would call on me.

"Don't they know where I am?" I wondered. I asked the nurses to pass them a message. It took many days before I was able to sit in a wheelchair and make my way to Akiki's bed. It was empty, the oxygen machine standing idly beside it.

"I would not search any further if I were you," muttered a patient in an adjacent bed without showing any emotion. "The news is not so good."

"What are you saying?" I asked him over and over again. At last I dared utter the dreaded word. " Do you mean... Akiki is... dead?" He refused to answer.

Hoping that she was still in a recovery ward I kept trying to find someone who knew. Only much later I bumped into her mother in one of the corridors. How different she looked now, so worn out and grey.

"What we feared all along has happened," she sobbed. "Your little friend wasn't strong enough. She did not survive the operation. The Lord has taken her home."

Long after Akiki had passed away I kept going back to the place of her bed. Just to check whether she might be there, but of course she never was. Akiki was the second friend I had lost. I still needed another operation and this prospect was now all the more daunting. Once in a while my ears picked up the sound of wailing and crying in the corridors, and I knew very well what this meant.

Yet, out of the deepening realisation of how nasty and painful life could be rose a growing strength. In Mulago hospital I learnt to see difficulties as hurdles. Every time the Lord helped me overcome one he proved to me that he could do so again. No matter how feeble my faith and how inadequate my prayers, I just needed to take all my worries to him. My destiny was in his hands. His love would never leave me.

CHAPTER 11

NOT FORSAKEN

"Though you have made me see troubles,
many and bitter,
you will restore my life again;
from the depths of the earth you will again bring me up.
You will increase my honour
and comfort me once more."

Psalm 71: 20-21

Months had passed since my operations. I was back in the polio hostel, learning to walk with callipers and crutches. By now I could manage short distances – to the end of the corridor and back, albeit at the pace of a snail and with a member of staff at my side to stop me from falling over. It was wonderful to be upright again, elevated to the same height as others. In the past this only used to happen when seated on the back of father's bicycle or when carried in the arms of an adult. How I wished my family could see me walk again. However, more than a year had passed since father and I parted, and no one had come to check on me in all that time.

Every day, after breakfast, I made my way to the bottom of the compound where I had last seen father, hoping that this was *the day* when he would finally turn up. From the shadow of the trees I expectantly peered through the fence that surrounded the premises, only briefly interrupting my vigils when it was time for physiotherapy or lunch. With a clear view of the road I could see everyone coming and going. The sight of a man with a black hat and bicycle set my heart racing. Sometimes I was so convinced it was father that I asked my friends to run ahead of me to the hostel reception and wait for him there. Often, when sitting near the fence with my callipers on, I called upon a passer-by to pull me up so that father would find me standing when he came. But he did not come, nor did anyone else from my family, not even anyone remotely connected to us.

The road leading to Old Mulago was steep. Buses took a long time to reach the bus stage near the summit, especially when fully loaded. Streams of people got off and dispersed in different directions – to the trading centre or to the various clinics. To pass time I made up a game called '*Guess where this one is going*', counting the score when I got it right, every new day trying to break my record. A woman with children was probably on her way to the Outpatients Clinic. Someone with luggage must have come from afar and be visiting a patient in the polio hostel or one of the wards. Whenever I spotted a woman in traditional Bahima outfit my anticipation soared. Perhaps she was acquainted with my relatives. She could tell me how they were and pass on news about me on her return. I was so eager to let my family know that I had been operated on and was now learning to walk again. If only they could see 'the new me'! It might inspire them to come back for me and take me home!

The doctors and staff at the polio hostel and clinic were conscientious, kind and caring. Although the treatments they put us through caused a fair bit of discomfort and pain we implicitly trusted they were out to do good. I especially remember Professor Huckstep, Miss Yield, Dr Bain and Mr De Souza. They showed such a keen interest in every patient and great devotion to our progress.

Professor Huckstep was a tall Australian man who tended to close one eye when emphasising something. He was the leading consultant at our polio clinic, a pioneer in new methods of treatment. Everyone looked up to him. His car, a Citroen DS, could automatically raise and lower its body. When it was time for him to drive off, my friends and I rushed to the car park just to witness this magical elevation. Then he smiled and waved at us, with one eye shut. Very occasionally I was allowed to sit in his car and accompany him and Miss Yield to some special function. These were usually held in posh places with lots of *Muzungus* who cheerfully patted me on the head while I marvelled at their smart clothes and inhaled the lovely, foreign scents of chocolate, cake and perfume.

Miss Yield was either a senior nurse or physiotherapist from Great Britain. To us everyone wearing a white uniform was simply a 'doctor' or 'sister'. She was very affectionate towards me, especially after finding out that my family lived far away and that I did not have a carer. Sometimes she drove me in her Volkswagen Beetle to her *Muzungu* home. This was a place very different from any I had ever seen. It had carpeted floors, fascinating furniture and a beautiful garden. She helped me indoors and put me in one of her large soft chairs. There I would sit like a prince, looking at colourful magazines and nibbling on biscuits. Her kindness and attention were a welcome distraction from the waiting for father and the endless pining for my family and friends.

Besides medical treatment and general care, the staff at the clinic and hostel went out of their way to give us all a good time. They showed us movies projected on the white-plastered walls of the ward. Those of us in traction had their beds turned so they could join in as well. Ward 7, vacant after patients were moved to New Mulago, was turned into an early learning centre and recreation area for us. Here we were happily kept busy for hours on end with picture books, pencils, paper and all sorts of materials for making handicrafts. Now and then strangers came round to find out how clever we were. While we did our best to impress them by carrying out given tasks they intensively observed us, making notes to write reports about our IQ.

Best of all was the outdoor play area especially created for us. It had a climbing frame, swings and even an old Peugeot 403 with seats that were worn to the springs. We were allowed to play in this car and try out 'mechanics' on what was left of the engine. Now, besides watching the road all day, I kept an eye on the car, ready to seize my turn when no one else was at the steering wheel. I spent hours frantically driving, making sure that my 'vrooming' noises were louder than anyone else's, until my lips were numb. My enthusiasm attracted the attention from carers and staff, often triggering a light-hearted exchange.

"How far have you gone now, Simon?" they would tease me.

"*Just passing Masaka,*" was my steadfast reply. "*I will be home soon!*"

Once in a while we were taken out on a trip. The prospect of being driven by coach, usually coupled with sweets and treats, was tremendously exciting. On those days a large red coach pulled up in our compound. After the wheelchairs and crutches were loaded, we merrily set off to join the outside world and admire the city views.

On Independence Day we went to one of the national stadiums to watch police and army bands on parade, as well as concerts, gymnastics, traditional dancers and many other spectacular shows. We visited Entebbe Zoo to see the animals on display. Some I had never seen before but the others used to roam freely around our rural settlement, only now I was able to get very close without any risk to my life!

We played on the shores of Lake Victoria, a vast water strewn with little fishing boats, canoes and posh *Muzungu* yachts, and afterwards enjoyed refreshments in the grounds of some grand-looking café. Occasionally a travelling circus erected the most gigantic tent in the centre of Kampala where we marvelled at acrobatic stunts, magic tricks and disappearing acts performed by seemingly supernatural people, just like the ones in our *Chwezi* legends. Some even did stunts with lions without getting hurt!

A highlight was definitely Christmas when staff and friends of the polio hostel organised a surprise party for us. Most of us had never experienced the *Muzungu* way of celebrating this event. We entered the coach with cheerful anticipation of exciting, yet familiar treats. What unfolded was way beyond our wildest dreams, keeping us talking for weeks on end. We arrived at a huge venue, stunningly adorned with glittering decorations. Never before had I seen such magical lights flickering in all different colours. Scores of people, some of whom I recognised, walked around with trays full of biscuits, cakes and sweets. They kept offering us more, saying we could take as much as we wanted! In the middle of the hall stood a peculiar tree, seemingly growing indoors with intriguing round sparkly balls dangling from its branches. I could not help staring at those deliciously looking exotic fruits, drawing closer to try and pick one.

"Simon, you can't eat from a Christmas tree!" a member of staff cried out, far too loud for my liking. Everyone turned round and stared at me. It was such an embarrassing moment that I quickly zoomed off with my wheelchair, a cheeky grin on my face.

In the midst of all this we were introduced to a special man called Father Christmas. One of my friends who was known to be very clever explained to me that Father Christmas was the Pope, the highest priest in the world who was sent by God only once a year to hand out gifts and treats. How amazing it was to meet this 'holy man'! I could not keep my eyes off him as he noisily chattered, his red face wrapped in white fluffy hair. When he took out a handkerchief and blew his nose I could not help feeling puzzled.

"Can a heavenly man really get ill, just like us? And why does he not talk about God like all the other vicars and priests I know?"

It did not really matter. We got presents and sweets, and everything was hugely exciting.

While the highlights and treats were a welcome distraction, they did not entirely stop me from feeling hopeless and lost. Each morning I wondered how was I going to face yet another day without seeing father. I began to believe what people said – that my family had abandoned me. I knew that this happened for real to disabled people in our society and then they resorted to begging. That seemed to be the only alternative way for them to survive. In the village I had heard people talk about "*masikini*" ("crippled beggars") but in the city I could see them for myself. They were sitting or lying near the bus stage with hands outstretched and a pitiful look on their faces, appealing to sympathisers to part with a coin. How I feared becoming a beggar. It almost became an obsession. Whenever a visitor offered me food, a sweet or a bit of money I instantly turned it down. I did not want to be seen living off other people's pity. Only if all the other children were included or if a gift came from someone acquainted to me who really insisted could I consider accepting it.

Uganda gained independence from Great Britain in 1962. The King ('*Kabaka*') of Buganda, Sir Edward Mutesa, became the first President. Dr Milton Obote from the north of the country was the Prime Minister. It did not take long before friction developed between these two over power and control. On 24 May 1966 Obote deployed the Ugandan army, largely recruited from tribes of the north, to depose his rival. Led by army commander Colonel Idi Amin, soldiers launched an attack on Mengo palace, crushing the King's Guards and overthrowing the *Kabaka*.

The Baganda were known to be staunch monarchists. They even had a political party called *Kabaka Yeka* which, translated from *Luganda,* means 'The King Alone'.

Fearing an uprising Obote sent heavily armed troops into the streets to quell any pro-Kabaka resistance and round up troublemakers. At the polio hostel we heard explosions and heavy gunfire in the distance but we had no clue what was going on. Then floods of casualties, mostly civilian, began to arrive at the hospital, and with them came all kinds of rumours.

"Mengo has been bombed."

"There are soldiers and tanks all over Kampala."

"They are trying to kill all the *Baganda.*"

Many times I had heard deafening blasts of thunder caused by the awesome power of a tropical storm. At home we used to duck for cover or fall on our knees for a quick prayer, not knowing where and when lightning would strike next. I had occasionally seen drunkards draw blood from each other on a market day or when a game of *Bahima* wrestling escalated into an angry brawl of stick fighting. Such sights had never failed to shock me! Yet, none of these had prepared me for what I was about to witness that day in Kampala.

Initially the fighting took place around Mengo Hill and the city centre. Then it spread to the suburbs. As the sound of gunfire and explosions came closer and closer, everyone at the polio hostel was hastily ordered inside. Parents and carers ran for their children, almost dragging them indoors. In no time the compound was empty, bar the odd crutch and calliper left behind in the rush. The doors were locked, the window shutters drawn. Mothers hugged their crying children, soothingly talking to them. Once again I could not help feeling that I did not have anyone close to me at a time when it mattered most. I examined the faces of staff members around me, trying to gauge their level of fear. Through cracks in the shutters we saw scores of people rushing towards the hospital grounds. The moment one started running the others aimlessly joined in , like a herd of panic stricken impala.

"The army is coming this way!" they cried. "People are being slaughtered in the city!"

Shops in the distance were swiftly closed. Traffic disappeared off the streets, something that normally only happened when a very important person came to visit Kampala. On such occasions a sense of excitement and anticipation hung over the city. Now the air was filled with panic and fear. Ugandans were not used to violence. We believed that the army was there to protect us. Never before had our government mobilised the security forces to terrorise and kill its own people. Terrified civilians sought shelter in respectable public buildings like hospitals and churches. They flocked into our compound, knocking on the doors and windows of the wards, begging to be allowed in. Those unsuccessful ran off to the next building. Military vehicles pulled up in the road. Soldiers jumped out, ready for combat with machine guns and grenades. On Independence Day we had seen soldiers discharge their weapons in salute as part of the celebrations. Now screams rang out when shots were being fired and I realised that these guns were actually hurting people.

"Watch out for stray bullets through the windows!" the warden cautioned us. Everyone ducked down. The door near my bed did not quite reach the floor. Lying flat on my belly I could see all the way to the trading centre. On the road, below the trees where I often sat waiting for father, a checkpoint had been mounted where soldiers stopped everyone trying to pass. People carrying a suspicious object like a *panga*, hoe or other working tool were interrogated and severely beaten. A gun went off and I quickly withdrew my head. *Help, the soldiers must have noticed that I am peeping at them. Now they are shooting at me!*

Eventually the checkpoint was removed and the sound of battle became sporadic and distant. We ventured out into the compound and curiously peered through the fence. At the roadside lay a bloodstained body. Further away, near the trading centre, more bodies down in the mud. A group of people had gathered around, some covering their faces in grief, others angrily gesticulating. Someone paid his respect by covering the bodies with grass and leafy plants.

Following the toppling of the *Kabaka*, Dr Milton Obote became our new president. He declared a state of emergency and put a curfew in place. Soon we learnt to recognise military vehicles by the sound of their engines and the reckless manner in which they were driven – without any regard for humps and potholes in the roads. *Kabaka* Mutesa survived. With the help of loyal followers he managed to escape to Britain where he was given political asylum and died in exile a few years later. In the wake of the attack thousands of his supporters were rounded up and shot, not only in Kampala but also in the surrounding villages and rural parts of Buganda.

I cannot remember exactly when father finally came but it must have been at least a year and a half after he had left me. It was one of those rare moments when instead of waiting under the tree I was near the climbing frame, playing with other children.

"Simon, you won't believe it!" one of my friends cried out. His voice sounded uncommonly enthusiastic. I looked up and there stood my father, right in front of me, wearing a hat and blazer. He knelt beside me and I threw myself into his arms.

"How are you, my child? You look so well. Haven't you grown a lot?"

I was well fed and dressed in smart clothes donated by charitable organisations. I showed him the callipers and crutches that I had just taken off to move about more freely.

"Look father, I can stand with these things. I can even take a few steps! I keep falling over though and someone needs to stay near me to help me back on my feet."

Father looked pleased but rather reserved. He gazed at me as I chatted away. Despite his composure his eyes could not hide a heavily laden heart.

"I'm sorry, my child," he muttered several times, gently interrupting my chatter. "Please don't think we abandoned you on purpose. Life has been very trying for your mother and me." I proudly introduced him to all my friends, their carers and members of staff at the hostel. *"Look everyone, this is my father!"* At last I too had someone who cared for me and who had come to see me!

Father was different from the way I remembered him. He seemed troubled and withdrawn and did not talk much about God. I took the hat from his hand and held it close to my face. It faintly reeked of alcohol, besides his familiar scent. He gave me a few *mandazi* and a soda. As I ate and drank he told me that mother and my brothers and sisters were missing me very much.

"Not a day has passed without them praying for you. We feared you might have died from the operations."

"Are you going to stay with me, father?" I asked him. "Will you take me home with you when I am discharged?"

"Not yet, my child," he answered, his voice sounding strangely weary. "I am on a journey now, perhaps on my return. I will tell you my plans later. Let us not think about these things. We must enjoy the time we have together."

It was not clear what journey he was talking about. He helped me up and I slowly took a few steps with my callipers and crutches. For a moment the shadow of unhappiness lifted from his face. In the afternoon he spent some time with fellow parents and members of staff.

"Has it really been worth it?" I heard him ask Miss Yield through an interpreter, as he wistfully glanced at children racing up and down with their appliances. "Will he ever be able to move around like that?"

"With further treatment, physiotherapy and a lot more practice he may stabilise and improve," she cautiously reassured him.

I showed father the place where we had last said goodbye so many months ago.

"There, under that tree, that's where I have been waiting for you every day, watching the road and everybody heading this way, but you were never among them!" As I spoke, tears streamed down my face. He squatted under the tree for while, head lowered, deep in thought. Then he told me in greater detail how difficult life had been and the purpose of his journey. However much he regretted what had happened to me, my waiting was not yet over. That very evening he disappeared for a beer in a nearby bar. Only then could he muster the courage to tell me that he had left home and explain the reason why.

"You know that your mother and I have gone through a lot. Over the years we have lost four children, while you, my son, were spat out by death and left incapacitated. Two of my elder brothers passed away and now my dear sister, your Aunt Miriam, has died in childbirth." Father paused for a moment before he continued, his features clouded with grief.

"You know very well how hard I have tried to care and provide for my late brother's son Rwesingo but he squandered his inheritance and has disappeared without a trace.

"Over the years I have had to sell many cows to deal with our needs, and many more have perished from drought or disease. As if that is not enough, our beautiful farm in Bweyale, in which we had put our all fortune and hope, is miserably failing. We have barely enough to eat, let alone any crops to sell. I couldn't even raise the necessary funds to come and check on you in Kampala!

"So you see, my dear child, it is pointless for me to go back home, only to be humiliated and see my wife and children suffer deprivation!"

These were hard and trying times for many Ugandans, and not just because of natural disasters. Following the overthrow of the *Kabaka*, President Obote had abolished all kingdoms in Uganda and turned the whole country into a Republic. Staunch royalists like father, who cherished their own monarchy and culture, were devastated, and the Christian faith of many had been affected.

I was largely aware of what father told me from the few words he had spoken to me that afternoon, but I did not realise the depth of his despair. His wealth had been depleted and his life turned upside down. The relentless trials and misfortunes had taken a toll on his faith. Worn out by the continuous battle of caring for his family he felt as though the Lord had abandoned him. And so he had decided to leave home to fend for his honour and that of our family. He would try and start afresh elsewhere and only return if he succeeded, either with a new herd of cows or to move our family to a different part of the country. I had heard of people resorting to disappearing in this way until their fortune changed. Some were never seen again. They usually went to remote areas, like Bulemezi, Bururi and Karamoja in north eastern Uganda, where the locals had tougher breeds of cattle that were more resistant to ticks and diseases than our Ankole cattle.

The journey was going to be gruelling and hugely risky. It involved the crossing of rivers and lakes infested with crocodiles and hippos. Without money to hire a raft or canoe, father would have to wade through such waters. Nature in those regions was largely untamed with many more dangerous animals, even elephants and buffaloes, still roaming freely. Some indigenous tribes were known to be hostile to outsiders, and their traditions generally more aggressive and warrior-like than ours. Bandits could be hiding along the route, ready to take advantage of solitary travellers, though father thought he might team up with other fortune seekers.

"Perhaps I'll find work on a large ranch," he tried to cheer me up. "They could pay me with cows instead of wages or I'll save up and buy them cheaply. Who knows, I may return with a whole herd!"

But I knew it was a desperate, almost suicidal mission wrought with risks and danger. Listening to my father I understood how distraught he was. Slowly my feelings of abandonment evaporated, only to be replaced with deep love and concern for his life. He left the next day, a broken man. I feared I would never see him again.

When the time approached for me to be discharged, staff at the polio hostel faced a problem. In the past two years my father had turned up only once. By now that was some six months ago and no one else had come to see me since. It was rumoured that my mother had been critically ill while expecting another baby and that someone called 'Petero Rumbeka' was killed on the way from Kampala to Karamoja. It sounded very much like my father's name, Petero Rutembeka. If both my parents were dead and I had been left abandoned to the care of the hostel, what should be done with me? In the end they decided to ferry me home by ambulance to try and trace any relatives remaining. Failing this I would be placed in a charitable institution, like the Salvation Army hostel for displaced, disabled children in Kampala.

Once again I found myself in the grip of that familiar sense of uncertainty and dread. What would become of me? I had so much to tell about my adventures and treatments and treats at Mulago, but who would be out there to listen to my stories? Who would look after me if my father and mother were no longer alive? Was this how disabled people ended up on the streets and became helpless beggars?

My going home was long overdue. Over the months many of my friends had been discharged, only to find me still at the hostel when returning for their periodical check-ups. The news of my departure had spread and many staff members, friends and other well-wishers gathered around the ambulance, smiling and waving at me.

"Simon, is it really happening? Are you going home at last?"

"I hope you'll find your family!"

"Bring us some milk and *ghee* when you come back for a review!"

The ambulance crew consisted of a driver, a hospital resettlement officer and another member of staff, one of whom was *Muzungu*. As the vehicle covered ground my eyes soaked up the scenery – small villages, the countryside, the equator crossing... Now and then we stopped along the way for a short break and a soda. The closer we got to Bweyale the more talkative I became, pointing at each familiar place and telling the crew all about it. I looked forward to showing them my beautiful home, but what were we going to find? The driver lowered the window to talk to a man on a bicycle.

"Could you tell me how to get to Mr Petero Rutembeka's farm?"

The man had never heard of my family. I tried to give directions, so far as my recollection could stretch. Although the location was familiar, at times I did not even know where we were. The area looked so different – so dusty, dry and bare! Slowly my anticipation turned into dread. What if something had happened to my parents? How was I going to handle it? *Please God, don't let me be taken back and put in an institution!*

After many wrong turns and dead ends we finally approached our home. There it lay before us... but what a sight of dereliction. Our once well-tended fields and gardens were overgrown with wilted weeds. The house itself looked rundown and deserted. Shrubs had sprung up all over the compound.

When the driver switched off the engine, a peculiar silence fell upon us. A shabby man emerged from the back of the house. He seemed startled at the sight of our vehicle.

"This place is now in the hands of different owners," he told us. "The previous ones left months ago. I have no idea where they've gone."

His words confirmed my worst fears. Our beautiful home in ruins and no family to greet me. There was not even anyone who could tell us where they were or what had happened to them!

"Simon, there must be people in this area who can give us more information," the ambulance crew interrupted my gloomy deliberations. "Please try and remember the names of any family friends."

Back in the village the driver got out to have a word with the locals. The more he found out the less eager he seemed to share his findings with me. I sensed a growing concern in my travel companions. An old acquaintance directed us to the *Balokole* settlement near Kikoma, some twenty miles away.

"I don't know anything about the child's father," he said, "but there they should be able to tell you the latest about his other family members."

The ambulance proceeded slowly, hampered by the rough terrain. At some point the crew even talked about turning back to Kampala. To stop myself from falling apart I decided to focus on the sights through the windows and any happy memories these evoked. If this trip was going to be no more than an opportunity to view a place from my past then I had better make the most of it. Whenever I recognised a familiar spot I asked the driver to slow down.

"Look, this is where father and I often used to pass on the bicycle," I told the crew with all the pride I could muster.

Eventually we reached the *Balokole* settlement – the very place where I had last walked with mother before succumbing to polio. Here Aunt Elizabeth had cradled me in her arms and fed me quinine. Curious faces turned towards the ambulance.

"Isn't that Petero and Rusi's disabled son? He has returned from Mulago!"

In no time a crowd surrounded our vehicle, calling out my name. A barrage of hands reached through the windows to greet us, taking us completely by surprise. We exchanged glances of delight and relief, speechless at this overwhelming reception.

"Simeoni has come home."

"Hey you, child, run! Go and tell his family!" A boy was sent ahead of the ambulance. We followed him slowly, accompanied by the entire crowd. We stopped in front of a small hut at the far end of the settlement. The crew tried to open the vehicle doors but it was almost impossible for us to get out with so many people gathered around. Eventually I managed to land my feet on the ground. It provoked a rapturous *Tukutendereza*.

"Everyone, come and see! Praise the Lord, the boy is standing."

Arms and chests smothered my face, pinning me against the vehicle, almost pushing me over.

"Poor Petero," I heard a bystander exclaim. "He should have been here to witness this special moment."

In the midst of this commotion my mother emerged from the hut with a small baby on the arm, behind her some of my brothers and sisters. Tears ran down her face as she embraced me.

"Simeoni, you are back," she called out. "O *Yesu*, I knew that you would bring my child home safely," drawing an even more enthusiastic response from the crowd.

"Where is father?" I anxiously asked her, but the mention of his name seemed to dampen her spirits.

"I'll tell you everything later," she promised, quickly changing the subject, "Aunt Elizabeth still lives here with her family and so does Uncle Thomas. Many of our old neighbours and friends from the time of the fires have settled in this place."

People dived into their huts, only to emerge with arms full of gifts as a token of hospitality and gratitude to the ambulance crew who had gone through so much trouble to bring me home. Shortly afterwards the ambulance departed, laden with pots of milk and *ghee*. Youngsters jovially chased after the vehicle. Everyone cheered and waved – the kind of African farewell normally accorded to celebrities and other prominent people.

Meanwhile father had gone to north eastern Uganda to try and change his luck. One night while camping alone in the middle of nowhere he suddenly heard a voice. At first he thought that he had lost his mind because there was no one else in the vicinity. Then the voice spoke again, loud and clear.

"Stop hurting yourself! Don't put your life at risk. You have been on the run long enough. Repent of your sins. Turn back to me and I will take care of your problems."

At once father abandoned his mission. He returned to Bweera, only to reach our settlement a few days after my arrival. News of his approach spread fast. *Balokole* from all over the region gathered to welcome him, singing *Tukutendereza* and praising God. All along they had been praying for father, and his return spoke more than words.

By the time he got to our hut I was fast asleep. Gently waking me up, he took me in his arms.

"Simeoni, I have come back to the Lord and to my family. When I visited you at the polio hostel I was not myself but now *Yesu* has lifted my burdens."

Father looked entirely different now. His body was straight, his face lit like a bloom opened up in the sunshine. His homecoming was a great blessing to us, especially to mother. Living with father had not been easy, the way he often felt depressed and frustrated, seeking solace in alcohol. Now his faith was restored and he had returned from a perilous journey. Surely the Lord would also make our home and family life whole again!

CHAPTER 12

THREATS AND THRILLS

*"So then, just as you received Christ Jesus as Lord,
continue to live in him, rooted and built up in him,
strengthened in the faith as you were taught,
and overflowing with thankfulness."*

Col. 2: 6-7

Soon life resumed to normal as though father and I had never been away. Everyone went about their business, looking after cattle, searching for green pastures and raising families. Meanwhile I spent the days around the home with my callipers and crutches, watching mother care for the latest addition to our family – a baby girl, born at a time of great anxiety and hardship. My parents named her Mary *Nuwe*, meaning 'The Lord is the One who gives.' Scores of visitors turned up at our home to witness the amazing transformation that had taken place at the hands of *Muzungu* doctors: the boy who once used to crawl on the ground was now standing upright, even taking a few steps! The *Balokole* praised God and everyone felt greatly encouraged that from now on my life would only improve.

While residing in Bweera I was privileged to witness spiritual life of enormous momentum, characterised by undeterred evangelism, inspiring worship, close fellowship and abounding love. The *Balokole* worshipped together at home and in churches. They also attended large rallies, such as the international Christian conventions in Kabale and Kawempe. Besides supporting their own dioceses and churches they hired coaches and travelled to different parts of the country to strengthen other congregations and evangelise in places where people had not yet received Christ as their Saviour. An important part of their worship was testimony time when they freely shared what God had done in their lives, speaking of physical and spiritual healing. Some testified how they had lost faith and how the Lord had picked them up and put them back on track. Many people, including children, questioned their own relationship with God, spontaneously repenting or pledging to dedicate their lives to serving Him even more.

When the Balokole convened in large numbers, exalting the Lord with boundless joy, the Holy Spirit was evidently present. At times it felt as though the earth was shaking.

"One of these days those *Balokole* will bring the heavens tumbling down on our heads," non-believers used to say to try and describe the impact of what they were witnessing. There was such deep love among the believers that when strangers looked into each other's eyes they felt at peace and totally accepted. After parting they would miss each other even though they had barely met.

Not only did the *Balokole* proclaim the gospel, they also lived according to the faith they professed. One evening a group of believers had gathered at home for a time of Bible study and worship. They were just about to end when a gang of armed robbers surrounded the house. The ringleader was the notorious Barinaba ('Barnabas') who terrorised the area with his men by killing, raping and robbing at knifepoint. *Balokole* homes seemed to be their particular target, with women who were virtuous and men who 'turned the other cheek'.

With eager anticipation the gang set upon kicking in the door. Noticing that some of the younger believers and women were getting anxious, the head of the household strengthened them.

"We do not know whether God will save us or whether the hour has come for him to take us Home," he said defiantly, "But we can be assured of his love and ask him to take charge of this situation. Let us pray to the Lord and praise His name!"

While the *Balokole* resumed praying and singing he opened the door for the gang and welcomed them in. For a moment the robbers stood motionless in the entrance, knifes and *pangas* in their hands, stunned to find such a display of peace and joy – nothing like the panic and fear they usually saw in their victims.

"You have overpowered us. We will not fight back," the head of the household submitted. "But before you carry out your plans please allow us to serve you some food and drink and afterwards pray with you."

Clenching their weapons the gang entered the home and sat down. Meanwhile the *Balokole* women prepared them something to eat. At last Barinaba could no longer keep quiet.

"I don't know what to make of this," he yelled frustrated and astonished. "We came determined to finish you off and take your belongings but it seems that your God has spared your lives. You have been very lucky!" For a moment he looked around with visible apprehension.

"I think your God is here now... with you... in this home..."

"If you accept him he will also be your God," the head of the household replied. "He loves each one of you. Repent of your sins and he will bless you. He will attend to all your needs without you having to harm other people."

They prayed with the bandits, asking the Lord to save their souls. After they had eaten and drunk like honoured guests the gang got up and left. Following this event the robberies in our area became less frequent. We later heard that several gang members had changed their ways. A few became Christian, others turned to trading while yet again others got arrested or killed.

This was a selfless, hands-on faith. The believers shared resources and actively looked out for each other. When anyone faced difficulties or challenges like illness, bereavement or faltering faith, they rallied round each other as long as was needed, offering support at home or arranging respite with Christian families elsewhere. There was no crime in our midst. No one ever used swearwords. Even we children modelled our playing on the life we experienced around us, thus imitating well-known preachers and taking our calves into the fields the way Moses once led the people of Israel out into the desert. Everyone felt safe and privileged to belong to such a loving and dependable community. Among the believers serving at the forefront were my parents, Aunt Elizabeth and Uncle Thomas.

True Christian life however never goes unchallenged. This also applied to the *Balokole* in Bweera. We depended for our daily survival on cattle, but widespread cultivation meant that there was limited land available for grazing. This, together with lack of water and inadequate veterinary services, made it difficult for us to keep herds. Even though God provided for all our needs, Bweera was heavily congested and eventually the situation became untenable.

Around this time we heard that the Government was distributing land from colonial ranches in Ankole, Western Uganda, where the presence of large public dams meant access to plenty of water for everyone. Several *Balokole Bahima* decided to return to their ancestral lands. Driven by the responsibility to cater for the welfare and future of our family father reluctantly followed. Moving away was a painful experience, especially for mother who thrived on being part of the community in Bweera, close to Kikoma, the very place where she and father had first met the Lord. Of course, there would also be Christians and *Balokole* in Ankole but they were perceived to be less devout – in the first place occupied with managing their farms and accumulating resources, and only topping up their busy lives with fellowship and faith. Not quite like the full and concentrated living for the Lord that took place amongst the *Balokole* in Bweera.

While father began the move to Ankole mother stayed behind. She needed more time to say farewell to the brethren and come to terms with being uprooted from the place where she belonged. Rather than leaving me with mother, father decided to take me to relatives further along the route. There I was to wait until he joined me with the rest of our family, our cattle and belongings. Once everyone had caught up he would take me again to relatives further ahead. This process was to be repeated until we had reached our destination.

The distance between Bweera and Ankole was not all that great but the move would take us ages. We needed to comply with cattle immunisations that were costly and required raising funds. Some areas were under quarantine, forcing us to divert from the direct route or wait for several months until the authorities allowed passage through. A system of formal clearance was put in place between counties to control the spread of cattle diseases. Only migrants with large herds were issued with a permit. This compelled people with a small number of cows to join up and travel together. Father teamed up with Uncle Musa ('Moses'), one of my mother's cousins.

In the end it proved very difficult for father to settle in Ankole. The process of government land allocation involved lengthy bureaucratic procedures, while buying or leasing land from a private owner required more money than we could afford. In the meantime we needed a place to live and so father decided to 'shelter'. This was an old *Bahima* custom whereby people in need were allowed to live on someone else's land, and benefit from the abundance of milk as though they were part of the household. In return they had to work for the host by helping him look after his cattle. My family settled on the land of a relatively wealthy rancher in Kazo.

Before we made the crossing into Ankole it was time for my first orthopaedic review at the polio clinic. Leaving everything in the care of Uncle Musa father put me on the back of his bicycle. We set off for the nearest railway station in Kabogore from where we would take the steam train to Kampala. Since it was impossible for us to reach the station that same day he planned to spend the night with Christian family friends.

I hated the thought of staying with strangers, dreading the way I would be received – stared at by adults and children. By now I had learnt that being disabled I could never take acceptance for granted. And the thought of crawling through a stranger's house! What if I needed the toilet? Moody and tearful I held onto father as he cycled along.

"Why can't we go straight to Kampala?" I whined. "At least let us stay with someone I know, like one of our uncles!"

"Brethren in faith are not strangers," father cheerfully replied. "They are like family. Just wait and see; let them prove us wrong!"

Years before I was born Mr Kaburuku and his wife had witnessed my parents' inspiring evangelism and selfless love. Although themselves now leading Christians they still looked up to my parents as elders in faith. They had not seen father for ages and greeted us with a joyful *Tukutendereza,* thanking the Lord for an unexpected reunion.

"Is this the child we have heard about?" the couple exclaimed. "How lovely to see you in person!" Their reaction took me totally by surprise. Instead of being put off or embarrassed by my presence they welcomed me with warmth and affection. They even shed a tear for me. *Kaaka* ('grandma') Kaburuku, who lived with the family, was already preparing a place for us to sleep.

"I want to talk with the boy and keep him close to me," she kept saying. "Petero, doesn't he look like you?"

Their children gathered around me, keen to know where we were heading and hear everything about my previous stay in Kampala. I mingled freely with them even though some were quite a bit older! No one looked down upon me. We just bonded like brothers and sisters. The love of that family was so great that it absorbed the other guests staying in their home. One of them, Theodora, remained a close friend of mine way into my teens.

The adults spent the afternoon thanking God and sharing testimonies of how he had kept them safe through trying times, only occasionally interrupting their worship with refreshments. As evening fell, the day was closed with Bible reading and prayers. The whole event was a wonderful example of how love should be among Christians: not just hospitality but a genuine, embracing love with unconditional acceptance. Our departure the following morning was moving as though we had been with them for months. I had made new friends and the experience of being loved and accepted outside my family was hopeful and reassuring. In the years that followed, family Kaburuku often sent us messages of affection and greetings while *Kaaka's* gifts of soap and toiletries kept coming long after I returned from Kampala.

From the age of eleven to thirteen I visited the polio hostel several times for orthopaedic reviews. These were meant to take place every six months or so but sometimes the gaps in between were longer if we did not have enough money to pay for the journey.

I faced these reviews with mixed feelings. It was exciting to see old friends again and have a chance of making new ones. I looked forward to being back with people of my kind. On the other hand, I never knew what to expect. Would they just check me over and discharge me or keep me in for operations or other painful treatments? I especially dreaded the traction as this meant being bed-bound for several months!

I had not made much progress with walking. Using my callipers and crutches had proven difficult in the rough terrain around our home. My way of 'walking' was painstakingly slow. First I placed one crutch in front of me and moved my hip on that side forward while sliding my foot over the ground. Then I paused to stabilise myself before repeating the process with the other leg. Indoors and on the relatively smooth surface in front of our hut I could just about manage like this but everywhere else the ground was ridden with obstacles and ditches that caused me to trip over. I was always covered in cuts and bruises and depended on other people to help me back onto my feet. Besides, our *Bahima* way of life dictated me having to crawl now and then. When needing the toilet, for example, I had to look for a bush away from the settlement. As I could never get there with callipers on I had to resort to crawling the whole distance.

Initially my family encouraged me to walk as often as possible and someone stayed around to help me keep my balance. Over time though I needed to learn to manage on my own. Everyone else had their own things to get on with. Eventually my zest for life got the upper hand. I did not want to be limited to taking a few steps in front of our hut. I wanted to take part in activities and be with the other children. So I undid the buckles, took off my callipers and crawled away to freedom. After keeping my legs bent all day it was painful to put the callipers back on again and I tried very hard to avoid it. The less I used my appliances the more my knees contracted. Sometimes my parents tried to straighten my legs by making me wear the callipers all day and night but this hurt so much that they reluctantly allowed me to take them off again. In the end I stopped using the callipers altogether, until the date of my next review drew near.

Father looked on as the nurse helped me onto an examination bed in the polio clinic. I was shivering. Was it the chill that rose up from the concrete floor or did I fear the outcome? Yes, I had resorted to crawling again. My knees and hips had contracted. Surely the doctors would not fail to notice it. I tried to stretch my legs as much as I could using my hands to press down the kneecaps. This was something I had been doing ever since my parents started talking about taking me back to Kampala. An orthopaedic assistant carefully checked me over and left to call the consultant. Whatever the treatment, it was up to him to make the decision. Now there was nothing else for me to do but wait and pray that my condition would not necessitate an operation.

When the consultant came in I could not help noticing the disappointed look on his face. Clearly my legs were not the way they should have been. Anxiously I watched him write something on my file before handing it to the assistant. Over time I learnt that doctors had a protracted way, somewhat like a ritual, of revealing what was going to happen, especially to young patients. They scribbled on your file and said things that were meant to be reassuring, like, "We are going to work on you... It won't be like last time... Soon you will be back on your feet again." And then they admitted you to the polio hostel.

This time father and I were told that I needed to stay in for an extended review while they decided on my treatment. We should be prepared for it to take months. Father was unable to stay with me. He had to go back to continue with the move to Ankole in search of a place where my family could settle. In the hostel I was assured of a cleaner, safer environment than my parents could ever offer. Grudgingly I had come to acknowledge this too but I dreaded being separated from my family. Having a loved one around would give me the peace I needed to appreciate the advantages of modern surroundings. On this occasion though my parents were determined not to leave me on my own in Kampala. Should I be kept in for treatment they would organise for someone to join me, if not my mother then most likely my eldest sister Phaibe.

I was admitted to a large ward with about forty beds and plenty of space in-between where carers could sleep on the floor. It was a lively place with lots of patients of different ages. Carers were usually mothers with their babies and toddlers or teenagers looking after a younger sibling.

Now came the best part of my stay in the hostel. Playing! Young patients made the most of this time before being confined to their beds by operations, traction or other forms of treatment. We dashed in and out of the buildings, wrestled and rolled over the floors and played hide and seek under our beds and blankets. Of course at the hostel we could not get away with crawling, but it was possible to race each other even with callipers still on by shifting ourselves along on our bottoms! When staff members were not looking, those of us finding it hard to use our appliances just threw them off and buzzed about. Sometimes our games escalated into quarrels and fighting – most likely when the vigilant eyes of our carers were closed for a nap in the heat of the day. One moment we were playfully wrestling, joking and teasing each other. Next we would be in one great heap on the floor, hitting each other with our orthopaedic boots and crutches.

In my ward were two nasty boys: a disabled one of my age and his older brother who stayed with him as carer. They both enjoyed bullying the other children and it seemed that especially the younger one liked picking on me. He often pulled my legs or jumped on them when I was crawling, causing me to fall on my face and hit my chin on the concrete floor. This always made him cry with laughter. The moment I tried to fight back his bigger brother stood up for him.

"Maasso mattu manene," they used to call me which, translated from *Luganda,* means 'Big eyes and ears'.

On one occasion I dared challenge the younger boy when he had snatched a toy from a child much weaker than him.

He grabbed my legs and I hit back with my crutch, the way we were taught to use our *Bahima* sticks at home. I was quite strong and agile and much more skilful in stick fighting than any of the other children. I hit him right on the head. Shocked by my unexpected resistance he crawled away crying. His older brother jumped on me and slapped me in the face. Him too I sorted out my crutch until the warden pulled us apart by the ears and confined us to our beds. From then on I became some sort of arbitrator amongst the children, standing up for the weaker ones and involving their carers before things got out of hand. The bullies listened to me knowing that when it came to a fight they could get a whack on their head with my crutch.

There was also a very pretty girl in the hostel. She had a beautiful upper body with elegant arms and shoulders, and only little stumps for legs. This girl could do anything she wanted – climb on the beds, play on the structure and walk upside down on her arms. I did not quite know what to make of such a noisy, dominating tomboy but she seemed to like my large, round eyes. Often she made me look into her face. Gradually I began to appreciate her cute and feminine features. Gazing into each other's eyes always made us giggle. Occasionally, when no one was watching, she pulled me onto her lap which felt very warm and cuddly. It gave a reassuring, yet exciting feeling. I kept looking out for her, wanting us to be close. By the time I went home the orthopaedic workshop was trying to make artificial limbs for her. During subsequent reviews I saw her again, still moving around on her arms and looking prettier than ever. We never had a chance to bond again. She was growing up fast and I was just a boy. A few years later I met her once more, now a blossoming young woman who had mothered a child.

Phaibe arrived before my treatment began. Some brethren dropped her off at the hospital on their way to a large *Balokole* convention in Kawempe. My sister was a keen Christian who even at boarding school used to team up with other youngsters to evangelise among fellow students and in surrounding towns. Later she became very active in our rural communities and churches. The hospital environment was a challenging experience for her, especially living among so many people with different behaviours and lifestyles. She seemed to find solace in the knowledge that, unlike at home, her little brother was not the only disabled person. The hostel housed many people with varying disabilities. My condition wasn't even the worst!

Shortly afterwards Professor Huckstep and Dr Bain did their usual round of the ward with a large group of medical students. This time they stopped at my bed to examine my legs and do the customary scribbling on my file. A few days later I was moved to a different part of the ward. A nurse began to wash and shave my legs, the way they did before an operation. *Were they really going to operate on me right here in the polio hostel?* Anxiously I asked Phaibe to find out what was happening. She tried to decipher my notes. *"Reviewable... traction... treatment"*.

The nurse explained that tractions were going to be used to stretch the joints in my legs until they were straight again. It could take several months depending on how well I responded. If this did not work, the doctors might have to resort to operating on me. With sticky tape an orthopaedic assistant fastened strings to my legs from my knees down to the ankles. Then he attached the pulleys and weights and mounted the traction.

Being stuck on a bed with my legs in the air was worse to me than any other treatment. Operations were nasty but at least I could race about in a wheelchair afterwards, even with my legs in plaster. The constant pulling of the weights was terribly painful, making it hard for me to sleep at night. I found some ways of easing the strain by resting the weights on my bed or tying the strings to the traction frame but of course that thwarted the purpose of the treatment. When the nurses discovered my clever scheme they explained to Phaibe that allowing this to happen would only prolong my time in traction. From then on, though very sorry to see me in pain, Phaibe prevented me from undoing the traction, which meant that I could only do it secretly, when she was fast asleep...

Never was I allowed to get out of the traction, not even for washing. I looked forward to the hour when the physiotherapist came to exercise my legs but immediately afterwards the weights were mounted again. Day and night, week in week out, month after month I was stuck to my bed, depending for all my needs on Phaibe. Sometimes nurses brought colouring books and pencils to cheer up the younger patients but often I was bored out of my wits, feeling miserable, tearful and moody. Eventually, like everything else, my time in traction came to an end. Next followed a period of intensive physiotherapy to rehabilitate my muscles. When it became apparent that my knees were very susceptible to contracting again, I was put in plaster for several more weeks.

Every morning and evening Phaibe read aloud from the Bible and prayed with me. She also did this when I was feeling miserable or could not sleep at night. Not everyone in the hostel liked her commitment to her faith and the way she freely spoke about *Yesu,* her Lord. One particular warden kept trying to flatter and flirt with her. He was deeply offended by her reply that as a Christian she could not indulge in such worldly behaviours. When she stood her ground he became very nasty toward us. In the morning he woke me up by whacking me in the face with his huge bunch of keys. When distributing sheets and laundry soap to patients and carers he deliberately ignored us. I dreaded making the slightest mess on my bed as he dealt with me much more severely than with any of the other children. He kept intimidating us and there was no way we dared speak out against him.

This time the lamenting and yearning for home were more on Phaibe's side than mine. Whereas I was quite happy to have my big sister around, she missed the regular worship with her *Balokole* congregation. Besides, the little money given by father had run out even though she had been very careful with spending. Patients and carers needed money to buy toiletries as well as snacks to keep themselves going during the long intervals between hospital meals. While Phaibe was more concerned about lack of essentials I craved for an occasional, tasty treat. Eventually Phaibe swallowed her pride and confided in one of the expatriate nurses. This lady was ever so friendly. After briefly disappearing she handed my sister a large paper bag full of 'goodies'. With great excitement I awaited my share of the treats but Phaibe was very secretive. She even hid the bag and refused to give me anything! I kept on moaning about it, saying how unfair it was. Surely the Lord would be unhappy with her for being so mean to me. At last she gave in and showed me the contents – nothing but toiletries and some odd boring things that women seemed to need.

My bed was at the very end of the ward, next to a door leading to the compound. The lawn here was often overgrown and through a small gap beneath the door mice, lizards, frogs and other crawly creatures could sneak into the ward, especially during the rainy season.

One night an *empiri*, a lethal snake, managed to make its way into our ward. It slithered over the slippery concrete floor towards Phaibe's mattress and curled up in the warmth of her bosom. There was only one source of light in the ward: a dim night-lamp with a large lampshade suspended from the centre of the ceiling. Sensing something cold against her skin Phaibe woke up and discovered the snake. One bite and she would be dead. Even the slightest movement could incite that horrid creature! Frozen with fear she prayed to the Lord.

"*Yesu*, help! What shall I do?"

I woke up from a light slumber at the sound of her whispering voice. We had prayed together before bedtime and I wondered why she was doing it again so late. As Phaibe kept on murmuring prayers the snake began to move, slowly uncoiling and slithering from beneath her blanket. Only when it had gone a safe distance she dared to jump up and warn the others asleep on the floor.

"Watch out. An *empiri*! An *empiri*!"

Everyone screamed and yelled. A warden rushed in. The full lights came on. The adults carefully combed the ward guided by the scanning eyes of bed-bound children. At last someone managed to locate the snake. To my great astonishment a heated argument broke out among the carers.

"Neither the girl nor we have been harmed by that creature. If we kill it now our actions might anger the spirits," claimed those who were superstitious.

"This has got nothing to do with spirits!" others insisted. "She has been protected through her faith in the Lord." The warden decided that the snake should be killed and eventually they did so with sticks. Everyone agreed how lucky Phaibe had been.

"Your prayers were not wasted," said the carers who appreciated that she was a Christian. Even those who used to giggle and smirk at the sight of her praying suddenly became more respectful towards her. The nasty warden heard the full story too. Although his attitude towards us remained cynical and uncaring, from that night on he stopped bothering us.

Radio broadcasts announced it, and everyone reiterated the news, *"The Pope is coming to Uganda!"* Pope Paul VI, Papa Paulo, the holy father! Could this be the real Father Christmas and not that noisy man I had met on Christmas day during my first stay at the hostel? Some adults went to great lengths to explain to us how special the Pope was – the holiest man in the Catholic Church. His importance resonated in all the preparations and upheaval. Soon in our minds the status of this man had surpassed that of the President himself!

This was a huge event for everyone, a great recognition for Uganda. Not just Catholics but also people from other churches and religions were excited. Among the places scheduled for a visit by the Pope were the martyrs' shrine in Namagongo (dedicated to the early Christian Ugandans who had been murdered for their faith) as well as our polio clinic and hostel. Now the national excitement spilled over onto us. We disabled children were actually going to meet the Pope! We were accustomed to painstaking arrangements prior to the arrival of dignitaries, usually government officials. However, no one had ever experienced preparations on such an enormous scale. The areas around the hostel and clinic were cordoned off, the buildings cleaned up and immaculately painted. Workmen spent hours slashing the overgrown shrubs and grass in the compound and clearing the paths leading up to our centre. Prior to the Pope's visit members of the security forces came to check out our place, followed by several groups of people from the Vatican where the Pope lived. There was a lot of protocol, most of which we did not understand. We were shown how to present ourselves to the Pope, where to line up, which side he would come from and who would stand where. To my great delight I was allowed to be right at the front!

Police bands played, choirs sang and scouts marched on that long-awaited day. Crowds lined the streets, rushing from one place to the next as the holy man slowly passed with his motorcade. A rapture of applause and cheers erupted in the distance, gradually moving closer. "Papa Paulo! Holy father!" No one had ever been received like this. Rooftops and windows were crammed with people. Some even climbed trees to get a glimpse of this special man. Masses of spectators converged upon our hostel, despite tireless effort by security personnel to keep them at bay.

In front of the building we waited in line, cleaned up and dressed in smart clothing, the inside of our bellies quivering with nerves and delight. Not only were we about to meet the Pope with his entourage but there were many other important people like ministers, diplomats and high leaders of the Catholic Church. A sea of vehicles covered Mulago Hill. Several makes and models we had never seen before.

My eyes were peeled wider and wider the closer he came. At some point I even started trembling. Papa Paulo made signs with his hand as he was being led along our line – members of staff first and after that we, the awe-stricken patients. For a moment he stopped in front of us and blessed us as a group. Then he came forward to greet a few individuals. He laid his hands on my head, murmuring words I could not understand. Afterwards I was on cloud nine for weeks. I felt so privileged. Everyone kept telling me how special it was to have been blessed by this holy man!

Some people said he had a fishbone stuck in his throat when President Obote was admitted to New Mulago. If that were the case, why then the sudden presence of military vehicles all around the hospital complex. Why the agitated mood amongst the numerous soldiers that had suddenly appeared? People at the bus stage started running in panic. Soon the streets were deserted, the shops closed. A sense of fear hung in the air, reminiscent of the time when the *Kabaka* was toppled. We hid inside the hostel where we sat down on our beds. But what had actually happened? Once again there were plenty of rumours and speculations.

"The President has been shot."

"He is dying. He may already be dead." If that were true then this was only the beginning. There would be repercussions, perhaps even a coup! Carers with transistor radios tuned in to hear the latest news. Everyone entering the hostel was questioned.

"What is going on outside? Have you heard anything?"

"There has been an attempt on His Excellency's life," a junior doctor finally told us. "He has been shot in the mouth after a party conference at Lugogo Stadium. Fortunately his injuries are minor."

The assassination attempt had been plotted by *Kabaka Yeka* supporters to avenge the overthrow of their monarch. Obote survived and he would soon be back at his duties. However, for now he was staying in New Mulago – in Ward 6C to be precise, the VIP suite on the sixth floor. Being so close to this important man was for curious youngsters like us a chance too good to miss. We had to have a peek at the President while he was still under our noses! I teamed up with another boy in a wheelchair and older one on crutches. Together we made our way from the polio hostel down to the casualty department. The entrance was guarded by armed soldiers. Outside the main gates I spotted several armoured vehicles and tanks.

"What are you doing here?" a soldier stopped us as we approached, his appearance imposing, his eyes unresponsive and red. It was rumoured that in times of crisis soldiers could be given certain drugs to make them feel aggressive and invincible. The man spoke in Swahili. Observing his dark and toughened features I could tell that he was a fighter from the North.

"We are on our way to the orthopaedic ward, Sir, to attend an appointment," I shakily replied in my best Swahili, "This path largely leads downhill so it is the easiest route for us to take with our wheelchairs."

To my surprise and disbelief the vicious looking warrior allowed us passage through. Beyond the hospital entrance everything seemed busy like normal. Or could it be that people knew what we were up to and was everyone staring at us? Determined to press on with our daring adventure we hurried to the lifts.

The sixth floor gave a different picture. It was strangely quiet here: no patients, just a few members of staff and not even a single visitor in sight! Cautiously we continued down the long corridor towards the VIP suite. Whenever a nurse passed we cheekily joined her, chatting and joking to make it look as though we were under her care.

The end of the corridor was guarded by heavily armed soldiers. Mustering up more courage we watched them from a distance and considered our options. Perhaps we could charm them with our innocent faces or my linguistic skills. From my experience people always liked to be addressed in their own language. The soldiers carefully checked the identity papers, bags and belongings of anyone trying to pass through. Those unable to satisfy their requirements were harshly dealt with and chased away.

"What are we going to do without papers?" I whispered to my friends. One of the armed soldiers spotted us. With an angry glance in our direction he alerted his colleagues. It was enough for us to concede defeat. From this point on we would have to contend ourselves with gazing at the windows. Many hours we sat in that corridor. Each time the curtains moved we held our breath; our hearts missed a beat when a figure appeared, but it was always just a doctor, nurse or soldier. No matter how long and hard we stared at the ward, there was no sign of the President himself.

Every so often I stayed at the polio clinic or hostel for an orthopaedic review. Phaibe only joined me on the first occasion. After that I was perceived to be quite capable of managing on my own without a personal carer. The place became like a second home to me and my stay there was always eventful – with plenty of scope for excitement and fun but also with unpleasant treatments. Sometimes I was only kept in for a couple of weeks, if the doctors felt that a course of intensive physiotherapy would suffice. Other times I could be there for months, with both my legs in plaster or wearing a cast from waist to toe, or a brace for supporting my posture and straightening my spine. Whenever I returned home from a treatment – legs nicely straight, callipers back on – my family and I faced a dilemma. With appliances on, it was impossible for me to take part in life in our rural environment. On the other hand, if I took them off, my legs would contract again. Ultimately the temptation to do without was always too great and I ended up crawling again.

CHAPTER 13

LIKE THE OTHERS

"The Lord will fight for you; you need only to be still."

Ex: 14:14

As if the orchestra of jubilant birds all around us wasn't enough, father burst into a hymn. His wake up call at the first sight of dawn. Mother joined in and soon the sleepy voices of everyone gathered in our home boosted the choir. The singing was followed by prayers. Once we had blessed each other with *'The Grace of our Lord Jesus Christ'* there was no turning back. A new day had begun.

By now the mooing of cattle had overtaken the twitter of birds – a reminder of the day's first priority. For a *Bahima* family like us it had to be milking time!

"Has the fire been made?" called father. "I don't see any smoke. How are we are going to milk these cows without a bonfire to repel the flies?" Suddenly the home was buzzing with activity. Everyone needed to help out. Youngsters carried out their chores early in the morning before setting off for school.

"Children, mind the time whatever you are doing out there! Don't forget you have to go to school," mother's voice rang out.

"Mama, can I go now? Yesterday I collected lots of firewood before breakfast and now I have a thorn in my foot so I cannot walk fast." That was my sister Miriam, as usual trying to get away with doing as little as possible.

"Shouldn't you wait for your sisters? They have gone to the well to fetch water."

Listening beneath my blanket I sobbed. I always did this when there was mention of my siblings getting ready for school. For me this meant only one thing. They were going, and I was being left behind.

We lived about three miles from the nearest school. Every morning my brothers, sisters and other children from the neighbourhood walked that distance over narrow, winding paths through densely overgrown terrain. In those days education was not compulsory, nor was it free. Parents often kept their children at home until they were able to cope with the challenges of nature. In fact, it was not unusual for children to start schooling at the age of nine or ten. And I was already eleven!

The return journey provided children with an opportunity to socialise and play. This was their time for talking, wrestling and searching for wild fruits. No one was particularly in a rush to get home quickly. How I looked forward to seeing my brothers and sisters come back from school. I listened intently to their stories and songs, trying to learn from them as much as I could. The alphabet, the times tables, a few simple sums. I even had my own exercise books in which I copied their work. I liked hearing them talk about their friends and all the things they were learning at school but it could never make up for my sense of loss. They were able to enjoy a piece of life that I could not take part in. I desperately wanted to go to school, even though there was only one way for children to get there. On foot.

Sitting on the edge of my bed I worked out a plan. My ears tuned in to father's whistle, the sound fading as he herded our cattle further away in the fields. The greater the distance between him and our home the better my chance of sneaking away unnoticed. Father had stopped me before. He was well aware of the dangers a young boy could encounter when crawling three miles through the wilderness.

I decided to make my way towards the workers busy cultivating the gardens of Mr Rupapiira, the owner of the farm where our family had taken shelter. In that way it would appear as if I were just looking for company. Then, very slowly I would move towards the well and disappear behind the bushes. I had not got very far when Stanley spotted me. He was the foreman of the gardeners.

"I know what you are up to," he bellowed, shaking his finger in disapproval. "Just remember, this time I won't be the one to nurse your wounds!" I responded with a broad, bribing smile, my usual way of trying to disarm him. His warnings never deterred me. One day I too would go to school. Who knows, this might be *the day!*

First I had to make sure no other children were in sight so that no one could make fun of me.

"Look, Simeoni is crawling after us again!" they would often snigger. I did not like meeting children along the way. Crawling through dust or mud – my bottom sticking up, thin legs trailing behind – I had become aware of their odd glances and occasional teasing remarks. At home I was surrounded by a loving family and Christian friends who accepted me the way I was. I did not feel any different from them. The Lord loved us all equally. One day he would save each one of us from imperfection and unfairness. Even some non-Christian visitors had come to acknowledge that I was not a write-off, seeing how cheerfully and resiliently I took part in life. However, twice my parents had taken me to church on father's bicycle, once for a special service and the other time to attend a cousin's wedding. On both occasions I had found myself surrounded by a crowd of curious children, gazing at me as though I were a strange exhibit on display.

Those who knew my family greeted me nicely but others stood by with pitiful looks on their faces which was very hard to bear. I just wanted to be accepted and supported in my efforts to live a normal life. There was no need for anyone to feel sorry for me. Several youngsters could not even hide their embarrassment at the sight of me crawling. They made it quite clear that they wanted nothing to do with me. Their attitude shattered whatever innocence I still had remaining. From that time on I got into the habit of trying to avoid everyone I did not know. If there was any advantage in my slow pace of crawling then it was that sooner or later I would have the path all to myself.

I had not gone far when I spotted a friend.

"Kezia, how come you are still here?" I called out. "If I could borrow your legs, no one would see me around here so late!" A young girl turned round. Her friendly face and beaming smile immediately set my heart alight. Somehow I never felt embarrassed in her presence.

"Ah, Simeoni, you can't be serious. You would not wish my legs if you knew what miseries they carry." Her otherwise enchanting voice sounded uncommonly troubled. "I'll do anything to avoid those nasty boys, even if it means getting late to school."

I silently wondered whether teasing boys were really her only concern. Perhaps she feared being sent home again. Everybody knew that her parents had difficulty paying the school fees.

"But Simeoni, it seems that you haven't given up yet!" Her face lit up again.

"Oh, forget about me," I answered vaguely, avoiding looking at her. "I am just passing my time here on this path. I've got nothing else to do..."

Together we moved on slowly but soon Kezia had to increase her pace and disappeared from sight. To keep up my spirits I decided to count how many trees and bushes I could pass without getting hurt, only occasionally stopping to examine my limbs, pull out a thorn and pick a leaf to wipe off the blood. I used these moments to talk to *Yesu,* asking him to give me strength and bless my attempts to reach the school that day. Suddenly I realised that Kezia must have noticed the cloth bag hanging around my neck, containing my exercise books. She must be aware of my intentions. Soon all her friends would know it as well! Hopefully the word would not spread to my parents when my brothers and sisters got home from school.

It was common knowledge within our family that some of us had special abilities or powers. We attributed these to our historical connection with the *Chwezi.* We could, for example, sense things we might experience in the future. In me this manifested itself in the form of strong premonitions combined with twitches on my face. Had I lived in the olden days I would probably have been earmarked for serving at the king's court as one of his royal advisers. Now, being Christians, we were conscious of the teachings of the Bible and dismissed the significance of paranormal phenomena.

As I crawled along the path I felt a twitch strike just below my left eye. In my experience this meant that something upsetting or traumatic was about to happen. Like all *Bahima* children I was taught that our environment could be full of nasty surprises. That is why I always dragged a strong stick along, clasped between my fingers. Living so close to nature our senses were sharp and kept on developing as we grew older. We were able to identify a wild animal merely by its scent. Early detection of a certain smell could mean the difference between life and death, giving us a chance to run for safety when lacking the strength or confidence to fight.

I had gone quite a distance along the winding path when my nose picked up an ominous smell. It grew stronger and stronger as I proceeded. I stopped for brief prayer, this time not just to ask for strength but also for protection. In my zealousness to go to school I had not given much thought to the dangers that I might encounter along the way. Now surrounded by tall grass and dense bushes I became aware of how vulnerable and exposed I really was.

The skies above were littered with birds. There was a lot to see, to distract my attention from my hurting knees and hands. One giant bird in particular was behaving very oddly. It kept flying in wide circles over my head as though it was preying on me. We called this kind of bird an *orokongoro*, a 'rabbit and reptile snatcher'. Wielding my stick to scare it away I shouted as loud as I could.

"Don't you have a go at me. I'm not a small animal!" But the giant bird persisted in circling above me. Deciding to ignore the creature, I kept on moving. A little further down the path lay something shiny in the grass. A large piece of snakeskin that had only recently been shed. Snakes discard their old skin as a new layer grows underneath. It confirmed what my nose had already detected. There was an *anchwera* – an extremely deadly, venom spitting type of black snake – very close to the path where I was crawling. The size of skin on the ground could mean only one thing. This snake was massive, far too large for me to try and fight off with my stick. By now the twitches were pounding my face but I forced myself to ignore them, the teachings of my parents echoing through my mind.

"Child, never believe in any power other than the power of the Lord. Those signs are nothing but superstition!"

Braving yet another distance I slowly proceeded along the winding path. To my excitement I had managed to reach even further than in any of my previous attempts. It inspired me to move even faster. Only by now I could no longer ignore my twitches…

"Yesu!" I cried out as my eyes landed on an even larger piece of snakeskin. Again that unmistakable smell, this time even stronger. *"Yesu, what shall I do? If I go ahead I could crawl right into the snake. If I turn back it might be waiting for me".* Wherever it was, it must be very close. The *orokongoro* I had

sighted earlier whizzed over again. It was nervous. This time it kept hovering right above my head.

"This can't be happening to me," I thought in a state of panic. "A giant bird is preying on me from the air while a massive *anchwera* is lurking in the bushes."

I had to come up with a plan. I needed to find a safer place, where I could work out what to do next. Any thoughts about reaching the school had vanished. All that now mattered was my safety. I looked around for an anthill to climb – anything to raise me up a little so I could observe my surroundings. Not far away was a sycamore tree, its lowest branches stretching out a few feet off the ground. I crawled over as fast as I could. Pulling myself up I prayed that the branch would take my weight. This was better than the path where anything could happen but my feet were still dangerously close to the ground. I managed to free a hand and pull up my legs.

Suddenly the giant bird swooped down into the tall grass, just yards from where I was sitting. A violent struggle followed. When it emerged again a monstrous *anchwera* was dangling in its grip. Wriggling vigorously the snake fought itself free and dropped onto the path, right where I had been crawling. I screamed for help. If only someone could hear me – perhaps one of the herdsmen on his way to water the cows. The enraged snake raised its head and flicked its tongue, spraying venom all around. Fortunately I was just out of range. The bird swooped down again only narrowly avoiding the branches. Once more the monstrous snake dangled above me, coiling with all its might. I brandished my stick (as if it would make any difference...). My heart pounded and I felt a little wetness in my shorts that was not entirely due to perspiration. If the snake fell on me now no one on earth would ever know what I had gone through. I called for *Yesu* knowing that only He could hear me. The spitting *anchwera* was just a few feet away from my head. Then ever so slowly, clasping its cargo, the *orokongoro* gained height and disappeared from sight. I was safe – rescued by the very creature that I had been wishing away. On the branch of the sycamore tree I shakily sang *Tukutendereza,* thanking my Lord the *Balokole* way.

Soon my tears of relief mixed with tears of resignation. With only one hill left to climb the school ever so near! Yet, after what had just happened I knew that it would be unwise to continue. Trembling all over I lowered myself from the branch and began to crawl the long way home. Any movement or sound in the vegetation along the path made me shiver. Now was the hottest time of the day, when snakes came out to bask in the sun and thirst made them fiercely aggressive. In my fearful imagination only an army of giant birds was going to get me home safely!

This time the path seemed much rougher than before. The soil was scorching hot and my throat felt dry. My knees and feet had been battered by stones; my hands were covered in thorns. Never would I want to go through such an experience again. On the other hand, how could I ever give up? Not even in my prayers for rescue that day had I uttered the promise to stay at home and be a good boy. As I crawled along slowly, leaving a trail of blood drops in the sand, I made a resolution.

"No matter what happens, my attempts will not be in vain. *Like all the others I too will go to school... I WILL!"*

My younger sister Peace came home from school, proudly showing off with her prize. A pencil. Last time she was given a ruler for having done well in a test. I looked through her exercise books: English words, some basic maths – none of it seemed too hard for me. Yet my younger sister was getting the prizes. This thought lead to an exciting notion: if I were able to understand these things without attending school, how well should I be able to do with a proper education!

My escapades had become more widely known, which had not only led to serious warnings from my parents but also to a wave of sympathy and support from neighbouring children. Several of them joined me in my cause. We often sat down together to work out different ways of getting me to school.

One day a bigger boy told me about 'the prohibited path'. The words sounded ominous but he was very convincing.

"The normal route is too long for you. Why don't you try this path? It really isn't as dangerous as the adults make us believe and leads straight to the school. One of these days you should watch me. I will prove to you that it is safe.

"But remember," he lowered his voice to a whisper, "it has to remain our secret. You are not allowed to tell anyone!"

I thought it over for quite a while. I had heard of the path he was talking about - out of bounds, densely overgrown, but a shortcut and therefore terribly tempting. I would only have to climb one hill. The school would be on top of the next.

A few weeks later, right after prayers, while my brothers and sisters were still doing their chores, I sneaked away from our hut. Crawling through the morning dew I met up with the boy and watched him climb a huge anthill. Somehow I managed to join him up there. He pointed at a narrow path disappearing in the undergrowth.

"Whenever I take this route, I first sit on this hill to observe the vegetation. If there is anything unusual I wait. Only if everything is quiet I run from here all the way through that very dense part."

For a brief moment we sat together, silently watching the surroundings. Nothing moved.

"You got to make sure that you are really fast," he went on to say. "When all is calm, like now, *it* is not around. Look out for circles of flattened grass. These are a warning sign that *it* is near."

The boy had to go; he was running late for school.

"When I have passed through the most dreaded part I will climb a tree and wave," he promised. He sprinted off and disappeared between the bushes. I waited for what seemed ages, feeling increasingly worried. A million thoughts raced through my mind. Surely, I was fast at crawling but never as fast as he could run! What if something had happened to him? I wouldn't be able to help him. I couldn't even call an adult because this was meant to be our secret and they would find out about my plan. How could I ever take such a risk when I'm already fearing for his life?

"No," I determined, "I will never use this forbidden path….. Well, at least not today…"

Finally I saw the boy frantically waving at me from a treetop. He might have been there for quite a while. I had just been staring in the wrong direction. That afternoon he told me how easy it had been.

"Really, only a small section of the path is overgrown and risky." Other boys were saying the same. Apparently from time to time they also took that path. Our parents had severely warned us never to take that route. Naturally we did not like to get punished. Yet, encouraged by my friends I could not stop thinking about it. Why not giving it just one try? I was not a coward.

One day after hearing my sisters recite a beautiful song that they had learnt at school, I could not wait any longer. The next morning I slipped out of bed very early, giving father a plausible excuse. "I really need to go to the toilet!" Of course, in our case that was far out in the fields. He gave me the milk from the very first cow and told my brother Sam to go with me. When we had gone quite a distance I asked Sam to leave me alone. He must have suspected something as he was quite reluctant to go.

"OK then," he agreed in the end, "but I hope that you are not about to try one of your crazy expeditions."

"If only I could…!" I answered with my usual vagueness and waited for him to disappear. I had to move slowly so as not to attract anyone's attention, taking cover in the tall grass whenever herders passed with their cows. Making sure that no one else was around I pulled myself up the large anthill. A few birds sat in a nearby tree, happily tweeting in the sunshine. The only things that moved were branches swaying in the morning breeze. There was no sign of danger.

I did not have much time to make up my mind. The longer I waited the more likely someone would spot me and the less my chance of reaching the school in time! I lowered myself from the anthill and, stick clenched between my fingers, I began to crawl like mad. Soon I was totally covered by tall grass and bushes. Unable to look around, my ears attuned to every sound. Insects, lizards, snakes, the pounding of my own heart... Only when reaching a less overgrown part did I pause for a quick break.

There, in the grass beside me, the unmistakable circular imprints of a huge python. This type of snake is known to kill by coiling itself around a prey, crushing its bones and swallowing it whole. Terrified I forged ahead, ignoring the obvious tracks, smells and hissing sounds of snakes everywhere around me. This route might have been shorter but it was infinitely more dangerous. I managed to reach the area described by the boys as 'safer'. No pythons here, instead the edge of a forest, a typical habitat for leopards.

"These animals usually don't attack in the morning," I tried to convince myself. I kept on crawling in spite of the many stones and thorny branches in my way. At the foot of the hill I briefly stopped, the corrugated iron school roof glittering in the distance.

It was early afternoon when I finally reached the school, only minutes before the lessons ended. My arrival caused quite a commotion.

"Look, Petero's son has come, the crippled one!" a few children cried out laughing. "He has been crawling all the way to school!"

My friends were delighted to see me but very sorry about the state I was in - petrified, exhausted and bleeding all over.

My clothes torn, my face scratched by thorns. The headmaster came over with a couple of teachers who were all very sympathetic and kind. I told them how much I wanted to go to school.

"I can learn, really I can," I tearfully pleaded with them. "I just need to be given a chance!" Breathlessly I recited the 'ABC' and the 'two times table' to show them how clever I was. For a moment they talked amongst themselves. I anxiously looked on, awaiting the outcome.

"Poor child, we can't just leave him. If only this were a boarding school, then we could have kept him here."

"Why don't we set up an arrangement whereby he can learn from home? We could send him homework and notes through his siblings and mark it when they bring it back." They agreed to give it a try.

That day I was taken home on the back of a bicycle, victorious, though exhausted and visibly shaken.

Naturally father and mother were furious but at the same time they felt deeply for me. They wished me to be educated like any of their other children. In general, *Bahima* did not see much need for girls to go to school, let alone disabled children. Christian families like ours were open to different ideas. We were hampered by physical and financial constraints. My parents could not possibly carry me to school every day nor could they pay for someone else to do this. They were earning hardly enough to make ends meet.

While still recovering from injuries and shock I waited for the promised homework. At last my mission had proven successful. Surely I ought to be grateful. Why then could I not stop thinking about the prohibited path? With hindsight it really was not all that scary. Next time I would know what to expect. If only I could leave earlier and crawl a little faster... But getting away from home was very difficult now. My parents and the other adults were keeping a vigilant eye on me.

The opportunity never presented itself for me to try the path again. A few days later one of the herdsmen came running towards our home, brandishing his stick in a state of alarm.

"Come and see this for yourselves! This is what we have been warning you about!"

He called all the children of the neighbourhood together and walked us to the prohibited path, right to the most dreaded section. There in the grass lay an enormous python, its head and upper body swollen like a huge balloon with two little eyes popping out on top. From its widely stretched mouth stuck the rear legs of a fully-grown goat. A poor innocent creature, swallowed up by that monster. The goat moved inside the snake. It was still fighting for its life. The goat was large, about my size, and could just as well have been a child... or me! The sight was so sickening that my friends and I glanced at each other. No words were needed for us to agree that this was really not worth the risk!

For a while the new arrangement worked. My sisters and brothers brought me notes and homework and took it back to the teachers for marking. However, over time this happened less and less frequently until it stopped altogether. All that I was left with were the exercise books of my sisters to look at but that was of no use. I needed teachers to give me explanations or else I could not keep up.

During the holidays I tried to forget about school. In the company of other children I was happy and did not feel left out. Only when they went back to school did the days become long and empty. Watching my siblings and other children leave in the morning, I spent most of the day staring at the hillside until they reappeared. How I longed to be with them and hear what they were learning, just to have a tiny taste of the life they were able to enjoy.

Soon I became restless again. At the sight of the python I had vowed never to take the prohibited path but there was still the other, longer route where I had once encountered the *orokongoro* and the *anchwera*. That route might work if I left earlier in the morning when snakes were less vicious and active. If I did not aim too high perhaps I might just be able to attend one or two lessons.

It was a glorious morning, a blissful blend of jubilant birds, crystal fresh air and sweet scented flowers. All of nature seemed to be cheering me on with a resounding proclamation. *Go, Simeoni! Get out and make the most of this day!*

Father was not at home. He had gone to try and buy a piece of land so that we would no longer need to shelter with a landlord. The brethren had found a potential place and they had set off together for an initial viewing. This made it easier for me to disappear. I got myself a new stick, larger than the one I normally carried. If now I stumbled upon danger I would be ready to fight like a true nature warrior.

The path was still fairly busy when I set off, the cloth bag with exercise books around my neck. When someone approached I got out of the way until I had the path to myself again. Then I crawled even faster to catch up on lost time. Before long all the children were out of sight. I was left on my own. Half way up the hill I could see our colourful Ankole cattle grazing, their long horns glittering in the sunshine. The grass was green and fresh, the air invigorating. A hunting horn sounded in the distance, gradually becoming louder and clearer. I recognised the high-pitched alarm cry normally used by hunters in pursuit. These were peasants from the same tribe as Possiano's, hunting with spears and large hand-knitted nets that they carried over their shoulders. When an animal took cover they surrounded the bush with their nets and flushed it out by making loud noises. Sometimes they showered a bush with spears before finding out what animal was hiding in there to prevent it from getting away.

As the hunters drew closer I could clearly distinguish their voices among the barking dogs. It was reassuring to know that the area was not totally deserted. As long as I was able to hear them they were bound to hear my voice. I could shout for help if in trouble. This realisation gave me the energy I needed to keep moving, in spite of my aching wrists and bleeding hands and knees.

A gazelle whizzed by, crossing the path close to where I was crawling.

"I could have been trampled," I grumbled. "I hope there aren't any more around."

All of a sudden a large group of hunters came running down the hill, yelling like a rioting mob. I was completely hidden from their sight by the dense vegetation. A couple of dogs jumped onto my path, chasing after the gazelle that had just passed me. Halting abruptly only a few yards away, they barked angrily in my face, their teeth bare, their mouths dripping with saliva. One of the hunters was now very close. I saw the tip of his spear move towards me above the tall grass. I screamed to attract his attention, striking the ground with my stick but the sound just merged with the turmoil around me. I did not know what to fear most – being torn apart by dogs or falling prey to this group of oblivious hunters. A tall figure loomed over me, poised to go in for the kill. Suddenly he froze with shock, his face startled at the sight of this cowering child at his feet.

"Hold onto your spears!" he yelled out to the others. "There is someone here on the ground!" His mate restrained the dogs and led them away to get on with the hunt. The others gathered around me. They were furious but their anger was mixed with shock.

"You shouldn't be here, you crippled boy!" they bellowed. "We could have mistaken you for the animal we were chasing after. You would have got us into serious trouble."

"I did not know that you were going to pass here," I tearfully defended myself. "I am only trying to get to school." The men were having none of it.

"You ought to be at home and be cared for by your mother!"

Numb with shock I tried to crawl away. My limbs just would not move. It was as though I was pinned to the ground. I wanted to pray but could not find any words. I kept on thinking, 'Why?' Of all possible dangers I could never have foreseen these hunters with their dogs. I could never be prepared enough for what might happen. What did this mean? Why was I being stopped all the time from going to school? The story spread fast. Stanley heard it from the hunters and he knew exactly what boy they were talking about. He told my parents who really punished me this time and made me promise never to crawl to school again.

It was one of the saddest moments in my life. Ever since contracting polio I had not been able to be a practical and useful son in the home. Yet I believed that going to school could change this. I had heard that education was a way of elevating oneself. Through education I could prove that I was still a valuable person, worthy of a place in our society. Besides, I had managed to reach the school once, even though tested almost beyond my physical ability and endurance. I had not failed, nor was I a failure!

My family was genuinely shocked by my recklessness and it was good to see their concern. At least my life and survival were still important to them. Of course I had known this all along but it was reassuring to feel their love and affection. It warmed up memories of other times when they had supported me in difficult situations and helped ease my disappointment and frustration. In the end something good came out of all my desperate trying. I had the backing of my family and was no longer alone in my wishes.

"Never give up hoping!" my parents counselled me often. "Only you must do this with patience and trust rather than by risking your life."

They encouraged me to start reading and copying words from our *Orunyankore* Bible. In this way I taught myself to properly read and write. The Bible became the foundation of my learning in terms of education, emotional support and spiritual growth. Over time I gained confidence to read from other sources – anything I could lay my hands on. It became our family prayer that God would work something out for me. Once father had bought us our own piece of land all kinds of new opportunities might be open to us. In the meantime I would just have to wait and believe that our Lord had the perfect timing.

CHAPTER 14

MOVING ON

"Humble yourselves, therefore,
under God's mighty hand,
that he may lift you up in due time.
Cast all your anxiety on him
because he cares for you.

1 Peter 5:6-7

Everything seemed to have ground to a halt, except for time which of course never stood still. Father had not yet secured our own piece of land. After years of setbacks we had insufficient cows left to raise enough cash. It also turned out to be difficult to find a suitable location – not too remote considering my needs and close enough to a school, church and *Balokole* community.

By now we were really quite poor. It was a daily struggle for my parents to feed and clothe all their children, as well as pay the necessary school fees. My only clothes were the ones I wore: a pair of shorts and a small shirt. If we were not so sustained by the grace of our Lord and by fellowship with other Christians it would have been a very despondent time for us all.

As for me, not only was the prospect of education waning, my social life was narrowing too. At the age of twelve I had reached a phase in my life when relationships between people grow rather complex. To adults I was no longer the cute and cuddly boy to whom they could freely show their affection. On my part I had also become more observant and reserved. One thing that especially eroded my confidence was a growing awareness of the changing attitude of my age mates towards me. When returning from school at the end of the day they preferred to hang out with "equals" – youngsters with whom they could go places and be physically active rather than stick around the home and play with someone like me.

Being unable to go out and meet people I depended for company on my immediate family and whoever dropped by, which gave me little chance of making new friends. The gap between me and my age mates was widening. Everyone seemed to be moving on while I increasingly lagged behind, simply because I was a disabled.

I did not quite know what to do with my days. There was not much going on around the home. During the day, when the other children were off to school, I copied words from my Bible or I watched the workers cultivate our landlord's garden. Sometimes I crawled into the fields to look out for the herders. Once or twice a week I covered the one-mile distance to the main road to see cars and pedestrians passing by. That was one of the highlights. I loved taking part in life, albeit from the roadside, as a spectator.

The crawling took its toll on my clothing. When my knees became too painful I resorted to shifting on my bottom, tearing large holes in my only pair of shorts. The moment someone approached I had to quickly sit down in the grass to conceal the exposed parts of my body and avoid embarrassment. Sometimes groups of teenagers passed on the path where I was crawling. They would whisper to each other and giggle at the sight of my thin legs, scratched by thorns and covered in dust or mud if it had just been raining.

It always made me feel awkward and shy to be seen in a scruffy, undignified state, especially if there were girls among them.

Our landlord had a daughter called Kevina who had left school prematurely to give birth to a child. Although now twenty and much older than me she seemed to enjoy my presence, perhaps because she also felt a bit lonely. Her little son liked my company too. Some days I played with him to enable Kevina to get on with her chores. This kept me occupied and gave me the satisfaction of doing something useful.

Kevina was very sympathetic towards me and we became good friends. Often she talked to me about her unhappiness of not being able to marry the father of her child. Then I would tell her about my experiences in Mulago. In one of our conversations I mentioned that during my stay in hospital a national register of disabled people had been set up. It was run by the Ministry of Culture and Community Development to ensure that disabled people who had not been able to attend school during childhood could eventually take part in a vocational training programme. Everyone on the register was given a Certificate of Registration. We children were urged to keep it until we were big enough to apply for a place on such a scheme. Father was looking after my certificate; he was very good at keeping things safe.

Every so often Kevina was visited by the father of her child. He was known as Mr Kagangure, a wealthy man by local standards, highly regarded and one of the very few *Bahima* in the county with a car. The Ministry of Health contracted him on a regular basis to drive medical practitioners to outreach clinics in rural areas. Whenever I saw his vehicle pass on the road I enthusiastically waved with both my arms and a beaming smile. That is how he got to know me even before we met.

A few times Mr Kagangure found me at Kevina's house, though the moment I heard his car approach I quickly got out of the way to give them some privacy together. He seemed moved by my situation. When Kevina told him about my registration certificate and how much I would benefit from vocational training he took it upon himself to make further enquiries. In this way we found out about the special training centres for disabled people that were being run in various parts of the country. Trainees could enrol by approaching their local authorities and convincing them of their suitability and needs.

Although this prospect was hugely exciting, my parents were unable to pursue it. They did not have the money for transport and a set of proper clothes for me. Kevina told Mr Kagangure about this, and the next time we met he gave me ten shillings. This was a considerable amount at the time, enough for a pair of shorts and a shirt from the local market. As usual I refused to accept the money, unwilling to rely on pity. He gave it to Kevina instead, urging her to talk me out of my 'stubborn attitude'.

"If the boy waits until his parents can afford it," he said, "it will take ages before he can join any scheme. Let them use this money to get him new clothes. Then I myself will drive him and his father to the local authorities!"

My parents were grateful for this opportunity and did not consider it improper for me to accept money from Mr Kagangure. He was a respectable figure in the community. They even allowed me to travel with him on my own. And so, when it was his turn again to ferry medics to a clinic in Kazo, Mr Kakangure took me along for a visit to the local government offices there. None of the personnel had ever heard of special schemes for disabled people but they took interest in my certificate and wrote a referral letter.

A few weeks later we took the letter to the county headquarters in Kiruhura. This time father came along too. The county chief was Mr Ntaama who knew all about vocational training centres for the disabled. Apparently one centre was only forty miles away, at Ruti near Mbarara, the main town in western Uganda. Unfortunately he was swift to inform us that these schemes were for grown-ups only. The training involved a lot of heavy physical work, like agriculture, carpentry and house building. He told father that the best place for a child like me was school, but of course that had proven impossible! I tried to explain this and pleaded with him. Father and Mr Kagangure joined in.

"This boy is so determined. He wants it so much. You should see what huge distances he can crawl!"

"He is agile and energetic, strong enough to make things with his hands. He really is a very deserving child."

Our insistence, supported by the referral letter from Kazo, eventually made an impact. Even though I was way below the qualifying age, Chief Ntaama gave me a Formal Recommendation for a place at the Ruti Vocational Training Centre, together with a free bus pass for me to travel with one adult to Mbarara. Now we no longer had a choice in the matter, as the Chief pointed out to father.

"Just remember," he declared with an air of self-importance, "Once the local authority has assessed a disabled child and decided to provide assistance, it has powers to impose action upon the parents should they fail to see it through!"

Father was only too happy to oblige. We had all been yearning and praying for something that would help me move on with my life and this seemed promising. While still rejoicing at this development my family received more good news. A farmer in Rushere was asking to meet with father with the view of selling him a plot of land. Father set off immediately. Some of the brethren went along to help negotiate the price. Finally, after several years of sheltering with a landlord and toiling for his gain, father was able to buy our own piece of land. It cost us most of our remaining herd but various *Balokole* and relatives offered to either give or loan us a milking cow thus enabling him to set up a farm. It was nothing short of a miracle. At last we were going to be independent again. The land even had a banana plantation so food shortage would be a thing of the past. We could grow our own, just as we used to do when living in our permanent home in Bweyale. And all this coincided with me going to Ruti, thus avoiding the usual problem of finding me a place to stay while the rest of my family moved and set up home elsewhere.

Father did not waste any time. The moment he returned from Rushere, he and I headed for the bus to Mbarara. Along came his trusted bicycle, as we were told that the training centre was several miles out of town. Saying goodbye to my family was hard. Everyone was very emotional. My parents had to remind us that this time I was not leaving home to undergo dreaded and painful treatments.

"This is an exciting opportunity," they told us, "a blessing that can only enrich Simeoni's life! Let us not be sad but thankful to the Lord!"

The Ruti Vocational Training Centre was situated on a pretty, secluded site along the busy Mbarara-Kabale highway. At the entrance we met several trainees with a variety of physical and sensory disabilities. Clearly, at the age of twelve I would be the youngest at the centre, the others probably ranging from nineteen to fifty. It was always exciting to see people in similar circumstances. Although a little insecure about staying behind in this unfamiliar environment I could not wait to get started. Father lifted me off the carrier and asked for the centre manager.

"What on earth is that child doing here?" I overheard the trainees murmur to each other. "Do they think this is a primary school?"

We were in for an immediate disappointment. It took just one glance for the manager to make up his mind about me.

"I am well aware that disabled people are entitled to vocational training," he stressed, "but this is not a place for looking after children! Here we train men and women to make things that we can sell to raise income for our centre.

Once their training has been completed they can use their skills to earn their own living. This boy is far too young to benefit from any of the courses we offer."

Father and I tried to argue my case. We both knew that anything would be better for me than hanging around at home.

"The boy is among equals here," father pleaded with the manager. "Yet you want to deprive him of this chance. He is probably even stronger than some of the trainees at your centre. If only you knew what he is up to at home! Please, try him out. Let him show you what he can do!"

"Besides," he added shrewdly, recalling the warning given by Chief Ntaama, "if I don't support my son in this matter I may be breaking the law..."

Reluctantly the manager invited us into his office. He rounded up some instructors as well as the matron in charge of residential care at centre. The matron thoughtfully observed me while the others debated my future.

"Really this child is far too young."

"He'll be taking the place of someone who could make much better use of our programme."

I was almost reduced to tears when at length she interrupted.

"Why don't we give this boy at least a chance? I will personally commit myself to looking after Simeoni as far as his residential needs are concerned."

In the end, with the backing of the matron, it was agreed that the instructors would test my abilities in the courses they thought I could handle, like leatherwork and tailoring. Mission accomplished father went home. I escorted him to the gate where he briefly spoke with the trainees we had met upon our arrival.

"I have brought you my young man," he cheerfully announced. "His name is Simeoni. He is very eager and resilient, happy to be back with birds of his own feather. Will you look after him?" They promised that they would.

Father handed me the small bag he had carried, containing a spare set of clothes that used to be Sam's, a hymnbook, a bed sheet, my exercise books, a piece of soap and a bit of money. I watched him cycle away. Parting was always difficult, both for father and me. Rallying my spirit I resolved not to feel sad. I was going to make the most of this God-given opportunity.

"Here I am," I said to myself. "Finally at Ruti. It is good to be in this place. I am all grown-up now!"

The grass near the entrance was green and soft. This was the place where trainees spent most of their spare time chatting and smoking. The road provided them with a never-ending source of entertainment – a variety show of life-on-the-move. Pick-ups laden with supporters on the way to a football match, chanting and beating their drums. Military vehicles and massive lorries heading for the borders with Rwanda and Congo. The old drunkard singing on his bicycle while trying to balance a calabash of *Tonto* without spilling it. A pretty young woman with a basket full of crops on her head, smiling and waving at them. This was also to become the place where I would often sit and remember seeing father off, feeling thankful to God as I reflected on how far I had come with my life.

The matron showed me the dining hall, the bathroom and my bed in the men's dormitory. I was introduced to my fellow trainees and instantly got on with them, making friends with the younger ones that very same day. We exchanged stories, joked and teased each other. They wondered how I was going to cope with all the heavy work that they were doing. That evening I got a new nickname: *Akoojo*, which means "Little boy!"

My classes started the following day. We had a highly skilled tailoring instructor who had studied fashion design in the UK. He could measure a person and make any outfit he wanted without the use of a pattern. At first I was told to watch closely what the others were doing. Over time I learnt to make trousers, dresses and shirts using a hand operated sewing machine. In the leather workshop I was trained in making belts and straps before progressing to bags and footwear. Eventually they also tried me out in agriculture, which proved physically quite demanding. After being taught the ins-and-outs of farming we were given tools and set to work on an allotment. Here we grew potatoes, maize and all kinds of produce for local sale and our own consumption. A really interesting course was 'Citizenship' which introduced us to the role of the state and our legal rights and responsibilities as citizens. It also taught us valuable life skills such as cooking and hygiene.

During one of our weekly assemblies the centre manager made an important announcement. Two volunteers from Norway would soon be joining us to help with creative activities and physical education. With great anticipation we witnessed the arrival of Miss Ursula and Miss Ulag in their Volkswagen Kombi. I cannot quite remember whether Ulag was her real name as it was also the first word of a song she would teach us later. Soon we found ourselves doing all sorts of exercises and games, no matter how disabled we were. We played football using our arms, fists, bottoms, heads and any other limb we could move. Everyone was able to take part and we had a wonderful time. We held drama and dance competitions between the various dormitories. Miss Ulag set up our own Ruti Choir that she accompanied on her guitar. They took us out on trips. We even went camping in a safari park up-country. Later, when Miss Ursula married a Ugandan college lecturer, our choir sang at their wedding and we were all invited to the reception.

The centre organised outings for us on public holidays and special occasions. On Independence Day we visited Kakyeka, the local stadium in Mbarara where we watched colourful ceremonies and marches. Sometimes our choir was asked to take part in the celebrations. We held plays and concerts for important guests, like ministers and district commissioners as well as for national and foreign donors. One day the Minister for Culture and Community Development, the Honourable Mr Katiiti, visited our centre with a group of MPs. We gave a concert not merely to raise funds but also to demonstrate to our guests the beneficial role a government can play in improving the lives of disabled people. Some visitors were so impressed that they placed orders with our tailoring workshop, including the Minister who asked us to make curtains for his new country home.

We communicated with Miss Ursula and Miss Ulag in English. In fact, my use of this language greatly improved because they always made a point of correcting me. Every so often they helped trainees with reading and writing, especially the younger ones who were keen on learning. I could not wait to show Miss Ulag the work I had done in my exercise books, every time asking her to write down new words. She was always ready to help, enthused by my aptitude for learning.

Amongst each other we spoke in our various local vernaculars, which was probably for the better. Miss Ulag wore a miniskirt that was regarded as shockingly revealing in our conservative African environment. It often made her the target of some rather crude comments and jokes. On one such occasion Miss Ursula asked me to interpret what the other trainees were saying. After some hesitation I did so, faithfully and in considerable detail. As a result everyone was furious with me: Miss Ursula and Miss Ulag for my impudence, and my fellow trainees for giving them away!

At Ruti I met Frederick, one of my fellow trainees. In the past he used to work as a foreman at the Kirembe Copper Mines in Western Uganda until one of the mines collapsed, injuring and killing scores of people. Fred was in his mid-twenties, tall, good-looking and now permanently confined to a wheelchair. Often he spoke to me about his traumatic memories of the carnage he had witnessed and how ambitious, outgoing and full of life he used to be. Before the accident he was popular and proud, feeling awkward when meeting disabled people, especially when accompanied by one of his many female friends. Never could he have envisaged himself as a disabled person!

Now everything had changed. Whenever he went to a club in his wheelchair, he was the one being looked down upon. Women stayed out of his way. These experiences left him frustrated and bitter, but more than anything he regretted his own past behaviour.

"How I wish I could turn back the clock," my friend was often heard saying. "Prejudice is hurtful. It makes life unnecessarily hard for people like us while we already have a lot to put up with." He desperately wanted to use his personal situation to enlighten others, to change their ignorance before it was too late for them.

On many occasions Fred and I sat by the roadside, philosophising about the world and sharing life experiences and feelings. We agreed that being disabled could at times be hard to bear, but gaining the acceptance of others was proving much more difficult. People, whose lives were intact, often did not realise how fortunate they were. Imagine if everyone would use their gifts and blessings to make a positive difference, however small. Even a simple friendly gesture could brighten someone's day. An example of this was the old grocery vendor who regularly passed our centre. One day he put down his heavily laden bicycle, wiped the sweat off his face and strolled across the road with outstretched, soil-stained hands.

"I have so often seen you here, sitting at the roadside," he greeted us with a broad smile, "and for long I've been meaning to stop and make your acquaintance." We had a cheerful conversation and, no doubt, when we parted, not only Fred and I but also the old man felt blessed and uplifted.

Away from the shelter of my *Balokole* family I was among older, more streetwise people. Many had very different moral standards which created a whole new kind of challenge for me. At the weekends they went into town for drinks, though they were not allowed to bring alcohol back to the centre. They also smoked, flirted and used swear-words. As a *Mulokole* I could not take part in these things. My composure made me the target of a fair bit of jovial teasing.

"Come on, *Akoojo*, your God won't strike you dead for a little indulgence!"

"A bit of smoking and drinking will make you a man among others."

"Look how sweetly that pretty girl is looking at you. Surely, a kiss can do no harm?"

"What else can you expect from an *Akoojo*?" I usually retorted. "This is a place of learning, isn't it? For the time being I will watch and learn from you. If I really must, I'll catch up when I am older!"

At home I used to attend Bible study groups and fellowship meetings but there was no chance of this while staying at Ruti. Some of the other Christians at the centre went to church on Sundays by public transport or on foot. I missed taking part in regular worship and often prayed that *Yesu*, who had enabled me get a place at Ruti, would provide for my spiritual needs as well.

One day I saw a vicar approach the centre on a bicycle. I thought that he was visiting a resident but his bag was bulging with Bibles and hymnbooks. He had actually come to hold regular worship meetings at the centre with those unable to go into town. Management approved of the idea and introduced us to Reverend Rujokyi. To my excitement he turned out to be a *Mulokole* like me. From that day on Reverend Rujokyi came to visit us every Sunday. Many trainees attended his services and benefited from them. Amazingly, he would later be posted to Rushere where my parents were now living and become the vicar of their local church.

I stayed at Ruti for roughly a year. It was such a happy time. No painful treatments or scary operations, just the buzz of learning, being productive and taking part in social life. It filled a huge gap in my longing for progress and soothed my regret of not being able to go to school like the other children I knew.

I acquired many new skills and discovered that disabled people did not always need to be dependent on the support and care of family or strangers. We could also achieve, even earn our own living! Miss Ursula told me about schools in her country for children with special needs. She knew a blind man who had become a successful pianist. Apparently in Europe there were many accomplished disabled people, owning properties and driving cars. I had witnessed something like that myself when staying in New Mulago. A senior medic had been paralyzed in a car crash and was given by the Ministry of Health an adapted car from abroad that he could drive all by himself. And his disability was much worse than mine.

I was inspired by such stories about resilience and success but they also touched on a raw nerve. While Ruti was a worthwhile experience, deep in my heart I was still yearning for education. I believed that life had more in store for me than ending up as a tailor or a shoemaker on a street corner. I just did not see the way in which this could ever materialise.

At the end of my training I was awarded a Certificate of Achievement in Vocational Training. I had made many friends at Ruti and we were very sorry to part. I never saw Frederick again nor many of the others. By now I had grown quite a bit and was no longer an *Akoojo*.

Miss Ulag drove me home in her Kombi. It was wonderful to be reunited with my family on our very own land in Rushere. Their lives had also improved in my absence. Once again they found themselves surrounded by a *Balokole* community. Moreover, with plenty of food to go round they were able to host again and help other people in need. I quickly found my place in this thriving community. It felt a bit like being back in the settlement in Kikoma.

There was only one thing that dampened my spirit and prevented me from fully enjoying the generally happy atmosphere. Being back home meant being stuck again, back in the waiting game. During the day my age mates were off to school and I just sat at home. The idea behind Ruti was that upon completion of the programme trainees raised funds for equipment and started their own workshop. My parents thought hard about getting me tools but it was not seen as a viable option. At thirteen I was too young to start out on my own. Besides, I knew little about setting up a business.

It was nice to have a certificate though. When other parents talked about their children's progress at school, mine could proudly say that Simeoni had just completed a vocational training course. My certificate proved my potential. I just hoped that one day I would be able to put my training into practice. For the time being though any thought of this had to be shelved.

My reading and writing skills had considerably improved during my time at Ruti and eventually I found a way of making use of these. Many of the older people in our neighbourhood were illiterate. Whilst their own children were away in town or at school, they turned to me for help, asking me to read out letters and write replies on their behalf. I also read to them from the Bible during their prayer meetings. Whenever the local village elders met to sort out issues and conflicts I attended their meetings, taking on the informal role of clerk and drafting simple agreements between the various parties.

Once upon a time people believed that I would die within seven years but against all odds God had enabled me to survive. As I grew older I longed to prove that other gloomy predictions about my future were also unfounded. The negative voices of the past always resonated through my mind. *"Poor Simeoni, he will never get married. He'll never be a useful person!"* It was true that within *Bahima* society marriage was very complex. It required the scrutiny and approval not just from the bride's parents but from her extended family, like all the aunts and uncles, and not everyone was filled with the spirit of Christian love and compassion. Flawless looks and health were essential to our people, as were wealth and status. Someone like me had virtually no chance of ever being accepted as a prospective husband. Yet, at Ruti I had met disabled adults from other tribes who were married and had children. Not one of them was rich. Some even moved around on hands and knees like me.

Having discovered that disabled people did not necessarily have to remain single, I wanted to find out whether it was possible for girls to reciprocate my affections. Would any *Bahima* girl ever be able to look beyond my disability? Could she ever like me for who I was? Naturally, in my early teens I was still too young to look for a lasting relationship but I was seeking reassurance. Meeting a girl with tender feelings for me would prove that I too stood a chance of finding love in the future. It would put my mind at rest.

As I began to 'test the waters' I quickly discovered that there were massive stumbling blocks to contend with. In the first place I was a *Mulokole* which in itself stopped me from being intimately close with a girl. Our faith demanded high moral standards, including total abstinence until marriage. Christian love and fellowship were regarded as more important than intimate, personal relationships. In fact, even a cuddle or a kiss was viewed as giving in to lustful temptation. *Balokole* of the opposite sex were meant to treat each other as "brethren" and that also applied to teenagers (although of course not all youngsters around me were committed Christians).

Secondly, I learnt that when it came to getting a girl's attention there was a lot of competition. In general, *Bahima* girls were attracted to strong and agile boys without physical defects. Compared to them I was no match. However, they did seem to feel safe in my presence and enjoy confiding in me. I heard many a story about their love for other boys or their heartache when they had been jilted. Drawing from my own life experiences I was able to give an encouraging word and help them deal with rejection. A very pretty girl once told me that I would have made an amazing boyfriend if only I had been 'normal'. All the girls would have been fighting over me! I would like to believe that she intended to give me a compliment.

I became something of a mediator between boys and girls, helping them sort out their differences and finding ways of bringing them together. After all, in the world of whirling teenage romance I was considered a harmless creature. A boy once asked me to set him up with a very sweet girl, knowing very well that she and I were growing close, as if I did not have any feelings! Often when a girl showed interest in me, boys got jealous and used all their tactics to sway her away, just to spoil our budding friendship.

"If that girl can become fond of Simeoni then I'll have an even better chance of catching her," I heard one boy snigger to another. "I won't waste time by just holding hands and praying together...."

Many girls found themselves attracted to my cheerful, friendly personality. They enjoyed talking to me but were embarrassed to do so in public. It needed only a bit of teasing from their friends – a comment like, *"She has got a crush on Simeoni"* and I was unlikely to see them again.

One day, when father and I were waiting for the bus, a group of teenagers passed by from a nearby school. Among them was a girl who had often poured her heart out to me when she was being bullied. I liked her a lot and she usually made a point of greeting me very sweetly.

"I'll just go and say 'Hi' to Simeoni," I heard her call out to the others. As she turned and began to cross the road her friends grabbed her by the shoulders.

"Why bother greeting this *ekyimuga* (meaning something like 'crippled freak')?" they sneered.

"But I know him well," she replied. "Simeoni and I are good friends!"

"Hush, don't let anyone know that you are friends with him. You should not be seen with that cripple!"

She looked back as they pulled her along and from that day on kept avoiding me. Hurt and angry, I said a swearword that we *Balokole* were not supposed to use. I must have picked it up at Ruti. My father was shocked.

"Where does that language come from?" he seriously reprimanded. "When something like this happens you should pray for your feelings rather than let them get the better of you. If you don't do this, Simeoni, you will end up a bitter person!"

More and more I began to realise that a full relationship with the opposite sex would be one of the hardest things ever to achieve. Only a strong, independent, open-minded girl could rise above the general prejudice and peer pressure. For the time being I had to be content with playing the role of counsellor and listening ear. It seemed to be either that or having no friendship with girls at all. Perhaps it was true what mother used to say when I was very young and unsuccessfully tried to turn wild baby birds into pets. *"Some creatures are best loved and admired from a distance. If you try to grab them they may not survive or fly away!"*

Over time I learnt to be patient and happy with whatever little I could get. This did not stop me from hoping, but the more I prayed the less worried I felt about the future. My very existence proved that nothing was impossible for God. He cared for me. As long as I put my trust in him he would attend to all my needs, in his perfect timing.

Once again father and I went up to Kampala for a review at the polio clinic. By now I wasn't even trying anymore to walk with callipers and crutches. The rough terrain around our home made me always fall flat on my back, like a tree being felled, which was not only risky to my weak back but also undignified and painful. As a result the joints in my knees and hips had contracted so much that putting on my callipers was no longer possible. After carrying out a series of assessments and tests the doctors decided against putting me through any further treatment. No more surgical procedures, no more physiotherapy and no more plaster casts or traction. Instead I was going to be given my very own wheelchair. I could not have been prouder. From now on my days of crawling in the dust would finally be over!

While staying at the hostel father and I heard about a vocational training centre for disabled people in Kireka, a suburb of Kampala. Here they offered a variety of courses that I had not yet tried out, like welding, umbrella making and office skills. There was even a chance of permanent employment as the centre had links with the business world and kept some trainees on in sheltered workshops. This was a promising new lead, definitely worth pursuing. The polio clinic employed a social worker, a certain Mr Ambrose, who promised to look into the matter and help me put in an application. Reassured by this prospect father went home. I remained in Kampala, ready to take on whatever life would bring next.

CHAPTER 15

A USEFUL SON

"Even though you are so high above, you care for the lowly,
and the proud cannot hide from you.
When I am surrounded by troubles,
you keep me safe.....
You will do everything you have promised;
Lord, your love is eternal.
Complete the work that you have begun."

Psalm 138: 6-7a, 8

Some four years had passed since father first brought me to
the polio clinic and hostel. By now Miss Yield and many other
Muzungu staff members had moved on. Even those replacing
them were about to return to their countries, leaving the
services and facilities largely in the hands of Ugandans.

While staying at the hostel, waiting for my wheelchair to
be made locally at the Old Mulago orthopaedic metal
workshop, I used every opportunity to share my wishes and
aspirations with the remaining expatriate staff. Although I
had applied to Kireka, there was always a chance of being
rejected if there were no vacancies or if they considered me
too young for a placement. Time and again I explained how
anxious I was about education or further training leading to
employment – anything really that would help me improve

or use my skills. I might have failed in getting back on my feet and walking again but I was desperate to succeed in my quest to make the most of my life.

The *Muzungus* at the hostel took time to listen to me and somehow felt compelled to help, even though I had exhausted all the usual medical treatment and rehabilitation programmes on offer. Before leaving Uganda, a rehabilitation 'sister' got in touch with other foreign nationals to see whether anyone would be willing to take me on educational outings and make a positive contribution to my quality of life.

I should have welcomed her idea as a great opportunity but oddly enough it filled me with dread. I was quite comfortable within the confines of the medical world. The doctors and nurses had earned my trust by accepting me and not considering my condition as a burden. How could I expect such an attitude from a total stranger?

One day the 'sister' told me that she had found me someone special.

"His name is Mr Martin Buckmaster," she said. "He is a prominent person, a UK Diplomat!" The title meant nothing to me. In fact, it only increased my apprehension. If this man was so important, how was I going to relate to him, and he to me?

From then on Martin Buckmaster came to collect me every Saturday morning to take me to a place of educational interest, like a museum, concert, Uganda State House, Kiira Harbour and Entebbe Zoo. Some days we just chilled out on the shores of Lake Victoria. Occasionally he invited my friends along, as many as could fit in his car. He had a limousine with a little flag for official occasions and a Ford estate car for casual use.

To my surprise and delight there had been no need for me to worry about Martin. Being kind and down to earth, he went out of his way to make me feel accepted. A devout Christian he had a special ability to connect with people who might be looked down upon by others. He did not even mind lifting me from my wheelchair and carrying me into his car in his arms.

Every so often we went to places further afield, like the source of the river Nile at Jinja with its massive hydroelectric dam. We visited the industrial areas of eastern Uganda where Martin showed me a sugar factory and explained how sugar was made. He was a knowledgeable man, fluent in several languages, including Arabic. On the way we would stop for refreshments – anything from an expensive meal in some posh restaurant to a soda and *mandazi* at a kiosk beside the road.

"What would you like to do next week?" Martin asked me after one of our trips. "Shall we go and watch the aeroplanes at Entebbe Airport?"

I had seen helicopters land at Mulago while waiting for my operations, but never aeroplanes and I wondered what they looked like. Whenever one flew over the village, high up in the sky like a tiny dot with a trail of cloud, we cried out *"enyonyi!"* – "bird!" Then all the children would come running out, twisting their necks and busting their eyes in the sharp glare of the sun just to catch a glimpse of this magical object. To actually see these imposing manmade birds stand on the tarmac was quite overwhelming. Breathless with excitement I chatted away, asking Martin all sorts of questions.

"Why don't they flap their wings? Is it because they have just landed? Have planes ever managed to fly into heaven? Is it safe for us to be so near?"

Whenever a plane landed or took off it made a deafening noise that boomed right through us, making the whole airport shudder. To me these planes were wondrous things, the way they moved through the air, as though propelled by a supernatural power, just like the Chwezi spears in our ancestral legends.

Eventually Martin invited me to his home in Upper Kololo, Kampala's elite area where many high government officials and foreign diplomats lived. We sat in his well-tended garden, had dinner or watched television. He even introduced me to some of his *Muzungu* guests. Martin turned out to be the First Secretary at the British High Commission. I did not grasp his position until quite some time later, when fellow disabled and even members of staff showed signs of envy at my acquaintance with him. Later in my life his status would become more apparent, when he visited my home as Viscount Martin Buckmaster, member of the British House of Lords. I was just glad to know a caring and generous person like Martin who took me on wonderful outings. He gave me many great stories to share with family and friends, and I cherish those memories to this very day.

Following the toppling of the *Kabaka* by Milton Obote in 1969 Uganda experienced a period of relative calm. Police kept law and order, the army stuck to their barracks, and gunshots were only occasionally heard at night when armed robbers made their opportunistic move under the cover of darkness. Sadly, on the evening of 24 January 1971 this peace was about to come to an end. We were getting ready for bed when a torrent of gunfire hit the city of Kampala, punctuated by massive bomb blasts. I had never heard anything like it before, not even during the shelling of the *Kabaka's* palace. Besides, in my young and excitable mind that had been a dramatic experience. I was quite a bit older now and much more aware of danger. The mayhem continued throughout the night, with heavy vehicles speeding past the hospital grounds amidst gunfire and rocket explosions. At times the blasts were so close to our hostel that the whole building shook.

With the national TV and radio stations off the air no one knew what was going on, but as morning broke the hazy sunlight revealed a terrifying sight. The streets of Kampala were littered with armoured vehicles, army trucks and monstrous tanks. Scores of heavily armed soldiers had spread out over the city to take up position outside every important building, mounting roadblocks along the way. On the road along our hostel a squeaking tank rolled by with a group of rowdy young men on top, chanting and waving machine guns.

"Look, isn't that Katumba?" my friend cried out pointing through the window. To our astonishment he seemed to recognize a member of Heartbeat of Africa, a well-known traditional band. Could this be true? Could almost overnight a singer and dancer turn into a fighter?

The shooting continued throughout the morning, only this time the soldiers seemed to be targeting each other and not civilians, as had been the case during the toppling of the *Kabaka*. Once we were absolutely certain of this our mood changed from alarm to curiosity. As a group of disabled youngsters we decided to venture beyond the compound and see for ourselves what was going on. It was rumoured that injured soldiers were taken to the New Mulago casualty department. If we were to have any share of the action then surely that would the best place to start!

We made our way to the medical students' quarters, a peaceful and secluded part of the hospital where a lovely "racing" ramp ran all the way from the fourth floor down to the casualty entrance. The hospital was heavily guarded and soldiers stopped us as we approached. After closely scrutinizing our wheelchairs and crutches, they eventually allowed us passage through. Some of my friends became anxious, wondering how safe it would be for us to move on.

"How could we ever be seen a threat," I tried to rally their spirits. "There really is nothing to fear. We are disabled. Besides, we look just like patients!"

A few of us turned back to the hostel while the rest took up position in the wide corridor leading from the casualty department to the wards, ready to dash forward at the first sign of commotion. Most casualties brought in were soldiers, armed to the teeth, with ammunition belts over their shoulders and hand grenades dangling down their chests.

Nearly all of them were covered in blood. One soldier sat on a trolley, clenching his machine gun while his severed leg hung on by the skin. A doctor tried to persuade him to put down his weapon but the delirious soldier was having none of it.

"Keep your hands off," he kept barking. "Not until I am in theatre will I surrender my weapons to a civilian!"

High on adrenaline the injured fighters threatened and bullied the medics who were getting visibly nervous. The more senior the rank of casualty brought in the tenser the atmosphere, until everyone seemed to be shouting at each other. Eventually we were spotted and chased back to the hostel. Timely really because by then we felt quite shocked at all the horror we had just been witnessing.

During the course of January 25th all gunfire died down and Kampala fell eerily silent. That afternoon Radio Uganda announced that Dr Milton Obote had been deposed in a military coup and power handed over to Major General Idi Amin Dada. A night-time curfew was put in place until calm had returned to the country. Amin seized power while Obote was in Singapore attending a Commonwealth summit meeting. He bitterly resented Obote for demoting him from the rank of overall commander of the Ugandan armed forces and for planning to arrest him for misuse of army funds.

At that time the Ugandan army predominantly consisted of Acholi and Langi, tribes from the north of the country where Obote was born, and of Amin's tribe, the Nubians, from the West Nile. After a brief but bitter battle between the different army factions, troops loyal to Obote were defeated. Obote himself went into exile in Tanzania where he would soon start preparing to stage his return.

Following the broadcast thousands of people emerged from their homes. Many were cheering and dancing. They blamed Obote and his government for being corrupt. He had abolished their cherished kingdoms and favoured his tribe by giving all the top jobs to his own people. In their eyes Amin was a liberator! Waving tree branches they took to the streets to hail their new leader, forgetting that it was Amin in the first place who had led the bloody attack on the *Kabaka's* palace. They began to tear down the posters of their former President and anything else remotely connected to his regime.

Before long the general euphoria escalated into looting. Asian property was the most obvious target. In those days Asians owned the majority of shops and businesses in Uganda and their dominance of the economy was another cause for growing public resentment. From the hostel grounds we saw an elated crowd thronging down the hill towards the city centre, only to return a few hours later bogged down under the weight of furniture and sacks of food. This, in turn, sent others running in the opposite direction to go and look for their share of the loot. The troops on the streets seemed to turn a blind eye, as though the unfolding lawlessness merely formed part of the celebrations – a way for civilians to let off steam after years of frustration under Obote. In fact, several people told us that they had seen soldiers take part in the looting.

After a while we dared stray to the roadside to join other groups of spectators. There we watched in disbelief how an unruly mob set upon the trading centre opposite our hostel and began to ransack the place.

Within a week of the coup Amin declared himself the new President of Uganda. He released scores of political prisoners, promised free and fair elections and, to please the *Baganda*, ordered for the body of their exiled *Kabaka* to be returned to Uganda and buried in state. Sadly, his honeymoon with the Ugandan people did not last long. Over the months that followed, many prestigious public buildings and residential homes were seized and turned into housing for army personnel. Numerous ministers and key players under Obote were killed and others forced to flee the country. Their positions were filled by high-ranking military officers who each had armed bodyguards and escorts. There were soldiers everywhere, ready to detain and beat up civilians and smash their property if they entered prohibited places or did not respond to orders. The streets of Kampala no longer belonged to the common man but to the army, and everyone made sure to tread carefully in their presence.

Of course, living in the polio hostel I only knew about these things from what I could see from the compound and from what other people told us. To me the large military presence in Kampala seemed incredibly impressive and intriguing. Something I was dying to have a closer look at. I was still waiting to hear from Kireka and could do with a bit of diversion. After all, nothing dreadful could happen to me. I was just an innocent boy in a wheelchair with nothing but the best intentions.

One of the most revered sites in Kampala was Bulange Palace. It used to belong to the *Kabaka* but had recently been turned into the new Army Headquarters. Everyone was talking about it.

"What if I try to visit that place? I may see the mighty Moses Ali, Amin's younger brother. People say that he almost single-handedly captured Entebbe Airport during the coup. Perhaps I'll even catch a glimpse of our new President himself!" Buzzing with excitement I shared this idea with my friends.

"But Bulange is more than three miles from here," they hesitantly objected. "You can never push your wheelchair so far all by yourself."

"The roads are very hilly... It will be dangerous!"

Their warnings, clearly well intended, gave me just the challenge I needed. I decided to do a few trial runs by wheeling myself to Nakivubo Stadium where disabled people were admitted free of charge to watch the games and events. Once I managed to cover this distance and back I would be ready to take on Bulange.

Situated on Mengo Hill, one of the seven hills of Kampala, Bulange Palace was a grand white building with a green dome-shaped roof. An endless stream of Landrovers, Jeeps and other army vehicles made their way up and down the long, steep road. The ones with flags and red number plates carried high-ranking officers, their shoulders and chests glittering with golden stars and other decorations. From my wheelchair I eagerly waved at them, occasionally getting a response. Most of the soldiers looked serious and mean, deliberately revving their engines as they drove past. I also saw black cars with long boots and dark tinted windows belonging to the newly established State Research Bureau. In the years to come these vehicles would be regarded as instruments for disappearance and death. However, for now they were an attractive sight and I waved at each one of them.

The exercise was taking a toll on my strength. I frequently had to pause to catch my breath. Now and then a pedestrian stopped for a quick chat.

"Hello *kijana* ('young man' in Swahili). Are you stuck? Do you need a hand?" Then I would quickly push my wheelchair a little further to prove that I could manage very well by myself. The area around Bulange was cordoned off and heavily guarded, yet scores of people were entering and emerging from the building, like a swarm of bees. From a distance I took it all in, ready to relay every detail to my friends at the hostel. Wondering what might be inside that fascinating building I slowly pushed my wheelchair closer. On the right was a small entrance where civilians entered to attend an appointment or to deliver goods. Not all of them were stopped and questioned. The odd wave and smile from the officers had convinced me that I would not get shot on the spot if I tried to have a peep inside.

A group of visitors approached the side entrance just as a high army official arrived at the main gate. With the guards momentarily distracted I decided to make a dash for it. The slope leading to the entrance was very steep. Someone behind me gave my wheelchair a push. All of a sudden I was inside the building.

However, from the compound I had not noticed the checkpoints beyond the entrance where guards armed to the teeth had been watching me.

"You there, stop!" they called out to me with a distrustful, scrutinising look on their faces. "Where are you going? Why are you here?"

Of course, the main purpose of my being in the building had been sheer curiosity. All I wanted was to explore a special posh place with very important people but I feared that saying so would not sound very convincing. I had to improvise quickly. Didn't I have a distant relative, someone related to my father, who was an army officer at the time Amin took control?

"I have come to see my 'uncle', Major Rwebigo," I blurted out. By now I was dripping with sweat, not just from the heat and strain of wheeling myself all the way up Mengo Hill but also from sheer trepidation. Soon I found myself surrounded by three heavily armed soldiers, firing all sorts of questions at me.

"Why have you come to these Army Headquarters?"

"Why did you not report at the main gate?"

"Why aren't you visiting your uncle at his home?"

How I regretted the folly of my actions. Once again my curiosity and eagerness to take part in life had got me into trouble.

"I don't mean to do anything wrong, Sir," I retorted. "I am Simeoni Ninsiima, son of Petero Rutembeka, and I have come here to see my uncle."

It struck me that even if this distant relative of ours were in the building, he would probably never have heard of me.

"Well, never mind," I hastily added with the most charming smile I could muster. "It is not really urgent. If it's too much trouble I think I'll better go home!"

But turning back as I pleased was no longer an option. The guards did not allow me to leave the building until they had fully established the reason for my entering, even though I was a disabled youngster who could not possibly do any harm. While I was detained in the corridor and later moved on to the main reception, a couple of soldiers were sent to look for Major Rwebigo. Over and over I had to repeat my story to different army personnel. I could see them getting increasingly agitated. Some even called me a liar!

Scary as the whole experience was, there was an advantage in being kept waiting. It gave me the chance to look at all those mighty military people. Their uniforms and caps were such a fascinating sight. And the way they saluted each other! And I, Simeoni Ninsiima, was among them, taking part in all this!

My 'uncle' Major Rwebigo happened to be in the building but of course he had no recollection of me. Fortunately he did recognise my father's name, Petero Rutembeka. Unwilling to come down to see me he sent a soldier back with a message.

"The Major says that if there is anything important the boy should ask his father to come here and make an appointment."

"Please, Sir, can I leave now?" I hastily pleaded with the guards. At last they let me to go, but not without a serious warning.

"You, child, don't you ever dare enter this building again unless you have formal clearance!"

I returned to the polio hostel with a very exciting story to tell, as well as with a little more caution. Being innocent and confined to a wheelchair did not necessarily mean that I could just go anywhere I wanted. No, from now on I would have to content myself with less risky undertakings. Like watching the officers as they drove past the polio hostel, escorted by military trucks with machine guns and rocket launchers. Instead of trying to enter contentious places I soon found myself a different kick – flagging down these vehicles to ask for a lift. Over time I actually became quite successful at it.

Meanwhile I was still waiting to hear from Kireka. Mr Ambrose explained that mature students were given priority. Only if there were any places left would they consider looking at my application. At every opportunity I pleaded my cause with anyone remotely in a position to influence the decision. Then, after months of waiting, I finally received the news I had been praying for. Kireka was prepared to take me on and offer training in courses deemed suitable for my age and physical abilities. I immediately moved to the centre and spent a few weeks umbrella making under a Japanese instructor. Next I did leatherwork and advanced level tailoring while being put on the waiting list for office skills and telephone exchange operation.

Kireka was one of the main rehabilitation centres in the country, making it a useful venue for disability activists. The Ugandan Association of Physically Disabled regularly met up there. Enthusiastically I attended their meetings, interpreting for fellow trainees and contributing by articulating issues that we disabled people were facing in everyday life. That year of 1971 was the early beginning of my interest and involvement in speaking up for people with disabilities in Uganda.

Soon it became clear that employment at Kireka was not guaranteed, nor were there sufficient work placements in the industries for disabled people. My instructors actually told me that the additional skills I was learning would not put me in a more advantageous position. Many trainees were sent home at the end of their course, even those much older than me.

Within weeks of arriving at Kireka I began to look out again for further training opportunities that would not just lead to yet more skills and another certificate but to actual employment. For a long time I had been eyeing the apprenticeship programme run by the Old Mulago orthopaedic

workshops. These predominantly trained and employed disabled people to make mobility appliances and aids. I was
quite familiar with the workshops. They operated in collabo-
ration with the polio clinic, and I had been there many times
to have my callipers and crutches adjusted. Several disabled
people of my acquaintance were taken on as apprentices.
Seeing them earn their own living, even being married with
children, was always a huge inspiration. Although my young
age would again be an issue, I had a Certificate of Achievement
from Ruti to prove my potential for progress and my
motivation.

Armed with my certificate I approached the workshops to
express my desire to join them. The management was not
interested, except for one senior member of staff. Wilson
Nsasiirwe seemed charmed by my enthusiasm and impressed
by my achievements. He was a supervisor and trainer in the
leather workshop where callipers and orthopaedic boots were
made. Coincidentally, he had trained at the same institute as
my Ruti leatherwork instructor! Wilson introduced me to his
boss who took a quick look at me and my papers.

"Your certificate is a prerequisite for an apprenticeship in
our workshops," he stated. "Even so there is no way we can
consider you for the type of work we do. Why don't you
come back in a couple of years when you are a little older?"

Wilson was undeterred. He promised to keep looking out
for opportunities and put my name forward until they were
prepared to try me out. He was a kind well-wisher who, over
time, would support and guide me as I moved towards
becoming independent.

After a few months my training at Kireka came to an end.
Armed with additional skills in making umbrellas and even
better leather bags I returned to the polio hostel, wondering
what life might bring next.

Shortly after my return, the hostel and clinic were thrown
into frenzy with a string of meetings taking place between

our staff and those of the various orthopaedic departments. The unusually feverish activity was reminiscent of the time when Papa Paulo came to visit. This time however we were not expecting a high spiritual leader but Uganda's first military Head of State – His Excellency Major General Idi Amin Dada. Once again I found myself caught up in the preparations as one of the few disabled youngsters to be paraded upfront.

During the Pope's visit security had been tight but on this occasion it was unprecedented. Armed soldiers swarmed along the roads leading up to Old Mulago and surrounded our compound and premises. The Military Police was everywhere, their red caps like bright flowers amongst the curious spectators. This police force was more powerful than the ordinary police. It had the authority to arrest members of the other security forces and their approach was usually much rougher. The moment a little skirmish erupted, such as a drunkard behaving disorderly or someone getting overexcited, they were pulled from the crowd and dragged away. As a result, everyone was on their best behaviour. No one dared to climb trees as they had done for the Pope.

Staff in squeaky-clean uniforms lined the path in front of our hostel, clapping and cheering as His Excellency approached, flanked by several high-ranking officers. Amin was a huge, imposing man who used to be the heavyweight-boxing champion of Uganda before turning to an army career. Upright in my wheelchair and bursting with pride I watched him get closer and closer – this important man everyone was speaking of and whom I was about to meet. I wondered what sort of character he was and whether to fear him or not. After meeting various hospital staff Amin stopped right in front of me and took hold of both my hands. Leaning forward until his face was very close to mine he chatted away in Swahili.

"Habari kijana, pole kwa wugonjwa." ("Hello young man, I am sorry about your illness"). Cameras flashed all around us. My hands remained locked in his as he went on to ask questions about my family. His big eyes lit up, his cheeks widened into a broad smile when he placed one of his large hands on my shoulder.

"Isn't Amin a charming person?" I vividly remember thinking. "He does not seem vicious at all. At least not towards disabled youngsters."

Little did I know what a ruthless dictator this man would turn out to be. One day, in preparation for an Organisation of African Unity summit hosted by Uganda, he would order the streets of Kampala to be cleared of 'unsightly beggars'. Many disabled people, including some I knew, disappeared never to be seen again, amidst persistent rumours that they were loaded onto lorries and dumped into Lake Victoria.

During all those months in Kampala and Kireka I never ceased praying to the Lord and asking him to bless my efforts. In return I felt a deep reassurance, even when there was no prospect of an apprenticeship or job. It was as though *Yesu* was saying to me, "It is only a matter of time. Look back at your life if you have any doubts. Is there not sufficient proof of what I can do?"

I began to feel an urge to venture into the wider community and mingle with non-disabled people. After trying out a few churches in the vicinity of the hostel I joined the fellowship group attached to the medical school. This group met for worship in the doctors' mess and afterwards went around the wards to pray with patients. I made friends with students, doctors and nurses, radiographers and other medical staff from all different tribes, only this time not as a patient but on equal footing, as a fellow believer. At home I used to be quite happy to remain in the shadow of older, more seasoned Christians, leaving it to them to lead the worship and spread the word of God. Now I found myself at the frontline. For the first time I was the one reaching out to others rather than being at the receiving end. I discovered that I had a lot to give. With my experience of disability and life with God I was able to support and encourage people in circumstances similar to mine! And so, by playing an active role in this fellowship group, I began to grow in confidence to stand up for my faith and call myself a committed Christian.

Meanwhile Wilson kept his promise and finally managed to convince his boss to try me out on their training programme. After a series of interviews and tests that went on for several weeks I was offered an apprenticeship at the orthopaedic leather workshop. Not having to plead and fight anymore was something I would have to get used to.

At the age of fourteen I had landed my first job. Now I could earn my own living and be independent! Martin was happy too, albeit a little apprehensive. Perhaps he thought that at such a young age I was not yet ready for working life. I was given a white uniform like the ones worn by medics, and it looked very smart on me. My training allowance was not enough to pay the rent for a place of my own but the polio hostel allowed me to stay on longer as an exceptional case. After a few months I became a fully waged employee and was allocated a room in the hospital staff quarters. These consisted of former Old Mulago wards, partitioned into small units by woven reed panels and curtains. My block housed approximately ten members of staff, many of whom had wives and children or other family members staying with them. My room had a bed, a small table and sisal mats on the floor for people to sit on. I cooked my own meals using a paraffin stove or a charcoal burner.

Being a 'young man of independent means' gave me a chance to make up for all the things I had felt short of in life. Like those delicious cakes and treats that used to pass my bed on hospital trolleys and that only people with money were able to get. Or like just plain sugar... At home mother always restricted our intake of sugar, as this was a delicacy we could rarely afford. If we had any in the house it was kept for guests and for special occasions. Sometimes Sam and I could not resist the temptation to help ourselves to a spoonful, cherishing the moment by sucking a few grains at a time, but if mother found out we were severely reprimanded. And whenever one of my aunts returned from the market with a couple of sweets, each was broken into tiny pieces and distributed among all the children, including those of the neighbours.

Now, at last, I had the means to make up for this 'deprivation'. This was my time to feast. With my very first salary I bought a large bag of sugar and a dozen *mandazi*. Back in my room I made myself a huge mug of tea that I saturated with sugar. Sitting comfortably on my bed I placed the bag of sugar on my lap and began to fill my cheeks. Munching the sugar and *mandazi* I meditated on the past. How desperate I used to feel when lying in the hut, unable to chase a fly off my face. Once upon a time I depended on others to come and feed me. Now I could prepare my own meals and eat whatever I liked in my own little place. People used to feel sorry when seeing me crawl in my torn shorts but against all expectations I had turned into a presentable 'young man' in a wheelchair who went off to work from Mondays to Fridays as an equal among others.

I ate spoon after spoon full of sugar, washing it down with the gooey tea and occasionally interrupting this process to stuff myself with *mandazi*. I had the time of my life, only wishing that Sam and my sisters could have joined in with me while celebrating this long awaited freedom. In one evening I gobbled more than a kilo of sugar and nearly all of the fatty cakes. In the end the inside of my mouth was blistering and my lips and tongue had gone numb. A sweet, sticky glue ran from my throat to my stomach. The following morning my head was hurting. I had severe stings in my stomach and chest. My body began to swell up and I had difficulty passing urine. Although feeling terribly thirsty I was too bloated to take any drink. I ran a high fever and eventually passed out. A neighbour found me in my room and carried me to the casualty department where my stomach was pumped out and I was put on a drip.

By now Wilson had become my mentor and good friend and I told him what had happened.

"Simeoni," he replied in a fatherly tone, "you are a very bright person but not yet an adult. There is still a lot of child left in you."

Being a conscientious Christian I also confessed my embarrassing indulgence to my fellowship group, among whom I was by far the youngest. They listened to me with solemn faces but somehow seemed to struggle not to burst out laughing, especially when I asked them to pray for me and ask the Lord to help me overcome my weakness in the face of 'sweet' temptation. I must admit that ever since this extravagance, I have not been too keen on eating sugary things!

With financial independence and a place of my own I was in a position to host other people, to look after those who had once cared for me. Uncle Daudi was one of the first to come and see me. I treated him with a visit to a World Wrestling Contest at Nakivubo Stadium. When he saw those mighty men take on each other he almost blamed me for bringing his past back to life. He used to be a magnificent fighter and might well have been a champion among those wrestlers had he not become a Christian.

My dear Aunt Mangyeri was so happy to find me in my little place. She was among the people who prayed for me night after night when I was troubled by terrible nightmares. She had never ceased to be hopeful and positive when others fretted over my future. Now, seeing me live independently, she glorified the Lord.

Sam came to live with me while attending a secondary school in Kampala. Schools in the city were much better than those in the village but boarding was very expensive. So he stayed with me and I contributed towards his school fees. One day he found out that Aunt Elizabeth was lodging somewhere in Kampala. I asked him to go and invite her and she joined us too. While we enjoyed the privilege of being mothered she could not stop thanking the Lord for what he had done in my life. Time after time she reminded Sam and me of how weak and helpless I used to be. She never thought to see the day when I would be hosting her!

Father also came to check on me quite often. On one of these occasions he was in a terrible state. He had been mugged on the streets of Kampala and lost all the money earmarked for paying the local taxes, something he had planned to do on his way back home. In those days local taxes were collected quite aggressively. People who paid were issued with a certificate that they needed to keep with them wherever they went. Local governments mounted surprise roadblocks to intercept defaulters. Anyone unable to pay was sent to prison. That day I gave father half of my wages, enough to cover his taxes. I also bought him a shirt and a watch from the local market. It was such an honour and joy to be able to do this for him. Countless times I had wished I could stand by my father – work alongside him in times of hardship, fight together when facing danger! Now, by God's grace, I could return the love and care he had shown me for as long as I could remember, but especially from the time I was struck down by polio. From now on we would be able to face all challenges together.

Upon seeing the money and gifts my father praised God, recalling the prophecy of the *hajji* spoken several years ago when he saw father toiling through Kampala railway station carrying me on his shoulders. *"God has a special purpose for this boy. Now you struggle under his weight but through his life you will be carried!"*

"Indeed the Lord has wonderful plans," my father rejoiced. "The child, whom everyone expected to remain dependent on his parents, has turned out to be a useful son after all!"

People came from far and wide – family members, relatives and acquaintances. Nearly all my earnings went on food for my guests. In the end I had to devise ways of diverting the steady stream of visitors and help them find alternative accommodation. Some came with the intention of seeing me while others needed check-ups or treatment in New Mulago. Many lived in rural areas and were unfamiliar with the hospital environment and procedures. As for me, Mulago was my world. I knew where to go or where to make enquiries. I could guide people through the maze of red tape and even interpret for them if needed. By just putting on my white uniform all doors were open to me within the hospital premises.

Many of those I helped were amazed to see what a disabled person could do. In fact, I became quite a talking point back in the village.

"If you ever need treatment in Mulago, go and see Simeoni, son of Petero Rutembeka. He will be able to help you. He may even put you up at his place in the hospital staff quarters."

"Isn't he that crippled boy who used to crawl in the dust...?"

There were times when people questioned God for keeping me alive. *"How can God be so cruel to leave a child in this terrible state,"* they used to say to each other. *"How can he allow such suffering? This boy would have been better off dead!"*

They challenged my parents for continuing to trust in God's unfailing love, even in periods of hardship, loss and pain. But the Lord is faithful in both the good times and the bad.

When we enjoy blessings, he is the one who gives them to us. When we delight in his glorious creation, he smiles upon us. When we face danger, turmoil, grief, abandonment or betrayal, he is right there with us. When we hit rock-bottom, desperate, lost in regret or shame, when we are weak or struggle with our faith, his hand still guides and sustains us. Even when the whole world seems against us, he sees the bigger picture. He has the bigger plan.

His love and grace are there for the taking, free to every person who chooses to believe.

I just hope and pray that my story will go some way towards demonstrating this.

More information on the author and this book
can be found on the following website:

www.simon-ninsiima.co.uk

Ingram Content Group UK Ltd.
Milton Keynes UK
UKHW042207080323
418239UK00001B/175